/ N A T I O N

Latin American Literatures by Women

Ileana Rodríguez *Translated by Robert Carr and Ileana Rodríguez*

DUKE UNIVERSITY PRESS *Durham / London 1994*

1000412357

¡Ay Nicaragua, Nicaragüita
la flor más linda de mi querer. . . !
—Carlos Mejía Godoy

What must be done so there is light, and the day breaks?
¿Cómo se hará para que aclare y amanezca?
—Popol-Vuh

Carlos

Santiago

Roberto

aurora beneath the closed door

Therese
Marilyn
Antonina
serenity, inner light

Contents

Acknowledgments xiii

Excursus xv

Introduction 1

PART I Gender/Genre/Nation/Ethnicity *The Masculine*

1 Transitions: Modernism/Modernity 23

PART II Nation/Ethnicity/Gender/Genre *The Feminine*

2 Teresa de la Parra: *Hacienda*/Nation—*Quid Pro Quo* 59

3 Dulce María Loynaz: Garden/Nation—
Parva Domus: Magna Quies 88

4 Jean Rhys: Island/Nation—*Hortus Conclusus* 108

5 Simone Schwarz-Bart: Provision Grounds/Nation—
Et in Arcadia Ego 132

6 Gioconda Belli: Urban House/Nation—Domi Nostre 165

Notes 199

Selected Bibliography 203

Index 217

Acknowledgments

This book was written at the Department of Spanish and Portuguese at the University of Maryland, College Park, during my tenure as a Rockefeller Fellow. I would like to express my gratitude to the Rockefeller Foundation, to the University of Maryland, to Saúl Sosnowski, Chairman of the Department of Spanish and Portuguese, to the professors at the Department, and to the Foundation consultants for funding my proposal to do research on "Gender, Ethnicity, and Nation in Times of Transition." Without their support, this book might not have been written.

I particularly wish to acknowledge with gratitude a special debt to Dr. Robert Carr, who patiently and selflessly applied himself to translating with care what he called, with poetic justice, my English phonemes into the standard vernacular, after meticulous consultation. The bond that we established will last forever. My thanks also to Paul Miller, a student of Comparative Literature, who walked the road with us for sixty long and not always pleasant pages, and to Dr. María Lima, also from Comparative Literature, who carefully read the manuscript lest Professor Carr be inadvertently seduced by my specialized dialect.

I am grateful as well to the students and faculty who attended my talks, conversed with me in the hallways, invited me to dinners and picnics, walked along the campus paths on tedious Sunday afternoons to find relief from the constrictions of the dorms—especially José Rabasa, Javier Sanjinés, Regina Harrison, Laura Martins, and Alberto Pinkas. And thanks also go to the administrative officers Kathryn Karam, Chanty Encarnación, Mary Jefferson, Allison Tucker, Rosana Morales, and Oscar Comulada, who responded patiently to each and every question and endured the occasional panic attack. And last, though by no means least, I am grateful to Patricia Herron, the Latin American Bibliographer at McKeldin Library, who carefully taught me how to use all of the library's data banks, thus helping and also accelerating my work considerably.

Production is always a collective enterprise. For that reason I want especially to acknowledge the labor of my colleagues Roberto Márquez, Ellen McCraken, Jean Franco, Doris Sommer, John Beverley, Marc Zimmerman, and Carmen Naranjo for reading the typescript and offering their encouraging comments, and the efforts of Elena Urrutia, who let me try out my ideas at El Colegio de México.

Among the people whose companionship has proved indispensable are Carlos Eduarte, whose serenity and resilience is a perennial source of bliss; Santiago Vega, whose birth filled my life with the purest imaginable joy; Roberto Guibernau, without whose love I could never have endured the course; Therese Meléndez, who mothered me during my most abrasive years; Marylin Cuneo, who held my hand while I blindly traversed the most dangerous waters; Antonina Vivas and Adilia Moncada, who in the middle of the war relentlessly taught me the art of the *dolce far niente;* and John Beverley, who always believed I could swing it.

Excursus

Traveler, there is no road:
we make the road as we walk,
the road is made as we walk,
and looking back,
we see the path
we will never walk again.
Traveler, there is no road:
only our wake in the sea.
—Antonio Machado
Sung by Joan Manuel Serrat
Translated by Susan Norwood

It was during the intense decade of the Sandinista Administration in Nicaragua that my interest in studying the intersections of gender, ethnicity, and nation in times of transition arose. My ideas for this book emerged from my direct participation in long and interminable meetings and debates over the material and spiritual improvement of everyday life, discussed in a pluralistic, multiethnic, multinational society.

The Sandinista electoral defeat in 1991 only rendered a process of economic deterioration evident. From 1986 on, a brutal monetary reform had underscored the severe fiscal crisis of the state. The progress of inflation had to be brought to a halt. Economic historians may trace the irreversible turning point of the social revolution under way to that year, in which retrenchment and the reallocation of state workers were to cause much distress. To political historians, true believers in the human agency of history, the final outcome is perhaps still pending.

I began to write this book at the University of Maryland after the Sandinista electoral defeat, away from the conflicts of the revolutionary transition taking place in that remote geographical area. The public plazas inflamed with the tumult of the masses became but a memory. The indigenous voices identifying the towns where the struggle had taken place, now printed in texts, joined the process of political reversal as they changed into poetry and rhetoric. Behind me was the thick forest, the impenetrable land. "Traveler, there is no road: we make the road as we walk." The words of Antonio Machado, sung by Joan Manuel Serrat, came back to me.

As a child I was trained in the impoverished official public elementary schools of postrevolutionary Mexico, where strongly nationalist policies did not allow me early access to transnational writings. In *belles-lettres* I remained attached to the land and circumscribed by the internal market. I was formed by the then-prestigious Latin American social writers. Reading *La Vorágine* as an adolescent, I identified, naturally, with Alicia, the woman Arturo Cova drags toward the thick forest in order to save his "honor." I never understood, in those days, the sense of shame that fell upon him but I always suspected it was related to class and to ethnicity, and that it was Alicia's otherness that made Woman deserve the first infuriating pages of an epic that seemed to me then the quintessence of passion. In Alicia's role I experienced the passionate rapture of *machista* invention. But, with time, I came to realize that my true identification was with Arturo. I wanted to live the adventure with him, to follow him and set off on the road to Casanaré and reach La Maporita, to hunt wild cattle, to go to the *cantina,* deep into the wilderness. I made his passion mine. I wished for myself his mobility, his sense of freedom, his possession of the landscape, and the construction of both his narrative and his adventure. *La Vorágine* was, therefore, in my adolescence and later in my adult life, the simultaneous realization of the masculine and the feminine tied to a certain feeling of continental regionalism and of yoking myself to the land, the country, the nation. It was, I came to realize, the formation of the nation that fascinated me, coupled with some kind of erasure of gender roles.

My first feelings were, then, regional, national, and continental, tied to the large expanses of land of the liberal horizon. I was born under those auras, fascinated by Arturo Cova, doña Bárbara, Mr. Danger, El Brujeador, El Cunavichero. Later on, at the university, I came into contact with the intelligentsia of the Spanish Republic, who schooled me in Marxism. Under the two hegemonies Rama alludes to between the lines in *La ciudad letrada*—Marxism and Neo-Positivism—I have read these texts.

In Strasbourg years later, on February 25th, 1990, at a United Nations convention on Women and Law, a Spanish representative notified me that the FSLN (Sandinista National Liberation Front) had lost the election. I remember distinctly that when Nicaragua asked for the floor at that time, in what is otherwise a most boisterous forum, the response was a profound silence. How ironic, I thought, that at its death the revolutionary state had left Woman located at the center. Gender and State were thus inextricably confounded, and for all present, as in *Iphigenia,* the result had been a quid pro quo. Woman was located at a crossroad, and had constituted herself a border between the Neo-Liberal and Marxist projects. Doña Violeta was the sign that one transition had come to an end and that another was awakening. Honoring our Spanish heritage, this new transition came to be known as *La Restauración*. Between empathy and criticism, the new administration began its course. Fortune has not furnished it with better winds to sail.

Violeta Chamorro, like most of the protagonists of the texts under scrutiny, is a "woman of porcelain," about which more later. Modernism, in the voice of its most outstanding poet and compatriot, Rubén Darío, would have sung to her as he did, in effect, to Margarita de Baile, relative of doña Salvadorita, the wife of Somoza, "*Margarita, está linda la mar*," or "*La princesa está triste/qué tendrá la princesa?*" ("Margarita, how beautiful the sea!" or "The princess is sad, what disturbs the princess?) The electoral campaign of doña Violeta is a lesson in the intersections of gender and ethnicity in times of transition. It was organized congenially and according to the size of Central America—as Henry Kissinger had advised. It put into play all the symbology of the Virgin Mary: Violeta as the Virgin, Violeta as a first-communion girl, Violeta as a saint on an altar. The icons reproduce a modernized version of Miller's *Daughter*, of Saint-Pierre's *Paul et Virginie*, and of Carolsfield's paintings, the alluring girl-woman images that seduced all but one of the women writers under analysis here: virginity, maternity, wifehood—the emphatic virtues of the Neo-Liberal horizon. Violeta belongs not only to the ancient oligarchy of the *haciendas*, "branded by the Chamorro iron" as she proudly asserted in her public appearances, but she was the wife of the national martyr par excellence, Pedro Joaquín Chamorro—owner of a country estate, the newspaper *La Prensa*, and a member of the most venerable conservative Granadian aristocracy. Her family was divided: a son in the *Frente* and a son in the *Contras*, a daughter at the Nicaraguan Embassy in Spain, and the other heading the opposition newspaper. In her, reconciliation and harmony converge: a *mater dolorosa*. Lord George, as she called former President Bush from her *hacendatario* horizon, gave her his *pláceme* and the popular vote put her in power. Daniel Ortega's campaign, on the contrary, utilizing all the symbology of *machismo*, presented him as a consecrated *gallo ennavajado* (fighting cock), and earned him his defeat.

Violeta is reminiscent of the woman of modernity in both its incarnations, although the modern women of the first half of the century, de la Parra and her generation, did not want to take power—they merely wanted to incorporate themselves into the liberal professions and be subjects of law. Tied more to Independence and to the Founding Fathers of the land, the modern woman finds that the only exit possible is through money. Capital/dowry provides the vocabulary for discussing the relation of marriage/

nation-state. Gioconda Belli posits money as capital in the second half of the century, in declaring that the three C's of women's success are *cara, cuerpo,* and *capital* (face, body, and capital), an aphorism that reproduces a masculinist thinking according to which, as Teresa de la Parra's Uncle Pancho puts it, "a woman is never poor when she is beautiful." Belli had already addressed the question of women's desire to be productive, and the convenience for the nation-state in incorporating women. Ironically, in Violeta, the Neo-Liberal woman, the representative of the *hacendataria* class, the woman of porcelain, marriages of convenience, and state participation syncretize.

It is not my intention to close by postulating that the incorporation of woman into the nation-state is a master's coup—which it is—but rather by signaling some of the most notorious maneuvers of the present decade: the appropriation of secular agendas, and the appropriation of women's power, to wield them against the subalterns—of race, class, and gender. In a kind of cultural *mestizaje* and ideological syncretism that Caribbean islands desiring to become nations deserve, postmodernism today, like doña Bárbara yesterday, is a voracious, multiethnic, androgynous being, at the moment of multinationalism, in a brilliant, open decade for the managerial class, perhaps at the twilight of the nation-states and the dawn of the open institutionalization of the corporate states.

Coming from an embattled past, I am indebted to Fredric Jameson for dauntlessly asserting the existence of history. He says:

> The sense people have of themselves and their own moment of history may ultimately have nothing whatsoever to do with its reality: that the existential may be absolutely distinct, as some ultimate "false consciousness," from the structural and social significance of a collective phenomenon, surely a possibility rendered more plausible by the fact of global imperialism, in terms of which the meaning of a given nation-state—for everyone else on the globe—may be wildly at odds from their own inner experiences and their own internal daily life. . . . There is, however, an even more radical possibility; namely, that period concepts finally correspond to no realities whatsoever, and that whether they are formulated in terms of generational logic, . . . or according to some other category or typological and classificatory system, the collective reality of the multitudinous lives encompassed by such terms is not thinkable . . . and can never be described, labeled or conceptualized. . . . In that case, of course, there is no such a thing as "history" either. . . . (282)

Introduction

I will walk again the streets
of what once was bloodied Santiago
and in a handsome liberated plaza
I will set out to cry for the ones absent
—Pablo Milanés

In this book my overall purpose is to study and analyze the intersections of gender, ethnicity, and nation in times of transition to Modernity in Caribbean narratives written by women. I have chosen the following transitions: Venezuela's transition at the beginning of the twentieth century as it is argued in the novel *Ifigenia: Diario de una señorita que escribió porque se fastidia* (1926) by Teresa de la Parra; the Cuban transition in Dulce María Loynaz' *Jardín* (1935); the Jamaican double transition (1832 and 1962) in Jean Rhys' *Wide Sargasso Sea* (1966); the specter of Guadeloupan transition in Simone Schwarz-Bart's *Pluie et vent sur Télumée miracle* (1972) and *Ti Jean L'Horizon* (1979); and the record of the Nicaraguan transition in Gioconda Belli's *La mujer habitada* (1988) and *Sofía de los presagios* (1990). Each of these transitions is signaled by a major difference: how the nation, and consequently the state, has or has not been constituted. My purpose is to unravel, expose, and analyze these differences, and to locate in each of them the assigned gender and ethnic positions.

In part one, "The Masculine," I work with two transitions to modernity: the first, at the beginning of the century, is carried out under the ideology of Neo-Positivism; the second, in the middle of the century, is under the ideology of Marxism. For the first transition, I take as examples of masculine paradigms the novels of nation-formation, and for the second, testimonial literature. In part two, "The Feminine," three women from the Latin American oligarchy—two working within Neo-Positivism and one within Marxism—speak of their nation; and two women, thinking of the histories of the transition between slave and free labor, speak of their islands.

Along the way we will discover the insidious presence of the market and of money capital and their seemingly immutable and irreversible laws; the multinational, global character of the social universe; and the insertion of nation-states into the dynamics of the world market. We will also find identities formulated by liberal Neo-Positivistic and Marxist thought, and even their convergence with tenets of enlightened conservatism, and realize, as Oscar René Vargas asserts, how amusing it must be "to the observer . . . [to] realize . . . how many things do not change with a revolution [and how] with the years they look like less spectacular social processes" (103). Or, in Rama's lapidary words, the youth of the '60s were Marxist because we arrived late to be Neo-Positivists.

In writing this text I have honored the terminology of the social sciences, and kept the names of Neo-Positivism and Marxism for the two master epistemologies. I recognize that the polemic between Modernism, Postmodernism, and Neo-Historicism, which this book cannot avert, constitutes a veiled discussion of Marxism, and that today's theoretical thinking would like to shorten the time span between Neo-Positivism and Neo-Liberalism, eradicating the mediation and influence of Marxism in the twentieth century. Two different epistemologies come to bear on this text. The literature calls them "systems," but what is at stake are "theories" and "moments of systemic change," that is, transitions.

Systemic changes, transitions, affect land, the geography of the national territory, and groupings and regroupings of people; consequently, they deeply affect questions of sovereignty and independence. On the Latin American mainland, at the beginning of this century, the ideology of Neo-Positivism emphasizes economic development, the rubrics for which are Progress and Civilization—or social order and the capacity of a people to govern themselves. It proposes a reorganization of property and the labor force. It craves productivity, foreign markets, organization, and the establishment of the Latin American "bourgeois" order as the law of the land. For Sergio Ramírez, Neo-Positivism, "the transformation of the country based on the rapid growth of export and the utilization of national resources," in Nicaragua is just an illusion, but for the men who conceived the project, say, of Venezuela or Colombia, this instant marks a transition (Las armas, 70).

Analyzing the change from the point of view of group formation, the ruling groups, the Independentistas, must undergo a metamorphosis—from warlords, caciques, montoneros, and idle señores into the "national" bourgeoisie. A good number of them demonstrate their readiness to take on the challenge. As Gallegos, de la Parra, and Rivera demonstrate, debate flourishes. A civil debate ensues, and reform rather than revolution is proposed. But the ideas of Civilization and Progress—the social bourgeois order—are an internal affair. Both are ideas and matters discussed in the inner circle, in the bosom of these oligarchic families, among the notables, the distinguished, and their allies. The battle for Neo-Positivist economic development has to be decided by whittling out, by separating the wheat from the chaff, as in the Gospel, by weaning out the *suntuarios* and luxury-oriented members of the founding families of the nation, the old *Independentista* stock, and by institutionalizing the survival of the fittest and constituting into law the productivity of private property, fencing, the labor order—in other words, by legitimizing and making viable the desired internal, national, primitive accumulation of capital. As it is registered in fiction, but guided by categories of the social sciences, I read the works of Gallegos and Rivera to illustrate this first transition in part one of this book, titled "The Masculine."

Much of this process of reaccommodation mirrors classical studies of English society at the end of the eighteenth century. Latin American societies, however, must deal with the different ethnic specificities of a non-homogeneous working class. Enclosures, foreclosures, and fencing in Latin America can easily underscore ethnic differences.

In the island nations (here, nations like Jamaica and Cuba), Progress, Civilization, and the social world order hinge on questions of Independence and the modernization of old plantocracies. Colonialism links their economies to the metropolis and makes the Neo-Positivist aspiration to Progress and Civilization, to political sovereignty, to primitive accumulation of national capital, highly mercurial. Benedict Anderson's facetious question about the concept of "the national bourgeoisie" is then very pertinent here. "Why is *this* segmentation of the bourgeoisie—a world class insofar as it is defined in terms of the relations of production—theoretically significant?"; why is there not any "serious attempt to justify theoretically the relevance of the adjective" 'national'? (Anderson, 4).

As for the planter class and the well-cultivated cane fields, Simone Schwarz-Bart carefully monitors them in her text, and all property, Great Houses, and Manors are in white French hands. Jean Rhys, too, everywhere addresses the question of the remodeling and revamping of island property. Antoinette's mate, the English protagonist, referred to only as "he" or "him," is one such new metropolitan entrepreneur allied to the new generic, modernizing, local and nonlocal planter class. Antoinette's stepfather and brother, Mr. Mason and his son, also belong to that group signifying modernization. Underlining the theses of my book is that without the primitive accumulation of capital—and hence the formation of a national bourgeoisie—the nation, a sovereign, independent territoriality governed by its own internal laws, is a contradiction in terms. In fact, the adamant and anxious discussion on law and order can be explained in these terms. The insistence of the "national" bourgeoisie to have their offspring study abroad, documented by Anibal Pinto for the case of Chile and by José Murilo de Carvalho for the case of Brazil, among others, profoundly underscores the necessity for the ruling groups of learning metropolitan economy and law. These are indispensable for the apprenticeship and maintenance of "international" law and order, which in turn sustains the global capitalist bourgeois world order at the local colonial and neo-colonial, imperial and neo-imperial levels.

However, in these narratives of nation-formation there remain loose and unclear ends. What is uncontestable is that everything is tied to the land, to agriculture, to lineage and family, and to the ethnic groups associated with them. "Land" is the yearning for nation and nationhood. Land, whose owners draw in and blur the boundaries between the *haciendas* and *latifundios* they inherit and sell, make and remake, and plot and till and replot, makes a history which is not the history of one narrative but of several, the history of an uninterrupted continental narratology, the history of a map of disputed borders, limits, and frontiers in the ever-polemical discussion of nation and nationality.

Thus, in all writings on "nation," there is a truth which some locate in the strict terrain of language and words, in "the narrative of the end of narratives," as Jameson has it, and which others, like myself, situate in the discussion of land, territory, and land tenure, that is, in the political arena of struggle, in the strength and funding of armies. Both theories, one linguistic, the other political, fight for the representation of nation. But this "nation," whether Creole, narco or begging, whether based on economic subsidy or linguistic unity, is a nation in which neither Indians nor blacks nor women have a space, or, if they have it, it is akin to *Costumbrista* literature where the rural world and the space of women are romanticized— arcadia without conflicts, the picturesque. Women and ethnic groups are characters, beings reduced to the category of living, transhumant organisms simply spread out across an immense geography, essential components of an ever-natural landscape governed by books of both law and literature.

Nation is *hortus,* land and ethnicities tied to civilization and progress, but also to social justice and well-being, to development, to poverty, to good or bad administration and government, the perennial existence of two or three or more republics in a history marked by failure and error and dread; the question of nation-formation always revolves around the concepts of ground, of agriculture and the distribution of agricultural land. It has already been established that the words "land-tenure system" signify abuse, harassment, battery, and the persecution of people understood as ethnic groups. The large *estancias,* productive or unproductive, in living or dead hands, are, to borrow Martínez Peláez' metaphor, *patrias del criollo* that stifle and choke and bewilder. The land-tenure system explains the Colonial Period and, beyond that, Independence and the Republic. In consequence, this history of centuries colors the process of Modernization and renders true Martí's dictum that the nation was born smothered by the colony.

Modernism, modernization, and modernist are thus highly problematic terms. Both Raymond Williams and Fredric Jameson have called attention to this, and I refer the reader to their texts for the discussion as it takes place in First World societies. In Latin America the issue is somewhat different, and I have been arguing modernization and modernism on the basis of the public perception of land and the land-tenure systems, as well as in reference to legality, to the extent that they affect women and ethnic groups in special ways. The land-tenure system is, and means, war. The ownership of land, real or imaginary, including its men and women and its ethnic groups, is also revolution, "the continuation of politics by other means," according to Clausewitz (62). In what other ways and by what other means is it feasible to restructure property? By what similar analogic theories can people overrun the fences, as Viglietti's song would have it? How can it be made known that the land is mine, yours, and Isabel's, as much as Pedro's and Manuel's? In these transitions there are people fighting and arguing, but who they are, as well as who the leaders and the army commanders will be, is up for grabs. Benedict Anderson warns us "that many leaders of the independence movement in the Thirteen Colonies were slave-owning agrarian magnates" (75). George Washington was first a Virginia planter and then a general in the army.[1] And what about Bolívar and San Martín, Morazán, Hidalgo, Morelos, and José and Antonio Maceo?

From this angle, plotting family and lineage is very relevant, and the women in this book argue their points concerning these issues very vehemently. In an enlightening study on lineage, the land tenure system, nations, and wars, Ramón de Armas confesses that for Cuba "the study of the true [political] representation and social background of the men of '95 . . . has not yet been done" (81). If this is the case, we cannot possibly know who General Loynaz is, a general whose daughter, Dulce María, in writing about a nation was to portray it as an immense garden by the sea. And in the case of Belli, lineage is illuminated by Vilas' study on families during the Sandinista administration. But properly to tie lineage, political representation, and ethnicities in Nicaragua, I must quote Lenín Cerna, former State Security Chief extensively. Speaking of the Juan José Quezada commandos, once they had successfully completed the rescue of a group of political prisoners and obtained a handsome sum, Cerna deliberates:

> One thing that caught my attention when they took off their masks . . . was the mixture, which had already been a source of distress for us . . . and which became concrete when we saw the faces of the blond people, side by side [with] the faces of the people we already knew. . . . As a matter of course, since we had already undergone a process of growth regarding a series of afflictions concerning the participation of the bourgeoisie within the movement in prison . . . *for when we in prison saw the pictures of Sandino . . . we looked at the sandinista generals and said the day our cadres look like this, we have reached the people* [emphasis mine]. . . . Then, when the comrades arrived, our attention, particularly mine, was called to the mixture of *fine people* as we called them. . . . These are *fine people,* poet! . . . but we also looked at Hilario, Picado, and Alberto's faces and even Clarita's . . . *because there it was interesting; among the political prisoners there, there was only one white, Jacinto. Jacinto was one way or another a mestizo.* In contrast, among [the members of the Commando] there were four or five whites, Eduardo, Joaquín, Javier Carrión, and Omar Halleslevens and Roger Deshon himself. . . . This mixture was very comforting and called to our attention the necessity of strengthening the ideological development at the bosom of the organization, so that from that union the Ideology of the Revolution emerged stronger. (197)

Naturally, the hiatus breaking the continuity of this narrative is clearly prompted by desire as much as by confusion, but mostly by duty. The fragment expresses first the desire that the political cadres—at least some, or a good proportion of them—be like those of Sandino's generals, that is, Indians or Indian-looking mestizos, that is, looking like the narrator himself, a strongly *aindiado mestizo,* the copper side of Garcilaso's countenance painted by Sabogal. To get an idea of what this means in the national vernacular one must read "Corte de Chaleco," a premier story of Pedrón, Sandino's deputy commander, narrated by Lizandro Chávez Alfaro, a Nicaraguan writer from the Atlantic Coast. Second, there is the confusion surrounding *mestizaje* but not *"fine people,"* a transcendental signifier in this fragment. *Gente fina* is a formula: white + lineage = government (rule, administration). Many *gente fina* were leaders during the Sandinista Administration. And third, there is the political duty signaled by the elliptical and somewhat obscure final phrase, a non sequitur indicating that ethnicity was a concern within the bosom of the Organization. Ethnic questions, conversely, were family questions, filial questions, tied to the land and to lineage before the takeover. These same discussions enjoyed a perennial life during the Sandinista decade in oral culture, in telling slogans such as "León contributed the bodies and Granada the ministers." Within Nicaraguan culture, León and Granada are cities associated with liberal and conservative political positions and with parties known as the "historical parallels," and to more or less popular and antipopular stances. The *Frente Sandinista* had strong supporters in León. This discussion, I must mention in passing, is totally absent from Belli's novels, although her witches and necromancers must belong to these ethnic groups. For her, to discuss ethnicities is then somehow irrelevant, a space reserved for psychic projections, and is exempted from her poetic narratives.

In this way I see how patriarchies and *patriciados* interweave. The presence of the notables, of familiar patrician names—Carlos Manuel de Céspedes for Cuba, and Joaquín Cuadra for Nicaragua at the turn of the nineteenth and twentieth centuries, respectively—signals the presence of a consciousness clinging to the local geographies and soil, to the physical ground called "national," which social history registers as glimmers, gestures, indices of a "national" bourgeoisie.

It is predictable, for example, that if there is a set of ideas favoring Arguedas' metaphor of a "wide and alien world," they are conservative. Within the modernizing horizon, these ideas belong to the oligarchy, or what Ramón de Armas has called the "non-national" and "anti-patriotic bourgeoisie," to the *testaferros* (figureheads), or *vendepatrias* (traitors), a rather small group of wealthy families, and to a dependent bourgeoisie, the *amaestrada* (attack dogs), and serve as a transmission belt, proposing syphon economies and local neglect.

If, on the contrary, the set of ideas favors small land holdings, wider distribution of the land, and mixed or state-owned forms of property benefiting the local inhabitants and promoting the development of an internal market, then we face a liberal, democratic, and nationalist project.

Ladino (mestizo, acculturated indigenous peoples, shrewd, crafty, sly) and *ladinizar* are two concepts I don't use in my study, although they signal transition and, as a metaphor, they could be extended to the formation of the nation and the state. To become *ladino* is to stop being one thing and become another: in Indian terms, for example, to put on a hat and begin speaking a foreign tongue. Martin Lienhard uses this expression to discuss the relation between literature and the state. For him

> the literary appropriation of "Mayan" culture in *Hombres de Maíz* also offers, on first sight, a certain analogy with the ladino appropriation, in the political world, of the historical figures of the [sixteenth century] Quiché rebel Tecún Umán: unsatisfied with having exploited and oppressed the Indians, the Guatemalan ladinos manipulate at will the memory of a hero who combatted their ancestors. (*Voz*, 319)

With some pertinent differences, the same argument can be applied to the instrumentalization of Itza, in Belli's novel, where the indigenous character and the indigenous people, the ethnic groups, become the cement of the revolutionary republic: here proletarian struggles are validated by the struggles of the indigenous peoples. Jaime Wheelock, former Nicaraguan Minister of Agrarian Reform, argued these ideas in his book on indigenous roots of social resistance. But what in fact happens, as Lenín Cerna implies, and Lienhard explicitly asserts, is that:

> The concept of the "*ladinización*" of the Indians confuses, in effect, different processes: the regional or national integration of the indigenous communities, their increasing social stratification and the appearance of the layer of merchants and *latifundistas,* the social mobility of young Indians thanks to education in the schools, proletarianization or, more frequently, the individual or collective subproletarianization of traditional Indians. (Leinhard, 124)

This structuring of literature and politics is pertinent to the nature of the nation-state and whom it represents. One difficulty in my readings, I must confess, is the difference historiography makes in calling some projects "nonnational" or even "antinational" but not others. It puzzles me, for the concepts of "national" and "nationality" in Latin America historically, in effect, have always been promoted and sustained by the "creolebourgeoisies." If, under this light, we take as examples the cases of Gallegos and Teresa de la Parra, we could perhaps distinguish, with a certain degree of confidence, Gallegos' handling of the promotion of "national" productivity "bourgeois" style—that is, Civilization, Development versus

Barbarianism—a style based on markets and marketability, whereas what we are dealing with in de la Parra is not that clear. Elizabeth Garrels' thesis on de la Parra's conservatism, however, seemingly argues a close relation between the two.

The large extensions of land—be they in the form of the transition from an unproductive *hacienda* to a productive *latifundia,* or from a sugar plantation to a sugar *latifundia,* the renaming and recomposition of the laboring class, but not necessarily mediating the extended improvement of their social condition—are the means by which the proprietary class consolidates itself or, in Marxist terms, by which it becomes, if it is possible, a class-for-itself, having a local and territorial, even a cultural, base but not, in their own terms, a national base. It is precisely the large expanses of land and their productivity, and the organization of the labor force, which make possible the grafting of the "national" bourgeoisies onto the global economies established in other territorialities, which could in fact properly be called nations. National development, political hegemony, and private accumulation of capital thus come together and mean one and the same thing. This process is related to what Marxism calls Imperialism, and what Neo-Liberalism calls the New World Order, that is, the authority and organization of the decentered corporate state becoming ubiquitous. The word "branches" or filials, used by transterritorial corporate societies, really reflects, in both its natural and genetic metaphors, the essence of their world order.

The word "treason," then, applied to the "national bourgeoisies," rests on the notion of another economic and political conception of nation and state in other types of narratives. In Cuba, for instance, the other notion has been clearly documented, and printed and reproduced in the form of a political and social *ideario*—in this sense a textual reality more befitting the type of imagined community of which Anderson speaks. José Martí's discussion of nation, understood as a project of national development based on small plots organized into a land-tenure system, makes the two propositions of nation and national very visible. In Nicaragua,

> Sandino's struggle acquires an anti-oligarchic character which in turn is anti-imperialist, for in Nicaragua [and in Cuba] there is an evident alliance between imperialism and the oligarchy, which is in turn an anti-popular alliance, and the only support of the Sandinista struggle is the popular support. One of Sandino's central propositions would then be to break away from the political dominion of the historical parallels as a creation of foreign dominion, and look for the forma-

tion of a third party which represents an alliance of peasants, artisans, professionals, small and medium-sized property owners. . . . (Ramírez 1987: 79)

In other words, in Cuba and Nicaragua, as elsewhere on the Latin American mainland, scholars must always go back to the original problem of digging into the documents that speak of building the infrastructure, or, what is the same, narratives of the social base, proposing to initiate the construction of a process of nation-building, of nation-ness, of nationalism. Discussions of sovereignty, national autonomy, and nationality also express social sensibilities, in this case a desire for internal development in general, a respect for the human person—"respect" translated into a set of structures ensuring the well-being of the people as a whole. Nation, then, for the poor is also a developmentalist agenda, socially democratic if you will, but spread out and all-encompassing, respectful of human dignity. Nation is therefore always a frontier, a vanishing point, a land for the landless and home for the homeless, for people "without a country, roaming their country's nocturnal paths" (1987: 40), a fatherland which for some means landlessness and for others just a camping ground—all these desires, notwithstanding the awareness of the lack of capital.

> In Nicaragua nobody thinks that in the future the country will not need capital for internal development, a program of foreign investment . . . and an orderly technological transference. . . . We only aspire to dignity, integrity, international respect. (1983: 54)

This is, in fact, the main dilemma for the second half of the present century, a dilemma which in truth is a carryover from the previous centuries, every one of which has had its leaders, politicians, and intellectuals, creators of alternative narratives of nationhood and nation-ness which, in their writings, incorporate the masses into the socioeconomic process, masses which are understood as laboring ethnicities and which José Martí, at a loss for words, called "the newly-born fatherland," "the natural nation," "the natural elements," "the nascent societies," "the new peoples," expressing far-fetched dreams of "Indian Academies," a thought rehashed by Ernesto Cardenal, who, in the middle of the twentieth century, in his famous *Canto Nacional,* willed "Ballet schools in Mulukukú." However, even in Martí, the ideal type of economic development could be located within Positivism, adding the adjective "radical" to situate it more properly and to distinguish it from that of, say, Alfonso Reyes or Leopoldo Zea. Martí wanted to see

Indian Academies; expeditions of cultivators to the agricultural countries; periodical and regularized trips with serious intents to the best
cultivated lands; impetus and science in planting; and opportune introduction of our fruits to foreign peoples; copious networks and road-
ways within each country, and from each country to the others; absolute and indispensable consecration of respect for others' thoughts. . . .
(25)

And Sergio Ramírez, echoing the same sensibility, expressed it as

a country full of children dreaming of being aeronautical engineers
and avant-garde poets, while legions of writers, philosophers, econo-
mists, engineers, painters, sculptors, civil engineers . . . had been left
wandering throughout the roads in the huge night of the landless.
(1987: 45)

In these projects, however, one cannot ignore Marx's warnings about the
concentration of wealth leading to monopoly capitalism. Neither must one
overlook Lerner's acrid sentence quoted below about poor societies seeing
in rich ones models for their own future. In order for this reformulation of
the *agro* to be possible, a series of anteceding distinctions had to be made:
first and foremost, the distinction between colonial and republican structures, between armed insurrection and the establishment of a new social
structure. "War is nothing but the expression of the revolution," Martí said
(Armas, 16). War (as in a war for Independence or the Revolution) is only a
means to dehegemonize and to redistribute, to become part of the political
play of forces; to be one among the groups making up the nation, so that
"the new elements," "the natural elements," could constitute themselves
into a government, into a class-for-itself. Cuban historiography agrees that
the conservative *Anexionistas* and the pro-Hispanic groups, contemplating
the struggle from the stands, let the Liberal Party and the insurgent masses
fight the war of Independence for them.

The republic [thus] excluded the Indian, the black, the peasant, when
the genius would have been to make them brethren and the necessity
of including the excluded, to adjust freedom to the body of those who
rebelled and overcame! (Armas, 16)

Ramón de Armas records the different instances in which the military
commanders were set aside by the more conservative elements, and Le
Riverend asserts that when the Spanish troops surrendered in Santiago de

Cuba, General Wood forbid the liberators to enter the liberated cities (17). As Marx put it, "a nation and a woman are not forgiven the unguarded hour in which the first adventurer that came along could violate them" (quoted in MacKinnon 1989: 155).

Pablo Milanés' song quoted above, although applied to another circumstance (Santiago de Chile), fits well here as it shows a reversal of meaning. Le Riverend's thesis is that Martí's death represents a rupture of a not-yet-consolidated equilibrium. The revolution was never the military insurrection, the battles in the mountain, but a social process that the civilian government practiced in the republic. Cuban historiography argues that the military commanders of 1868 were the best guarantors of an all-encompassing national representation, one including the masses of the people. Their intervention and representation would ensure that the insurrection would make the republic. But however much this may have been desired, there was a proviso: the ideological *mélange* came out as ethnic misgivings, and it was not clear what kind of representative force was held by

> the great leaders of '95—Antonio and José Maceo, Máximo Gómez— nor to what degree each one was a political commander as well as a military commander. The same holds true for the great military leaders—Quintín Banderas, Augustín Cebreco, Pedro A. Perez, José María Capote—who were invariably relegated in all matters not exclusively military. (Armas, 81)

If ethnic misgivings are in the foreground in the composition of the army, and a split between politics and arms is articulated, the political representation of the Government Council (Creole and Hispanic whites) leaves no doubts. Their attempts to obtain hegemonic leadership and unrestricted control of the elements located around the nucleus of the military apparatus is uncontestable. Early in the game, the Council constituted itself as the deciding body confirming military ranks, from Colonel on, to ensure that civilian and military agendas would work in tandem. The most important posts were assigned to professional people—as in Gallegos, to physicians and lawyers. Maceo's phrase to Salvador Cisneros is very telling:

> the humbleness of my cradle forbade me locating myself from the very beginning at the same height as those *who were born* commanders of the revolution. (Armas, 84; emphasis mine)

Maceo's diary reveals his bitterness: his subalterns disobey his orders and are inclined more and more to proceed out of political and not military considerations. The old *autonomista* politicians, the Creole and Hispanic bourgeoisie, had secured for themselves the leading positions in government.

From this we can gather how problematic it must have been for a woman poet like Dulce María Loynaz, a woman who had been born in 1902 and therefore belonged to what Le Riverend calls the "clean" generation, to come to terms with the republic. Since she was born into an *Independentista* family, she could not help but have received from her father, General Loynaz, some of the bitterness left over from the discussions surrounding the formation of the republic.

The same narrative holds true for Nicaragua in the present century, where the defeat of Sandinismo meant the defeat of the revolutionary process, the struggling "to the death for the Nicaraguan nation" (Ramírez 1987: xxx). The counter-revolutionary tactic was

> to contain and stop the process, freeze [the Sandinista's] determination, derail its path and transform its tactical apparatus into strategic frustration, dissolve the organized mass support of the neighborhood organizations, peasant organizations, and trade unions, at the same time enhancing the immaculate democracy, the infallible kingdom of unique and efficient private property because free enterprise doesn't admit administrative challenge and the state takes everything to ruin. (96)

In the Neo-Positivistic order, then, land, cattle, rubber, and also women and the labor force, are enclosed, fenced in, and bound, tied by the new law. Placing women and laborers on the same semantic plane as land, cattle, and rubber—making them chattel, items on the agenda for the new ruling group, serving as means for the primitive accumulation of capital—de facto denationalizes them, for they are not written into the Constitution as subjects of law. As Francine Masiello argues for women, neither women nor laborers have constitutional rights. They only have responsibilities, obligations, duties. They are possessions, private property belonging to either the family of the *hacienda* or the plantation or both. As Josefina Ludmer has demonstrated in the case of Argentinian literature, national literature in general, the national *belles lettres,* fiction, has been greatly troubled by this process and has done its best to document it.

First, literature has coded it as a debate, that is, as dissonance, polyphony, and dialogism in the formation of patriotism and the establishment of the fatherland. My readings, I hope, demonstrate that there is not a unified fiction constituting nation in Caribbean Latin America. There is

instead flux and flow, a discrepancy in what the referent nation is supposed to become. As Doris Sommer has argued, the literature of national
foundation could be called fiction, giving to fiction the nuance of invention
that idealism gave to visions of the world in order to dismiss those words
(nation, for one) whose referent, like Lewis Carroll's Chesire cat, was forever becoming a metonym of itself, or, as Benedict Anderson argues, had
created an imagined—meaning a written—sense of community.

In this discussion of nation, male voices predominate, but there are mestizo and women's voices as well. And to the degree that Latin American
literature is truly polyphonic, as, according to Bakhtin, all enduring literature is, in the interstices there are also black and indigenous murmurs
spoken through the mouths of those mestizos and white males and female
writers who need to register discrepant points of view, if only to use them
as grist for their mills. Naturally, in order to unravel these murmurs, the
reader must, as Ranajit Guha has recommended, read those few textual
moments backwards.

In the literature under scrutiny we find the anxious disputes concerning
national state-formation and, as Lucien Goldmann suggested, the splinter-
ing within ruling groups and their projects, propositions, and postulates,
as we saw in the case of Cuba. Such discrepancies and dissonances, unfortunately, at times unacknowledged let alone resolved, pass from one
transitional horizon to the next: thus are conservative ideas carried over as
ballast from past into future radical agendas. Perhaps this is the main thrust
of Benítez-Rojo's metaphor of "the repeating island" or González' "mon-
stered self." Accordingly, the propositions of private property, of land, of
its productivity—foundational pillars in Gallegos' narrative—are reproduced by Belli. The myriad ways in which the ideology of Neo-Positivism
is incorporated blindly into the revolutionary transition are also something
I want to account for, and my readings of *testimonios* in part one pursue
this question. Literature thus enables the inquisitive scholar to tease out
the hidden duplication of ideas and the reproduction of mental structures,
the carryover of epistemes from one system to the next.

We must then expect the second transition to stand on the shoulders
of the first, however much it defines itself in opposition to its predeces-
sor. Haunted by Neo-Positivism, the revolutionary transition defines itself
as its antithesis and targets private property as the source of all evils, the
clog that jams the engine and explains "the exploitation of man by man."
The revolution during the transition undertakes the elimination of private
property, consequently eliminating the past division of society into classes

by institutionalizing state ownership, the vehicle for the democratic distribution of social wealth. The key words of the Neo-Positivistic horizon, Civilization and Progress, are replaced by Sovereignty and Independence as preconditions of social justice, social justice constituting itself as the paramount goal. The "bourgeois" nation, it is claimed, is a dependent nation, and the ruling group, in Günder Frank's extreme phrase, is only a "lumpen bourgeoisie." The new nation would be a workers' state, hopefully within a new working-class world order, and the constitution of the new Republic, the new law of the land, was for the first time to constitute workers as central subjects of law. This new state promised, in Nicaragua,

> a program of democratic vindication leading towards the organization of a democratic state of social justice. [The] Government [was] to de-Somocize the army, giving it a professional and democratic content and structure . . . ; to struggle to return trust to all sectors in the country, to create sources of jobs, to foment agrarian reform based on the land expropriated from Somoza to achieve advances in education, health, housing and an orderly economic development. . . . (Ramírez 1987: 55)

However, in this transition, as in the previous one, once laborers were constituted as subjects of law, the only remaining excluded social groups were women and ethnic groups. As is evidenced by the debate, neither women nor those constituted as ethnic groups felt represented in the supposedly all-encompassing category of "laborer." At the close of this century, feminist scholars have demonstrated that the concept of the "working class" is yet another essentialism. As with the concepts of people and social bases, the concept of the working class has men as its referent, and not men *and* women; it has whites and perhaps light-skinned mestizos or ladinos and mulattoes—in Schwarz-Bart's terminology *macaques,* and in Rhys', "white cockroaches"—but not ethnic groups per se. Throughout my readings of these texts I have tried to unravel these terms, basic components of national censuses and terms for mapping the population in the constitution of the "official nation."

I have divided the book into two parts. Part one is titled "The Masculine," and part two "The Feminine." The preface, Beatris Pastor taught me, is always written at the end, and so I wrote the first part last, when I reached the conclusion that without the dominant principles of masculinity, the feminine debate limped along. For the women in this study argue with concrete, real men, and it is against men's positions that they fiercely debate. The masculine is dedicated to consecrated male ideas that men have attributed to men—Gallegos and Rivera (Güiraldes), Cabezas, Borge (El Che)—Founding Fathers of the Americanist tradition in one case and of revolutionary Latin American letters in the second. They are made to speak for the continent—a unit larger than the nation, the vast geography across which men bond, weld, and lock gender solidarity within male-dominated epistemes. The Americanist traditions of the novel of the land and of guerrilla literature, at both ends, openings and closings, fulfill similar functions in cementing the state.

It is not within my cultural traditions to preface my arguments with the verb "to argue." This is not to say I am not developing ideas and therefore knitting arguments, following the rules of logic. My method is feminine, and as Mary Louise Pratt asserted some fifteen years ago, it works by accumulation and often makes its point at the end, when the overwhelming accumulation of evidence proves my point for me. I select main statements, ideologemes, hypograms, and draw out their diverse and controversial meanings. A typical example is the word "ethnicity," which, written as "ethnos"—a word not found in most dictionaries—or as "ethnia," a Hispanicized version of the word, in previous drafts elicited much comment from readers. Ethnicity is defined in Webster as "of or relating to races or large groups of people classed according to common traits and customs," or "a member of a minority ethnic group who retains its customs, language or social views" (1974: 247). The contradictory description given by this citation already proves my point, but my point, I hope, is much more variously hued. For in the literature I am reading here, *peón*, or laborer, for instance, could mean poor mestizo, indigenous mestizo, black or mulatto, or ladino—mestizos and Castizos simply defined by Alexandre Valignano's dictum that "the more native blood they have, the more they resemble the Indians and the less they are esteemed by the Portuguese" (Anderson, 59). The same problem applies to any and all categories of labor.

All labor categories are tied to ethnicity, and ethnicity is therefore a constant. I have always been struck by the enormous diversity of such categories—*medieros, aparceros, colones, esquineros*—as I have been by the ethnic categories of blacks, two of my favorites being *tente en el aire* (keep yourself still in the air) and *salto atrás* (a jump backwards). Although ethnic components of labor categories are never clear and never explicit, their use, their inclusion as a social category, indexes transition and rubricates democracy. For instance, it is most likely that the laborers populating Gallegos' and Rivera's literary topography are indigenous mestizos, but in

Pobre Negro there is room to argue that they are mulattoes. In *La Vorágine*, rubber-plantation workers are indigenous mestizos as well, but the indigenous peoples populating the national frontier are nomadic groups, non-Westernized, unacculturated ethnic groups, transhumant peoples fitting the second meaning of the term given by the Merriam-Webster dictionary. Mestizo Indians or Indian mestizos means a larger or smaller percentage of white or native American "blood," or more specifically the presence of a phenotype stressed by those who would legislate difference—in noses, lips, and cheekbones more than in, but not to the exclusion of, skin color. Purity of blood is what is referred to by *mestizaje* and it expresses racism, a living ideology of the official nation-state. Lesser or greater percentages of "blood" slant the meaning toward the primary or secondary definition. Whites, then, are also an ethnicity, depending on geographical and cultural location in the diverse scholarly universe of printed political worlding.

In all of the texts under scrutiny here, ethnicity means service, obedience, servitude, subserviency, self-obliteration, abdication of civil and human rights. The laborers in the plains of Arauco as well as the workers on the rubber plantation of *La Vorágine,* and the live-in maids and nurses—Laura, Gregoria, the haughty and self-possessed Christophine, Ma Vitaline, Ma Eloise, Queen without a Name, Lucrecia, and Flor—all belong to subordinated cultures, subordinated texts that, out of self-interest, I read against the grain.

When ethnicity appears as overt self-affirmation, as is the case in Simone Schwarz-Bart and Jean Rhys, a vindication is taking place and a sign-shift is engendered, plotted, or imagined. When members of the service sectors—maids, nurses, or secretaries—not only begin to lead but simply become repositories of the most elemental common sense, ethnicity begins to show upward mobility, and a democratic horizon is in sight. Movement, transmutation, and visibility do not necessarily imply erasure, or, as Gioconda Belli once put it, the end of self-projection.

Insofar as ethnicity, gender, and nation are concerned, then, I try to draw out the different and major components of a hypogram. But I must warn the reader that some components are more visible and direct than others. In mestizo and mulatto republics, ethnicity is always a threat, a lurking phantom, a fluid term shot through with fear and signalled in some cultures, as in Cuba today, without words, simply by rubbing one's right index finger over one's left forearm. The only fixed terms are the extremes, where biology banishes all doubt, as in blacks, whites, and "true-blooded Indians," but mainly in non-ladinized people, where culture and phenotype couple.

The indigenous peoples as transhumant groups and frontier peoples in *La Vorágine* could be considered a sample of "true-bloodedness." And "jet" black characters like Christophine, Telumée Miracle and her mother Victoria, or the African Wademba, are unequivocally black. As white women, ladies of nacre and porcelain, with lily-white hands, adorable little angel cameos are unequivocally white. Fiction is dead set on textualizing these differences, and in Teresa de la Parra, Dulce María Loynaz, and Gioconda Belli, they come very close to race. But ethnicity, like gender, goes beyond physiology and biology. Since they imply culture, they cause havoc and set the whole conceptual world awry. For calling them cultures and making them into epistemes is already to transform them into something else. In these texts culture carries a very fixed meaning. It evokes metropolitan areas, almost invariably Europe and most specifically France, with its touch of Orientalism, as either Darío or Said have articulated it. Culture means books and learning, poetry, table manners, taste as in wine, food, and clothing; it means sensibility as in racism and in the fabrication of myths, including that of culture itself, with its industry and technique. It is not what it means in ethnology, in the areas of marginality, oddity, poverty, mores, habits, patterns of daily life. Calling gender and ethnicity culture is, then, for dominant epistemologies, to invoke entropy. As in the case of the concept of *desalambrar,* to disarticulate this well-established and normed universe of meaning is quite a task. Nothing ensures that my reader will not read ethnicity as race—for instance, that culture will not be automatically replaced by biology in an unconscious renaturalizing of discrimination.

Aside from ethnicity there is the idea that woman has no country. It is distressing for me to call this fiction or imagining, because for me it is not fiction, although it has been written into fiction and is debated through fiction. Catharine Mackinnon, for instance, is one who has much to say on the subject. Citizenship, as a legally constituted condition, is at stake here, and for us, women, citizenship begins at the level of legalized biology, in the recognition of the full control of our bodies, and this is what I see these women writers adamantly arguing for.

At the level of "body" politics, all hell breaks loose. Teresa de la Parra, for instance, fiercely argues the ideas of marriage, inheritance, and wealth in her book, such as they relate to the ties that bind women, men, and the state. She discusses women's access to education and to the practice of the liberal professions. Jean Rhys' discussion of patrimony, land and nationality, *arraigo,* one's rooting in one's own place, and English law fall directly into our purview: her turf a debate on nations as they relate to each other and to women as registered in the books of law. Belli's insistence on women's participation in the military struggle prior to the seizing of state power by the revolutionaries reveals the perception that women's place within the newly constituted state, "at home and in the senate," is decided then and there. And indirectly Loynaz' protagonist's solitude, and Schwarz-Bart's portrayal of abandonment, desertion, and dereliction is related to the way in which women see themselves in consonance or dissonance with the constituted or unconstituted state, and the state's administration of its laws. "House," "garden," and "nation," then, constitute some of the terms a disenfranchised majority employ to enter the ongoing struggle and to signal the appropriation by women of ever-larger social spaces in the organization and reorganization of privatized spaces and in the territorial administration of the globe.

PART I

Gender/Genre/Nation/Ethnicity

The Masculine

1 / Transitions

Modernism/Modernity

The texts of Rómulo Gallegos and José Eustasio Rivera, as well as the texts of Ricardo Güiraldes, speak of a geography without limits. Across vast and ill-charted plains, at high altitudes where the lines of the horizon can barely be discerned, in regions populated by cunning natives, disturbed only by the thunder of enormous herds and limited at their borders by the human frontier of ethnicity, the nation-states are postulated at the beginning of the century. The lights of Modernism begin to flicker. If in Rivera the signs of a modernist aesthetics first scintillate, in Gallegos only the final gleamings can be discerned. This shift in semantic planes we call transition.

The feminine boudoir of Mercedes Galindo and its Oriental flavor in Teresa de la Parra; the Parisian taste her wardrobe displays; the languid, sensual posture she adopts on a divan; and her well-appointed dinners and her Baccarat glassware all recall a modernist aesthetics. But the after-dinner conversations on oil extraction, marriages of convenience, and alliances between professionals, *hacendatarios,* and founding fathers already belong to the horizon of Modernity. This shift is also an index of transition.

Transition is thus a generous concept. For when the impoverished daughters of the original plantocracy, without a name or recourse to the law, are taken hostage to the metropolis; when they languish in solitude in gardens reverting to jungle; when women of porcelain and women of ebony[1] occupy the same discursive plane, and the daughters of the "commercial bourgeoisie" are shot by the army, we are also facing a transition.

The Spirit of the Law

Transition is the limit and the threshold: it is a border, a deep divide between two alternative modes of thinking, affecting one's self, the world, conversations, kinship and labor relations, table manners, peasant behavior, and the words appropriate to addressing subalterns. But it can also be a wound, a deep wound, an amputation, bloodshed.

Insofar as it postulates change, transition is related to utopia. It articulates desire and hope. This century has developed around utopian ideas of social health, "progress," and/or social justice, ideas of revolution. In the horizon of literary modernity at the beginning of the century, in Gallegos for instance, to progress is to civilize. Progress and civilization constitute a copula. The history plotted in *Doña Bárbara* is the history of an obsession: to civilize is to tame, to vanquish, to coordinate, to kill—in short, to constitute the masculine agencies that support rational production, progress. The Neo-Positivist spirit of Santos Luzardo, the hero of *Doña Bárbara,* pronounces itself against all barriers to progress and civilization: idleness, barbarianism, the misuse of time (capital), the stagnating and unproductive accumulation of money, the mismanagement of land and its wealth, and the poor habits of the labor sector—in short, all that comes to impede the primitive accumulation of capital.

The concepts of progress and civilization also imply the displacements of hierarchies and hegemonies (men/women, master/peon, white/mestizo, mestizo/indigenous peoples). *Doña Bárbara* diagnoses the problem, and the prognosis for recovery invokes the spirit of the law as mediation. To rewrite and to recodify the law is the only way to regulate the exchange between the unequal terms of the social equation. In Gallegos, the judicial argument is the vehicle for administering progress and civilization, the dominant discourse in the constitution of the productive nation. The plains of Arauca are the geography on which matters of property are proven; and the plains' extension, government, yields.

Here, two problems of Neo-Positivistic, liberal desire will be addressed: to make civil law valid over custom, and, consequently, to reconceptualize legal prose—sales, litigations, territorial extensions, accounting—as an interaction between master and peon. The concepts of "custom" and "law and order" are thus recast. As Hobsbawm has argued, customs, the mundanities organizing everyday life among the subject-peoples (women, peons, mestizos, indigenous peoples), the residual cultural norms of ethnic groups vanquished in the constitution of nation-states, are recast as folklore; and law and order, the means to transition, are incorporated into the newly modified structures of government. The method of personally exercising authority and exacting punishment on the flesh of the subaltern by administrators in societies of extraction (plantations and mines) is replaced by the depersonalized forces of the army, the custodians of frontiers (borders and limits as geographic and legal concepts) for the nation-state.

Governing and government are politico-economic concepts. Politically, they rest in the army; economically, they are understood through the paradigms of development and underdevelopment. In terms of the conceptualization of spaces and institutions of organization and control, "transition" could then also be understood as a euphemism for development. The nonnegotiable term in the transition to modernity is thus progress constituted as civilization. To advance. To move forward. To reach. In Daniel Lerner's paraphrase of Marx's thought, it is the fact that "more and more developed societies present to less developed ones the image of their own future" (Schiller, 140).

Productivity is progress. It is politically legislated civilization, the constituted state or the state about to be constituted, that which regulates the social behavior of productive beings. Santos proposes to fence, to shoe, to order and educate as conditions of progress. Reading Santos against the grain, it can be argued that progress is the institutionalization of society through a series of dualities: men's hegemony over women, the master over the peon, whites over other ethnic groups. The metaphor signifying transition is inscribed in woman in masculine terms: in the heroine doña Bárbara as repression/dictatorship, and in Marisela as affection/democracy. On the bodies of women, class, ethnicity, and gender converge.[2]

The transition to modernity is, then, not only the articulation of desire, the constitution of national projects, the proposing of programs; it is also a method. A close reading of Santos' strategic activities reveals Gallegos' reliance on the culture of the oligarchy as the paradigm of civilizing culture, on elegant speech as a method of progress. In his grammar, phrasing, and vocabulary, in his knowing how to speak well, and in the "respect toward others" latent in his words rest his superiority over the whole peonry. His impeccable culture is a weapon for defeating the concept of power envisioned by the subaltern groups. The educated voice of the white man is thus to be established as hegemonic in the social and literary text. From polished oligarchic white men's speech norms are established. Bad behavior, pride, cunning, and bad government are defined as progress' adversaries. The internal market where all possibilities are negotiated becomes, in this new light, chaos and disorder, and barbarianism (the culture of indigenous peoples, women, peons, mestizos—the irrationality of centaurs) is constituted as its limit. Barbarianism as a signifying chain must be codified, and norms and pathologies established in race and blood, as in the indigenous peoples'; in feelings, as in women's; in pride, banality, and manliness, as in deviant subaltern behavior; in avarice, as in money that does not produce capital. Indigenous people, cantankerous women, laborers, and the oligarchy must be rewritten according to the new spirit of the law.

To Civilize—To Progress/To Kill

These structural modifications imply from the very beginning a reimagining of space and place, a geography, a people. A few days after arriving at the Altamira cattle ranch, Santos Luzardo visits his cousin Lorenzo and offers his friendship. In this conversation between two cousins, a drastic split in the oligarchic conceptualization of the nation takes place and a transition between a before and an after, a pre- and a post-, is established. The dialogue between the two men, one a lawyer and the other a doctor, seals a family reconciliation. The family bond is written as a metaphor when Lorenzo, speaking from the bosom of the medical profession, advises Santos to kill. The discursive field here registers modern and ancient epistemologies as oppositions in the binary "plain/city" as much as in "barbarianism/civilization."

The principle of change (progress/civilization) along with the advice to kill as male bonding are inscribed as memory, as writing, and as history and ideology. Lorenzo's patriotic speech commemorating independence embodies the will to kill, and so the terms of transition as a military concept are established. Significantly, the mythical figure of the centaur, an indigenous interpretation of the Spanish invaders now reversed and extrapolated to define the inferiority of the mestizo peonry and the indigenous peoples themselves, is the axis on which the passage between literary/textual Modernism and economic modernity turns. The centaur as self (in the self of ethnic groups signaled by the narratives) is the semantic plane in which the discourse of history is filed:

> [T]he centaur is barbarianism and, therefore, we must be done with it. I knew then that with that theory, which proclaimed an orientation more useful to our national history, you have created a scandal among the traditionalists of the epic, and I had the satisfaction of rati-

fying that your ideas had created a new epoch in the manner in which our *independentista* history was evaluated. I was already of an age to understand the thesis, and felt and thought in agreement with you. (Gallegos, 69–70)

Addressing each other in the familiar, the consensus among "us," as well as the distance between "us" and "them," is established. The discourse on the centaur illustrates the split between traditionalism and modernity, between "him" as a metonym (him = men and women) and "him" as a metaphor (him = him), between the interpretation of the new and the old histories, between a modernist aesthetics and a modernizing one, between beauty and utility. Nation, in its transition to modernity, is overwhelmingly an economic concept. But the distinction between traditionalists and moderns marks yet another split: the disagreement over historical hermeneutics, the interpretation of the historical fact of Independence.

Here a gap between the Venezuelan men and women writing the nation opens up. The voice of Teresa de la Parra represents, in women's writing, the space previously held by the "traditionalists of the epic," a movement toward the conservative in this historical discourse.[3] *Mantuana*, an aristocrat, a defender of her clan, of her relatives, the orientation which, in her, contributes to modernity, is not found at the ethnic-group level, nor at the level of the nation, but at the level of gender. In her *Ifigenia*, Teresa de la Parra moves the concept of barbarianism from mythology (the centaur) to law (regulating feelings); from aesthetics (*Doña Bárbara*), to the spirit and the letter of the law, the civil code. She collapses the mythologic and the generic, placing legalized male barbarity, marriages of convenience, and benefits for the nation-state on the same plane. The name of Ifigenia, is, in this sense, as telling as that of doña Bárbara. In the figures of these two women and the mechanics of their construction, the polemics of gender, ethnicity, and nation in times of transition in Venezuela are embodied.

From the Beautiful to the Utilitarian

At the beginning of this century, the process of transition toward modernization in the cultural arena was designed through an enlightened, positivist epistemology that ideologically willed to modernize. According to Subercaseaux, it expressed itself

> economically by structural incorporation into the capitalist world market, socially by massive immigration and the presence of new

actors, and politically by the inauguration of theoretically liberal re-
gimes, which in practice were strongly restrictive. (145)

The mid-century revolutionary processes were oriented by the principles
of Marxist epistemology, which proposed a change of the social agents in
power, a state-owned economy, and a struggle against imperialism. This
was illustrated by the revolutionary thinking inscribed in testimonial texts.
In this sense, in the first transition,

> the liberal and enlightened elites fulfilled a fundamental role. Besides
> being carriers of the ideology of lay-progressivism, and of economic
> liberalism, they mediated between Frenchification (and Europeaniza-
> tion) in the most diverse realms: fashion, languages, food, art, de-
> sign . . . [a] project which, in the last instance, pretended to model
> society in the image, and to the liking, of the norms and values that
> that very same sector paraded. (174)

And in the second transition, the wretched of the earth, as Fanon will
call them, or the semi-proletariat, constituted the social agent. Its enormous, volatile potential in poor, peripheral, or developing societies, given
the productive profile of such societies, was responsible for revolutionary
projects to reformulate, in a "profound manner,"

> the external articulation of their respective societies, and to increase
> the capacity of political self-determination of the nation-state. Social
> revolutions . . . always group three basic questions: transformation
> and economic development, democratization of political institutions
> . . . [and] national self-determination; for this reason . . . they involve
> an ample spectrum of classes and social groups. (Vilas 1986: 18)

Dilettantish, sybaritic, consumer-oriented, frivolous, urban, acratic, orientalist, *fin-de-siècle,* the Modernism of Mercedes Galindo and María
Eugenia Alonso represented by Teresa de la Parra does not avoid polemi-
cizing against the dictums of masculinist modernization, with its emphasis
on labor, savings, productivity, and science and technology. In the merely
economic sense, elements of this argument could be incorporated into the
debate on the second transition of the century. Speaking of Modernism
in the voice of his generation at mid-century, Angel Rama actualized this
counterposition. Referring concretely to the life of the artist and the split
between material life and literary creation, he considered the incursions
of transnational capitalism into the economy detrimental to artistic pro-

duction and dissemination, and gave us a concrete example in the case of Rubén Darío (Rama 1970, *passim*).

In this same spirit, in his book Subercaseaux rescues a thought according to which Modernism formed a part of the

> great *fin-de-siècle* controversy between utilitarian and mercantile modernism which does not leave a space for "the life of the soul," [a position] that conceived art and beauty as the foundation of an urgent and necessary spiritual renovation. (179)

Feminist narratives were not alienated by this discussion even though they differed in their wording. The polemics of Galindo and Alonso against the rest of society, which serves us here as a paradigm, could be spoken of in these precise terms. The discussion of the transition toward modern statehood on the basis of modern-versus-ancient habits, and the construction of the modern nation, can be seen even in the much-mediated case of the debate over England in Jean Rhys. England as a constituted nation, as a political fact, as a spirit of the law for the colonizer, as an invention in the social imaginary of the colonized, and as a forum for discussion of the dowry (English man-Caribbean woman—which invokes the mediation of the spirit of English law) can all be read in terms of the upsurge of nation-states in the Caribbean, in their secularization and entrance into modernity.[4] As I will argue later, modernization in the Caribbean possessions of France is plotted around Africa, an Africa constituted very differently from the Africa at the beginning of the century. In many ways the literary reconstruction of a mythologized, tribalized Africa comes coupled with the signs of visible change—in the introduction, for example, of electricity and drinking water into the huts of the peasantry in Guadeloupe.

The controversy between the desire to follow the road of developed societies versus the awareness of the social costs that such a choice entails appears in women's literature of the twenties and thirties as conservatism, as an adhering to the concept of the fatherland of the *Independentista* generals. In the particular cases of Venezuela and Cuba, it appears as an affirmation of the spirit of Bolívar and Martí, as a prolongation of the spirit of independence, and in the person of the *aristos*. Disenchantment in Loynaz' *Jardín*, for instance, could be attributed to a rejection of the outcome of the struggle between minor and major founding fathers, the minor being the *Machadato*, who negotiated the Republic differently from the manner in which it was conceived by the major, the *Independentistas* of '98, several of whom—Generals Loynaz, Mendez, and Cabrera—retired from public

life and returned to the practice of their liberal professions.[5] And even Gioconda Belli, whose radical horizon is more evident in creating the figure of
the grandfather, returns to the border of the *fin-de-siècle* and deposits in
his person socialist utopian thinking: a world of "benevolent" landowners
who desire a different order based on "distributive" class harmony.

The conceptualization of the nature of the state is what ultimately seems
to be in question in all these writings. Ethnicity (or gender, for that matter),
as an agent of change, is not in itself sufficient to explain the normative
process of such polyclassist phenomena.[6] As before, in reading Gallegos,
to imagine a world in which everything is changed (for the better) implies
a rethinking of macro, mundane questions such as the type of state and its
legislation, the form of government, property statutes, and codes.[7]

Seen from the point of view of the nation-state, transition can be limited
to its political meaning and refer to a change in form of government, the
change from dictatorship to "democracy," for example. At the beginning
of the century, this proposition was formulated as a dilemma, as a position
against *caciquismo*, against the abuses of the paramilitary groups and their
cabecillas left stranded after the war of Independence.[8] Lacking legitimized
state power, we see them cross the literary text searching for territoriality,
a search manifested in the taking of land and of power over people. They
are the feared mestizos of de la Parra, of the nation-building novels.

But the transitional change can also be understood in its productive
meaning as formulating a change of systems, for instance the transition
from capitalism to socialism (cum communism). In the middle of the century, texts registered the entrance of the mountain men, the bearded ones
who banished themselves to the forest to conceive "the new man" and plot
the takeover of the nation-state. This new social subject repeats the history
of his ancestors in indigenous and black maroonage and propels them from
the borders of the plain, the high plateaus, or the terrifying wilderness, to
situate them at the center.

States/Zones/Populations

In the decade of the twenties, José Eustasio Rivera, Colombian writer
and inspector of oil fields, member of the commission to mark the frontiers between Colombia and Venezuela, published his novel *La Vorágine*.
According to the critical tradition—Angel Rama, Rodríguez Monegal,
Ernesto Mejía Sánchez, Anderson Imbert[9]—this novel, together with those
of Gallegos and Güiraldes, marked the birth of an Americanist tradition in
Latin American literature.

Reading *La Vorágine* as *testimonio,* we find a narrativization of nation as country, and consequently of the Americanist tradition of the nation-building novels as a moment in the historical constitution of the nation within the realm of modernization.

In this first horizon, the horizon of modernization, the limits Rivera traces between zones call attention to themselves. A zone is defined insofar as it comes close to or moves further away from central power, as the relative presence or absence of government and law. A zone is also constituted in terms of a productive character and the capacity to generate cultural practices. The ensemble of zones forms a coherent image of a multilingual, multiethnic nation, with common habits, which by adding and constituting and constructing narratives begins to form the male image, or the meaning that men make of nation.

To this wide and heterogenous territoriality, the designation "nation" can tentatively be given simply because the narrative "I" has two points of reference clearly defined: (1) the remote and faraway city, the capital, Bogota, and (2) the constituted government. But in its variety, as much geographic as ethnic, the vacillation over the limits to which this nation is confined becomes visible. The (capital) city, Casanaré, La Maporita, the plains (savannahs), the river (the indigenous people), and the wilderness are in the style of regions, provinces, districts, and counties that, as I have said, denote not only the heterogeneity of the nation but also, for that very same reason, the difficulties in constituting it as a coherent totality. Together the ensemble achieves the status of what Benedict Anderson has called an "imagined community" (46–49).

I have given these spaces a variety of names in order to distinguish them from each other, to evoke a series of referents, and to signal their status as spaces and frontiers, limits and beyonds, in which aesthetic and national identity is in the process of constituting itself. The macroworld, the macro-space, the place of the macronarrative, is put together as a matter of course, beginning with the concept of horizon within the geographical terrain, a territoriality. Nature is the assigned hegemonic term in the constitution of the nation simply because liberal criticism has emphasized its natural character, wilderness and land.

But in *La Vorágine,* other limits are clearly distinguishable. They are inevitably inextricable from the geographical, and they are always concerned with the constitution of a concept of nation: the family of Arturo Cova, the (white) protagonist, lives in the city, and his living in the city is invoked as lineage—a hypogram made up of house, the garden close to the room, the son's wetnurse, and literary success. The concept of nation as (white) ethnicity, ascendancy, rank, tied to family and the city of Bogota, however, already distinguishes itself from the concept of the lineage of the founding fathers, represented, let us say, in *Sangre Patricia* by Manuel Díaz Rodríguez, but it also moves further away from the indigenous peoples. The indigenous people are represented as a hunted animal and confused with wilderness. He is at the other extreme of the concept of nation, as excluded from, or a problematization of, nation. The "Indian" is the bush/wilderness, at best the guide in the wilderness—even in guerilla literature. Wilderness is the end, the horizon, the limit, the border of the plain.

The plain and the river (El Vichada) are two contradictory terms of territoriality, equivalent to those of ethnicity. The plain is the place of the native (already a mestizo); the country, as in *pays* and country, a geography and social organization not yet part of the state. On the plain, Arturo Cova (urban, citizen) learns to be a man, learns to desire as wife a woman who was his mistress, and dreams of building his house (as in woman, a nation)—another territoriality, another concept of the family unit, and another frontier. He dreams of these

> fascinating plains, living with Alicia in a smiling house, which he will raise with his own hands on the bank of a creek. . . . There, in the afternoon, the cattle will be gathered, and I, smoking on the threshold as a primitive patriarch, my bosom softened by the melancholy, I will see the sunset on the remote horizon. . . . I would limit my desire, my wish to take care of the land my eyes survey, my pleasure in peasant labor, to my consonance with solitude. The cities, what for; perhaps the fountain of poetry was in the secret of the untouched forests, in the caress of the winds, in the unknown language of things. (Rivera, 103)

There is, naturally, a feminine sensibility akin to de la Parra's and Rhys' in the contemplation of nature as country, a conceptualization Belli cites and discards in her first novel, but bends to reproduce in the second. The position of the subject contemplating this nature is lyrical, poetic, literary. It is, of course, as Raymond Williams suggests, the vision of those who see it and not of those who labor upon it, or what is the same, of the one who enjoys it and profits from it. In the case of women, it is melancholic memories, folklore, that is, remnants of the marginal culture that survive as a reminder of the decimated groups (indigenous peons who cultivated their fields and provided luxurious life-styles, a pastoral); and in the case of men, as a locus of desire (indigenous peoples and peons to be broken into productive agricultural workers to accumulate capital). In both cases it is the position of the owner, and, for that reason, poetic. Nature as landscape, we could almost say as garden.

Nevertheless, in all cases, the meaning of the nation is modern. On the narrative margins, the recognition of the state, of the political body that represents the supreme center, a government in common and a constituted territory, is being admitted and confirmed, albeit precariously, by the literature of this same decentralized state and its inhabitants, conceived, with some difficulty, as a totality. The equation that liberal thinkers, according to Hobsbawm, make between nation, state, and people (sovereign) ties nation to territory. In the narratives of the beginning of the century, the definition of the state is essentially territorial, and must therefore be consolidated on the geographical terrain. As in the case of European states annexing other European states, assimilating the smaller into the bigger, the Latin American nations initiate a process in which the macrostate and the macroculture swallow up the microcultures, and in which the diverse ethnolinguistic units (constituted as culture or as ethnicities) are incorporated into the nation.

The three notions of the constitution of the nation pointed out by the English historian have been fulfilled. First, there is the union of nation and state, coterminous with the appropriation of the people who inhabit it, constituting the state as people. Second, there is the establishment of a cultural elite with a written national literature enforcing the vernacular, reducing everything that is not of the dominant ethnolinguistic group to the category of folklore or ethnicity. And third, there is the proven capacity for conquest—a proof, according to the British, of the evolutionary success of the social species. Nation as progress was equivalent to the assimilation of the smaller communities into the larger. Nation thus represents in human societies a stage of human development. To establish this particular nation-state is to demonstate an aptitude for evolution and historical progress.

Seen from the perspective of the constituted state and the spirit of the law, we have in Rómulo Gallegos the classic case of a male narrative of the transition to modernity. More within the perspective of the landlord, Gallegos metaphorizes the nation, as the Altamira cattle ranch (private property) situated in Arauco (region = country), and the families (Luzardo and Barquero = the law). For these reasons all the major conflicts and tensions of *Doña Bárbara* occur around private property, its extent, and its government. When there is some misunderstanding over questions of heritage and borders, the family resolves them.

Under the *cacicazgo,* the family is the fountain of law and fulfills the functions of the state. In the modern state, the law is represented by its interpreters. But *ab initio* the interpreters are members of the founding families. Santos Luzardo is a lawyer and Santos' grandfather, El Cunavichero, was a *cacique* and a *montonero.* As the process of modernization deepens, the system takes, and there is an abundance of lawyers mediating between the state and the individual, interpreting the spirit of the law to the benefit of property owners. In this moment, the moment of *Doña Bárbara,* the family clans are in the process of being displaced as a source of law, and the family ceases to be directly constituted as a metonym for the state, even though the fountain generating law continues to be private property.

For these reasons, modern state-building deconstructs its metonyms: cattle ranch = plain = country = rent = family = affection = nation. Property represents at the same time the soul of the plain and rent; capital, or the soul of the plain and feelings, as well as the family, constitutes nationality as well. The cattle ranch itself will be reconstituted and defined as a productive unit, as a center generating capital and surplus value. The fundamental shift is not readily apparent, for what is in question is changing the concept of rent for the concept of surplus value (from idle property to productive property), for which it is necessary to remodel the social landscape and, above all, to stop "enriching" the overseers, the administrators of the cattle ranch, in the absence of its owners.

The overseers are now held responsible for unproductive idleness. They are, like the attorneys and agents administering the English plantations of the Caribbean, scapegoats for the irresponsibility and absenteeism of the owners. But the real reason for the growing antipathy is that the overseer, more so in the case of the representation of the nation as private property, implies the constitution of another social, and in some cases ethnic, group.

The values attached to the formation of this new social group are displaced from economy to ethics—hence the concept of honesty that tarnishes the semantic field, of not touching what is not yours, articulated also in monogamy and virginity. Honesty and fairness in poor men means working for others without asking for just compensation. It is to keep, meaning to maintain and guard, what others have and what one does not. In this sense it comes close, and is related to, subalternity. The concept of the administrator is going to change. The administrator is no longer placed at the center of economic productivity. The transformation of land into productive private property now directly concerns the owner. Thus the formation of the national bourgeoisie begins.

In this masculinization of the state and its metaphors, doña Bárbara poses a question to be solved. As a woman and as a mestiza, she is one of the central poles. On one side is the nation and on the other, Barbarita. Bárbara is a hypogram; she is labor, desire for wealth, sexual cravings, feelings, profit, virgin land, plain. However, in spite of her apparent clarity, her figure is much more obscure than that of Santos. Constituted as desire and rape, as lack of love and feeling, repression and desire (the symbolism of country and plain) converge in her. Plain and Bárbara carry identical adjectivation; they are one and the same. Doña Bárbara is, then, on the one hand, a concretization of a masculinist feminine sexuality, a fear of women, as in the myth of the guiablesse in Schwarz-Bart with all her incantations. She is also a masculinized woman, one in whom heterosexuality is very much in question; perhaps she doesn't like men—that is, perhaps she is a-sexuated; perhaps she likes women. She is a syncretic being who unites, at the symbolic level, a feminine sexuality rendered masculine by men, and the eroticization of force and masculine virility. She is also the exacerbation of a fear of losing power, of a surrender before sensuality called "lechery." The sensual feminine in the masculine imaginary is a vortex, *La Vorágine*, untamed nature, wilderness, not power. A man's desire for women is his worst enemy, a paradoxical sign of men's weakness, coupling the sensual (lechery) and territoriality, sensuality (lechery) and privatization.

The hatred that she embodies (woman/devourer/doña Bárbara, the feminine masculinized) is the uncontrollable desire for territorial accumulation both as nation-formation and as private property, in the form of latifundia. The loss of emotional control is coupled with the loss of economic power, and with this, in turn, political danger. For by her own means Barbarita has attained the co-optation of the state, and she has made it work for her. Her image represents all these and more: the taking of economic control by the mestizo and the implantation of a mestizo culture, which, for whites, real or imagined, is equivalent, without any question, to barbarianism. When the mestiza controls the state and becomes Cacica del Arauco, that is, Law, men tremble. Bárbara, on the other hand, represents tradition. It is through an indiscriminate and brutal takeover of lands, a lack of respect for fencing, that great cattle ranches and great landlords are formed. Thus it was that, like doña Bárbara, El Cunavichero, Santos' grandfather, formed his patrimony. And Luzardo is afraid that she, woman, possesses "the same vices as entrepreneurial men."

Nature/Indigenous Peoples: From Ideals of Progress and Civilization to Ideals of Sovereignty and Social Justice

A simultaneous reading of Central American guerrilla and testimonial literature marks the break in a reformulation of nature establishing the horizons between the "liberal" sensibility of José Eustasio Rivera and the "revolutionary" sensibility of Omar Cabezas, Tomás Borge, Mario Payeras. . . . Wilderness in the former was represented as state eating state and as globalization. In Rivera's own definition of nation, insofar as it was indigenous, wilderness was not only an obligatory national frontier but the border of the nation imposed by the transnational rubber plantations. In national terms the plain, the savannahs, the grasslands, the ensemble of cattle, and the ensemble of peons are greater than the wilderness. La Maporita (already a place and not the wilderness) represents nation, occupied by more "modern" concepts of space. In contrast, in testimonial guerrilla literature, mainly in Central America, the road is inverse. As a place unexplored and uninhabited by the enunciating subject, the mountain, substituting wilderness, is the space that comes to define an initial national moment. Later guerrilla literature changes its route to testimonialize the city. The mountain is also adventure and emotion. As a dream and from the city, this is the way this realm is projected. Up close, it is "dense bush you cannot penetrate" (Cabezas 1982: 28). It is counterpositioned between the enunciating subject and the enunciation, for the peasant can walk through. For his mountain is not for him "a wall . . . a great obstacle . . . fucking grassland . . . but small mountains the size of this house, not yet immense trees" (67, 68). As in the earlier narrative, the encounter is strange: it causes disgust, irritates, changes personalities, and alters the relationships between people.

A distinction between genres is pertinent here. In contrast with novels, it is said that testimonials

> document spheres of reality . . . that dominant discourse usually ignores, hides, or falsifies, and what is at stake is to restore and explore, to insert them in the absences and the blind spots of the social discourse, dominant or not . . . [and that] the subject of enunciation is usually at the same time a witness and an actor. (Perus, 134)

What is argued here, then, is that there is not only a split in the structure of the discourse (dominant versus marginal, novels as testimonials) but also

in the position of the subject. The concept of frontier, however, is similar
in both. What is added to the natural definition is that the mountain is not
only an immense green steppe, nature, but something larger. That "something larger" could, in the first instance, be a myth, the myth of power, of
the unknown and of the mysterious, a symbol of the new nation and of the
constitution of the new nation-state and revolutionary power.

This nature is not yet a poetic object. It is not postulated as the contemplation of the spirit, or as the projection of a subjectivity, as in *La Vorágine*,
but as a terrain traversed by obligation, a place still inhabited by discipline,
a uterus in which the new man and the new nationality gestate. For that
reason common language simulates difficulty with rhetoric or erudition:
trees are trees, bush is bush, big is big, and small is small. There is no attempt to metaphorize, for what is described is not nature but the effort and
human will:

> [so] dense you cannot see the ground, neither can you see the sky, or the
> treetops appear to kiss each other; and the rains continue, beginning
> before we start. (Cabezas 1982: 71)

In testimonial literature, nation is land and territory together with the
transformation of man. A space fit first to acculturate oneself, to season
oneself, to know the terrain, to tread on it as if it is one's own:

> I didn't hear any noises, except those of the . . . mountain; I learned
> to distinguish clearly a strength as when a fruit falls in the mountain,
> when it falls to the ground from a tree, as the noise of the wind when
> it comes from afar, and comes closer and then passes, and then when
> it passes by where you are, the current of wind and its distance . . .
> or the sound of a woodpecker, the footfalls of a squirrel, when a cow
> walks, or when a bird is scared by another animal, or the noise of
> water when it rains far away. . . . The same happens to your sight on
> seeing the same so much. I knew by heart all the trees, their forms, the
> shades, the effects of light that at different hours are projected within
> the mountain. . . . The same with smell, you learned to smell every-
> thing. . . . But the mountain is only a school where many *compañeros*
> of the city will come to form themselves and then they will have to go
> down. (1982: 153)

This speaking voice is that of the mestizo of de la Parra's horizon, come
into the land of the indigenous people at his own invitation. There is primi-
tivism, a return to the original and then to communication with nature as

school and learning. But mountain is also that piece of unknown country: a territory only pro forma incorporated into the nation, inhabited only by residual people, indigenous people and peasants. In this sense, Payeras' enumeration is one of the more comprehensive. The indigenous people

> form a numerous familiar nucleus of self-consumers, isolated by many hours walk from the closest market. . . . Throughout the years they built the basis of a self-sustaining economy . . . [which] reduced itself to the production of corn and a bit of sugar cane and plantain around their houses, and some grains and fruits. . . . The large majority of their household artifacts were made by them. . . . Money was obtained through the production of straw in the mountains of the zone. This form of production had its psychology and simplified their vision of the world. For them, men did not differentiate themselves in relation to material goods, but more by language and customs. . . . The existence of only one or two surnames in those mountains indicated how close they were to the gens society. . . . Knowing nothing more than a part of that small reality, they lost themselves in the particular and understood only with difficulty the general concept. (75)

Rigoberta Menchú gives ample evidence of this ethno-nation of which Payeras speaks, an ethno-nation which is at most an unincorporated part, a (precariously national) ethnicity, and which the new national horizon wants to incorporate as masses.[10] But these indigenous people are not seen from the liberal perspective; they are not the small units who can be devoured by the large ones. They are precisely the opposite.

Patria Is a Question of Balls

Well, guys, what is Nicaragua's problem? Is it a question of men, of balls, or what?
Wait a minute! Problems of men and balls, we don't have.
What is it that you need then?
What we need is a bitch of a lot of weapons.
(Martínez, 214)

In this dialogue between the guerrilla commander Francisco Rivera, alias "the Fox," and General Torrijos, the revolutionary transition in the constitution of the new nation is immediately postulated as a male organ. As in the Neo-Positivistic horizon, which only showed men laboring arduously, in this dialogue the historical subject and his country are also constituted as a question of "grown up men" (45), of balls, the body organ par excellence, the metonym for the fatherland, the stud.

The revolutionary horizon desires liberation, independence. The non-negotiable terms are freedom and social justice. Consequently the nation's revolutionary transition is predicated on armed struggle. The revolutionary transition is a military fact undertaken exclusively by men. It proposes the integration of the nation as territory and geography into the nation as people and ethnicity. Ethnic groups have a place secured in the holy war of revolutionary narratives, for geography bestows a location for the guerrilla subject, and geography is ethnicity: "In some indigenous languages [Martínez cites Torrijos] 'I' is said 'here,' 'you' is said 'here,' 'he' is said 'there.' One identifies oneself with the place where we are, with this site, with the space one occupies" (Martínez, 56). People are a subject: an eye which looks at, and not an eye which is looked at. "Eye because it sees you, not because you see it," as Antonio Machado said (Martínez, 65).

Country, nation, and national subject are constituted simultaneously as ethnicity and as maleness in the history of male representation in testimonial literature. Later, as in Neo-Positivistic novels, this construction merges with the concept of the revolutionary intellectual and the creation of a new culture. The historical record as expression of desire has its space in letters. José de Jesús Martínez tells us that when General Torrijos discovered that he was trying to enter the army as a draftee, Torrijos commented that clearly Martínez "was looking for a theme for writing a novel" (Martínez, 19). In contrast to Gallegos, first as a novelist of a constituted state and later as a president of that state who knows that he has access to an ample discursive field, the men who write testimonials know that their prose is the only discourse witnessing the unconstituted state.

But to distinguish between "literature" and "reality," between "fiction" and "politics"—and I suppose also between the artistic and the ethical, the masculine and the feminine—Martínez draws again on heterosexual gender imagery: more than discovering reality, unveiling it, subtly raising the veil that covers it, as suggested by the Greek word for "truth," *aleteia*, which means "un-covering," he was "manfully falling upon it, penetrating it like a plough, to impregnate it with events" (34). And later he manfully asserts that "revolution is a question of men. Not of angels or faggots. Of men" (154). It is not surprising, then, that in the face of this masculine conceptualization of masculinity as a foundation in nation-building, during the morning drills the draftees sing the following couplets:

Por las buenas/o las malas
por razón/o por la fuerza
de huevo a huevo
soberanía o muerte.

[For better/for worse,
for reason/or by force
from ball to ball
sovereignty or death.]

Or

Viva, viva la jarana
a las seis de la mañana
Yo me culié a tu hermana
en casa de doña Juana

[Long live, live the spree
At six o' clock in the morning
I fucked your sister up the ass
In the house of doña Juana.]

The crudity with which the founding of the mestiza nation/fatherland on male genitalia is expressed leaves no doubt that the new nation is again predicated on the exclusion of women. Signed by the same inclusion of male anatomy as a metaphor or as a metonym, woman is not an essential constitutive element, or worse, if she is, she is included through the image of rape. However, this conceptualization puts the male/female relationship in a predicament, for we must remember that the nonnegotiable term of this transition is liberation. Thus, even if the phallocentric principle of testimonial writing is hegemonic, women travel in the geography of the revolutionary fatherland, and the principle of the feminine has at least a foot in the door, for liberation, freedom, and social justice willy-nilly also embrace gender. But, as I will argue later, since this concept of the feminine is defined on the basis of the masculine, it has its problems. As in Loynaz, women in guerrilla literature continue to be a memory, words in a letter, images on the glossy, printed paper of a photograph. Women are not given the textual freedom of becoming a "new woman." Yes, they are harangued in these matters, and yes, they are much appreciated when they acquire dexterity with weapons. But, as Martin Leinhardt says, the operation of writing is taking possession, and male writers are taking possession, recuperating the categories of thought (among them, women) inscribed in the cultural landscape.[11]

Payeras, for instance, mentions women a mere twelve times, only once in the plural—as women in arms—and the large majority are wives, *compañeras,* teachers, someone's wife, someone's girlfriend, sitting, or with a toothache. The only one who has a name is Tita Infante, because she is Che's girlfriend. Omar Cabezas mentions women fifty-nine times. As family members—wives, girlfriends, daughters, and mothers—they appear twenty times. The rest are anonymous beings: the little old lady, the woman fixing lunch, two despondent bourgeois women whose skin, fingernails, hands, and hair they like to look at, the feminine voters, the *compañeras,* the woman with an embittered face, 'new girls,' 'she whom we told that,' 'she who works there,' 'the fat ones with an apron,' 'the domestic ones,' nurses, teachers, 'the big-bellied woman.' Or they are known by given name and surname: Marta Harnecker, the *compañeras* Doris Tijerino, Gloria Campos, María Esperanza Valle, Tita, Monica Baltodano. Or as objects and expressions of desire: 'to be a hero of,' to 'not say anything like a woman;' 'there it's harder to light a fire than a woman;' the loneliness— 'they look like little women or faggots.' And as something to forget about— not to think about, more literally. Of all these expressions the only one that shifts is *compañera*. Like the sign /balls/, the sign /*compañeras*/ shifts, meaning comrade, as in arms, and sexuality, as in mistress, lover, wife.

The Fatherland: A Love Song for Men

The construction of the revolutionary fatherland as armed struggle excludes the principle of the feminine, or includes it tangentially, as a literary fact, as metaphor. In the words of a peasant, the image is of the Edenic couple: General Torrijos is not dead, he is "hiding in the mountain with a woman." In other words, woman, who will later be the mountain, physical geography, the site of insurgency/ethnicity, is in this citation the *compañera,* the couple, male sexuality within the womb of the guerrilla nation-state. But grammatically she is only an adjunct, a man's companion, family—this, as we saw, is the way she appears in the guerrilla texts.

The myth of the hero, the "man who never dies," the mountain as representation of nation, and of woman as adjunct, deputy, subaltern remains fixed in these images. Nature is still covered by men: "instead of seeing an enemy landscape, a hill that had killed him, I saw that General Torrijos had spread the wilderness, that he was everywhere and that he was everything"

(Martínez, 261). In the original Spanish, "to spread" is a synonym for "to spill," an expression for ejaculation.

The conflict between the masculine as a representation of the revolutionary nation and the feminine that is excluded from it tries to arrange itself, resolve itself, by means of two concepts: ethnicity and class, where supposedly woman is included.[12] For Martínez, Torrijos' thought was directed toward one single social category: that of the people. The poor and the people were, in his mind, one and the same. The indigenous people were something else; they were ethnics, the Other of one's self. Indigenous groups belong in the mountain, people in the city.

People have no sex. People have no nationality either. People have a trade. Women can sneak into this conceptualization of the people without being taken into account. This grammar is men's traditional way of coming to terms with an undesirable equality. Mountain people (men and women, peasants and indigenous people) are people without property to defend, without property onto which they can project their own egos, without property on which to posit their ideas of development, their national utopias. Mountain people have no territoriality. In the former horizon the mountain people as wilderness are the indigenous people as plain; they are the mestizos represented as peons and as fugitives, workers on cattle ranches belonging to whites, and persecuted by the law. The geography of the revolutionary transitional horizon at the middle of this century cannot therefore naively be established as an undisputed economic or legal fact. The geography of the mountain people is an armed geopolitics.

Within these highly diversified territorialities in which nation is understood as an armed struggle, the "new man" is wrought. And the "new man" is again understood as metaphor and metonym. The "new woman" is a "new man," a woman with balls, meaning a courageous woman, balls being the signifier of value, a *compañera*, as in comrade-in-arms. But since balls are also the masculine signifier par excellence, the term slides from one meaning to another to suit the convenience of male power: the conflict in the semanticization of a woman/man who must be—but cannot be—like Che also reminds us of the woman-man doña Bárbara embodied in the liberal horizon who must be—but cannot be—like Santos Luzardo. The new woman in the mountain has incorporated all the male attributes: she is a ballsy woman who is brave, ready, audacious—but she is not yet a man.

In Martínez the distinction between woman and guerrilla-woman, between woman and militant, already exists. Gender equality is predicated on the basis of political-military identification, and the political-military i.d.

is male. In this connection several women are mentioned by name, since military comrades deserve to be mentioned by name in the revolutionary unit. Women appear as respectable examples in the text only when they are mentioned as political-military subjects. In several cases their rank in the army of the poor is respected. Miss Guatemala, for instance, is "a very beautiful university girl, as much on the outside as inside, for she was in the left" (115). Of guerrilla leader Ana Guadalupe, Martínez says she is sweet with the sweetness that guerrilla women have. And of Patricia Hearst, he says that she is "an interesting woman. . . . Small, very pretty, and very intelligent. I remember that one time she asked to see my machine gun and she disarmed and armed it with professional dexterity" (220). He naturally admires this surprising delicacy among "those women who know how to hold weapons" (243).

Beauty in women is never superceded; it is always an object of male desire. Doña Bárbara is a very handsome woman. And women's sweetness and tenderness are qualities guerrilla men want to incorporate into themselves. This is apparent in Omar Cabezas' testimonial *Canto de amor para los hombres* (A Song of Love for Men) (1989). Desire in men is postulated as feminine. But in this new masculine rapprochement with the feminine, the principle of women's rebellion is recognized as valid only if it is framed by the group organization.

There is an attempt to distinguish between the feminine and woman in these texts of revolutionary transition, but the distinction is not an easy one. Women and the feminine are a riddle. The embodiment of Woman itself is no longer folklore, whether she is a guerrilla fighter, a popular woman, an Indian, a beauty queen, or a true queen like a Farah Diva, "natural, modern, easy to be jealous about." But the feminine continues to be an ironic object and an object to be disqualified, a metaphor for men's uncontrollable desire for women. We will see in Schwarz-Bart the feminine expressed as desire/terror, a fear in men of their own feminization. Sensitizing oneself is tied to impotence, that is, to the loss of power. The counterposition of native woman and foreign woman, or porcelain woman and ivory and ebony woman, also intensifies the narrative of gender. The place of distinction occupied by the women of the founding families in the former transition is taken by foreign women who come to replace them in mestizo republics. Remember that in *Memories of Underdevelopment* the German Anna was the paradigm for woman, overriding all other ideas of women including white, upper-class Laura, the protagonist's Cuban wife.[13]

The testimonial women are not the modernist women of alabaster and porcelain, but there is one who is, *compañera* Claudia Chomorro, whose pseudonym is Luisa. Because of her whiteness, she is called a Yankee. In Rivera's testimonial she is the only one physically described: "the peasants were astonished by her beauty. . . . Tall, blond, cat's eyes" (127). Throughout literature beauty is an attribute of whiteness. The admiration for white women as superior to colored women is clear in the textual privilege granted to her, even though beauty is politically qualified. She is beautiful even though her mentality

> pissed me off. . . . She was a high-life girl from the oligarchic Calle Atravesada families of Granada. . . . But she began to change. . . . Soon she abandoned all the habits of a spoiled lady, assimilating teachings. . . . Learning from everyone in conversations and discussions far advanced in military training. . . . After forgetting all her idiosyncracies, she held the peasant boys, and talked to the women in the huts, helping them with their tasks as if she had always been one of them . . . surprising everybody with her serenity and courage. . . . And I remember her now as a brave woman, decidedly heroic at the moment of combat and negating the moment of [her] dying, already wounded, to retire so that I would retire.
>
> . . . .
>
> That's why I insist that she was a woman the likes of whom have been few. Braver at the time of combat and at the time of death than many men I've known, and they have not been few, the ones I have known. (128, 131)

Male Sensibility

The testimonial that contains the definition of male sensibility consonant with the mountain is, however, the first text by Omar Cabezas, which defines what it means to be like El Che. The situation is classic and reminiscent of the tears of a Homeric hero, of Achilles for Patroclus, let us say. Crying is the act through which the protagonist of a military action finds the limit or limits of his troops, brigade, column, or army, and harangues: "you are little women . . . you are faggots, shitty little students, good for nothing" (106).

According to male sensibility, Tello, the commander who knows how to be strong, indomitable, how to push himself to the limit and cry, finds himself facing a rejection, a negative, established by the limits men define as physiological. They lack physical strength and their will is undermined. Tello changes his strategy and counterposes violence and denigration with persuasion, substituting the images of little women and faggots with the new man:

> "*Compañeros*," he says, "have you ever heard of the new man. . . ? And you know where the new man is? The new man is not in the future. . . . You know where he is? . . . He is there, on the fringe, on the top of the hill that we are climbing. . . . He is there, catch him, find him, look for him, get him. The new man is beyond the normal man. The new man is beyond our tired legs. . . . The new man is beyond our tired lungs. The new man is beyond hunger, beyond rain, beyond mosquitos, beyond solitude. The new man is there in the extra effort . . . where the normal man begins to give more than the common man . . . to forget fatigue, when he begins to negate himself." (106)

Naturally, newness is postulated here to overcome and castigate the body. It is the body, physical resistance, that has to be extended to survive in the inhospitable conditions of the mountain. Perhaps mental condition emerges as a corollary, the corollary of the extra effort; perhaps it is a precondition. In any case, there is a change in mental attitude, which has as an operative center the body in heavy training, in the mountain, in the terrain of war, in not being a woman, a faggot, an intellectual.

We have already noted that the birth of the new nation, the gestation of the new nation, is predicated on armed struggle. It is a military struggle. Its death-defying space in the first moment is the mountain, the heavy conditions that require definite physical fortitude as masculinity. Therefore armed struggle in the mountain is a question of men, or, as for General Torrijos, of balls. Consequently the sensibility to develop is in accord with it. If, as Gioconda Belli relates, at the time of repression men do not let themselves cry in the bedroom, in the mountain, even though it is forbidden, they do. The guerrillas express their essentially male sensibility in tears, visible only in the relationships among themselves, when a column or a member of the column surrenders to the effort he has put into it, when the group succeeds, or when a man falls:

> May 17, 1979, we say farewell for good . . . for this old, stubborn man, hard and dark, a cane cutter from his miserable childhood, a founder of the *Frente Sandinista*, fighter of a thousand battles, proletarian hero, curser and joker as only he himself could be, brave to the

limit, frank, transparent, whom nobody could shut up, was killed in the capture of Jinotega that he dreamed of. (Rivera, 244)

This is the way Rivera relates the death of El Danto. And, for his part, Omar Cabezas is overtaken by emotion on meeting his friend:

> It was about three in the morning and I approached the hammock of the Cat . . . and then I see the Cat's machine gun. . . . I place myself beside the Cat and I smell the same smell that I had, the smell in my backpack, the smell in my hammock and my blanket . . . and, let me tell you, I was nervous. For I didn't know if the Cat was going to be happy to see me, I didn't know if he was going to feel what I felt, and I was nervous, for I didn't know how he was going to react, for if the Cat only said "Hi!" to me. . . . Then, after a while during which I was observing the hammock and smelling the smells and inwardly remembering a thousand things to tell him: did you see what we got into, or did you see how far we have gone, I touch him, I tell him "Ventura . . . Ventura . . . Ventura," and the Cat wakes up; "Ah!" he says. "Ventura, it's me, Eugene." When I said "Eugene," the Cat rose up violently and then was still, sitting in the hammock, half-awake. . . . "Cat, it's me, Eugene," and I take his head like this in the dim light of the moon, and then he says . . . "Skinny one," he says, and he embraces me, and I embrace him and the Cat falls from the hammock and we fall embracing. (150)

The expression of sensibility is not related to woman, then. It is a developing sensibility, without being or corresponding to the change in sensibility that women argue for in men. Woman does not show disdain for sensibility itself as an expression of the heroic spirit, but asks for inner fortitude acquired through the recognition of personal vulnerability in the face of desire. In the recognition of emotions, such as they are, there is a sadness, fragility, vulnerability, powerlessness, tenderness, shyness. . . . It does not, then, have anything to do with physical fortitude, the physical resistance necessary for the mountain. But yes, it is articulated with the feelings of love that men manifest for men, for *compañeros*.

There is a way in which both sensibilities might coincide, in which extra effort could be based on transcending the emotional, after recognizing a sensibility as one's own and in a bodily discipline, after having acknowledged sensibility as a limit, and fragility. The development of male sensibility, or the feminization of man, has a correlative in the development of feminine independence, doubt reflected in the phrase "perhaps I was a man with the body of a woman. Perhaps I was half-man, half-woman" (Belli 1988: 122).

Belli's woman, like Schwarz-Bart's, suggests Plato's androgynous beings, his idea of the means, beginning with her change, her fracture, her weakening, her living in "the parallel world in which she was born," as "a romantic heroine from some novel," in this "false-bottomed city," and accepting that "to be born is taking a terrible chance." She had to become accustomed to being a trinity, three people in one: "one [person] for her friends and her job, another for the Movement, and a third for Felipe" (131). And finally, she is another person, "a woman in the middle of the national territory, a farm lost, abandoned to the ghosts, and to the dreamers ready to change the state of being, alert, a young Quixote with a lance at the ready (229).

Transition: The Language of the Social Sciences

In its political dimension, in the *fin-de-siècle* as much as on the revolutionary horizon, transition is a secularization. Insofar as it imagines the vanishing of the principle of centralized authority and precedes the institutionalization of open societies, transition could be considered a feminization. This is not Gino Germani's interpretation, however.[14] When he speaks of modernization (and for him modernization, transition, and secularization are synonyms), of the "great transition" to the creation of the modern industrial society, he refers to the emergence of the modern nation-state of industrialized countries from whose models he adjusts categories to systematize transition in nonindustrialized nations.

From this perspective, the transition at the beginning of the century in Latin America corresponds to the impact of the industrial revolution in these territories, and to stage three of his scheme: "dual societies and external expansion." The representation of societies in Gallegos is homologous to this concept and belongs to narratives of intersection. At the beginning of the century, the narrative of modernization proposed by national bourgeoisies, in its different moments and styles, also narrativizes women, though more carefully. For it is evident that transition in these documents has as fundamental protagonists the state and its institutions, areas under male trusteeship for the security of the state, patrolled by armies. They also deal with the social sectors that constitute it and thus center themselves in the concept of law. Women's narratives heed the signals of "no entry," but they penetrate the institutions at their weak points. Woman argues from the bosom of the family, and comes to debate questions of legislation and customs as a means of influencing habits and mores, in kinship or in interethnic or polyclassist social relations.

Ordering societies anew presumes thinking on the one hand of the social costs, and on the other of the political control needed to destroy the indigenous forms of socioeconomic organization. Unless they meddle with the state, women's narratives find themselves at a disadvantage, for in this century the highest priorities are nationalism and protonationalism, polyclassism and even anti-imperialism, the image of the future, indicated above by Lerner, in which the primitive accumulation of capital is condition *sine qua non*. The political sophistication of Gioconda Belli takes her to postulate her subject-position as a struggle on two fronts: the everyday life of the family, and the struggle against the state. The collapsing and converging planes defined by the authorized prose of the social sciences are economic transformation, democratization, and national liberation.

Essentially, the construction of the paradigm presupposes the sense of a limit with which the desire for, and the illusion of, change must dialogue. In this sense, the limits could be the structural matrix of marginal societies, international relations, or simply the masculine sensibility which encompasses them. The desire for independence, and proposals for getting out from under the controls of tutelage and services; beginning to govern one's own house, to create and recreate that domestic space, that dominion and control over one's self; and the aspiration toward development so as to generate and administer productivity and the territorial budget could be—and in fact is—applicable to the house and to domesticity in a literal sense.

Societies must also have ideas of the social cost and of the crisis inherent in certain types of productivity. Oftentimes, in the seduction that metropolitan societies exercise, in the representation of the spatial organization of the city, and in the apparent distribution of its wealth, consideration of the costs incurred in the will to make is glossed over.[15] Impatience and the desire to make is often translated into willfulness in the prioritization of the subjectivity of the high-command elites in the transitional process, and into the subordination of economic circumstances to political and ideological arrogance. Revolutionary literature provides ample evidence of this kind of development.

In the testimonial by José de Jesús Martínez on General Torrijos, for instance, one can observe distinctions in the perception of the human horizon. He insists that Torrijos never deceived himself about the limitations of his best cadres, nor about the opportunism he necessarily had to expect, as it was rampant at all levels. He was never deceived about the deformations the enemy caused his people. In service countries, the mentality of the citizen is that of the "waiter," and of the soldier that of the "raving dog, do not enter, private property." He invokes the famous historico-geographic servitude, the domestic trade union, for which "to say imperialism and oligarchy is a redundancy, for they are the same" (30–31). Neither the oligarchy nor the people had nationality. That is why he established distinctions using, as an example, the difference between rank and hierarchy:

> To be a macho is a rank . . . to be human, a hierarchy. . . . Rank is given by decree. Hierarchy is conquered through exemplary action. . . . Reason has rank. Necessity has hierarchy. . . . And in Panama the maximum hierarchy is that of hunger. (25)

In this light, and in referring to the literature on revolutionary transition, Vilas invokes Marxism as "left developmentalism." When talking about backwardness and the nature of transitions, he refers to restrictive factors like the subjective aspects of the class character of the leadership, and he wonders if, in the case of the revolutionary transition, it

> would not be perhaps premature, the intent to undertake socialist revolutions in backward societies resulting from the radicalism and impatience—at base, the psychological characteristics—of the petit bourgeoisie more than the needs and objective possibilities of the society? (1989: 8)

That is why transition is economic, political, and social; but it is also cultural. For Vilas, transition is the expression of the contradiction between productive forces and the relations of production—property relations in its different legal and subjective expressions.

"Attending only to material necessities produces in a new society an old man" (Martínez, 75). Class struggle is given at the level of the personal, in everday life. To privilege only the external articulation of transition to the detriment of the cultural articulation is to reorder a type of institutional state/national integration above other social conflicts. Revolution and transition are synonyms. Socialism is the expression of the development of peripheral societies in their transition from capitalism to socialism and even communism.

In both cases, the transition is violent, even if the former wants to interpret itself as a legal debate, as a slow alteration, and sees social change as a secularization. But seen as modernization or as revolution, from one or the other end, the viability of transitional projects resides essentially in the manner in which the question of development, the administration of social chaos, is faced, whether it is considered a movement toward development or from underdevelopment.

In both cases, transition is an accumulative structural change. The components of the process are economic development and political and social modernization. It is an undeniable principle that pacts established with the elements of the former horizon brand transitions indelibly. External interference is also a determining factor. The flags of national independence and social justice borne by the emancipatory projects of the transition of the last quarter of this century, or the ethical arguments made at the beginning of it, form part of the sensibility through which the social protagonists express themselves in any narrative.

The proposed problem deals in our case with the construction of a narrative of intersections: how gender, class, ethnicity, and nation are intertwined. To this end we must borrow Germani's concept of secularization—that is, *"the change in attitude and mentality in relation to the norms of interinstitutional and interpersonal exchange, mental structures valuing more the change than the tradition"* (1972: 7; emphasis mine).

Economically this means a more equitable distribution of what is produced, that is, a class recomposition of society. Politically it implies a democratization, that is, an organization of the state such that it incorporates stability and marginality. Socially it refers fundamentally to structural rearrangements in the systems of stratification—divisions, mobility, visions, forms of participation, "particularly to the ostensible and the social rights of the lower strata" (5). In education, it refers to a sense of participation and identification. All of this is to "diminish differences (ethnographic, economic, and sociocultural) between strata and social groups, urban, rural, and regional" (6).

And that is why the projects of transition are violent and must have "the capacity to originate and observe structural changes in [all] spheres," and count on "some type of political participation of a large majority of the adult population" (5). Understood as modernization, transition tends, therefore, to reformulate the elite nation-state as an ideal, and theoretically to incorporate social sectors known as ethnic groups and those who form the ethno-nation.

Concerning an earlier horizon, when choosing his most dramatic formulation Hobsbawm posits the following:

> As modern war illustrates, state interests now depended on the participation of the ordinary citizen. . . . The degree of sacrifice which

could be imposed on civilians had to enter the plans of strategists. . . .
Obviously the democratization of politics, i.e. on the one hand the
growing extension of the (male) franchise, on the other the creation of
the modern, administrative, citizen-mobilizing and citizen-influencing
state both placed the question of the 'nation,' and the citizen's feelings
towards whatever he regarded as his 'nation,' 'nationality' or other
center of loyalty at the top of the political agenda. (83)

That is, on structural questions, Germani and Vilas, coming from two
different conceptual positions, agree in their appreciations of transition
and development; and the thesis according to which economic expansion
is undertaking only a small social mobilization of the population and is
tied to ancient lateral forms does not have a major impact. This is what
can perhaps be seen in slave or plantation or mining economies, of which
Schwarz-Bart speaks so much. From the plantation system, dual economies and societies develop, profoundly split between the archaic and the
modern, everywhere apparent in island literatures. While if change impli-
cates great sectors at the lower and middle occupational levels, the internal
market grows and there is an effect of expansion and economic development.

Even if the theory of transition does not specifically include the category
of gender in its vocabulary, to the degree that it requires "social mobilization," urbanization, an increase in the life expectancy of the people and
"*structural changes in the family and in the internal relations of the nuclear
family as much as in the kinship groups and family modifications of the
stratification profile and its systems, a reduction of the medium traditional
groups and expansion of the modern ones*" (Germani 1972: 7; emphasis
mine), it does in fact involve gender.

Where the elites were inefficient and did not want to go beyond their
own myopic interests, Germani argues, referring to Latin America in its
previous horizon, modernization stops short, and the opposite rewards
those who decided to push the frontiers.

Facing this idea of a transition that belongs to the public sector and of
spaces dominated by the masculine principle, the feminine imaginary produces another type of reconstruction. Its terms leave traces of erosion and
subterranean spaces. Women's narratives take care of the transition from
the bosom of personality itself, and from the smallest institutional unit that
society recognizes, namely the family. They postulate changes beyond this
social nucleus, changes in the ego that simultaneously unveil the indige-

nous forms of organization and the multiethnic, polyclassist nature of the state of the common social space, and of the feelings and the psyche that accompany it.

Feminine Narratives Choose the Family

The feminist counterattack to the configuration of nation seems innocuous by comparison. For, in contrast, the social feminine imaginary deals fundamentally with the small, and is concerned with only one of the components of change, that which deals with the family and kinship groups, and subordinates or repeats from a conservative perspective all the other questions, mainly those of class, as we saw in the case of the peons, *haciendas,* cattle ranches, and the ethno-nation. This is to say that with respect to ethnic groups, feminist narratives share the same conservative position as liberal groups, and, insofar as the narratives of revolutionary transition are concerned, they seem identical.

In the five narratives that I have selected, the figure of the nuclear family has been displaced. The father and the mother as leading forces and reproducers of social behavior have disappeared and have been substituted by aunts, uncles, grandparents, and servants. Mothers have gone crazy, have prostituted themselves, or are dead, leaving the protagonists in a state of social orphanhood, which serves them as a platform from which to launch their projects of emancipation. And in the two cases where there was a brother, both have died, leaving the protagonist an only child and therefore heir to any patrimony. The right of male primogeniture is finished, and property must be transmitted to women by right of inheritance. But it is precisely property and inheritance that are in question in at least two of the narrative cases.

Tending toward solitude as a possible emotional horizon, these protagonists end, however, in monogamic couplings, with husbands national (in de la Parra, Belli, and Schwarz-Bart) and foreign (in Rhys and Loynaz), around whom the function of wealth is worked out. Curiously, none of them progresses into the new horizon: all die or become widows. Thus, for the most part, inherited or transferred wealth reverts back to male hands. Unlike de la Parra's protagonist, who is kept waiting for marriage as if it were a sacrifice, Loynaz' dies when a garden wall collapses on her; Rhys' commits suicide; Schwarz-Bart's is left living alone, like Fanotte, the woman who inspired the narrative, selling peanuts on the Church doorstep; and Belli's perishes in an urban guerrilla operation. In other words, the traditional family is obliterated, and, in retrospect, the radical vision of Teresa de la Parra postulates a brand of traditional landowning family that is already passé. The implosion of the traditional model of the family narrativized by women writers is total.

It is evident that the other pole of interest related to the family is that of servants and peasants. The ethnic questions and the question of the nation-people are also analyzed here. The romantic relationships that all of these white protagonists establish with their black servants are the expressions of social pacts proposed by the elites, realized with greater or lesser democratization depending on the author. Without question, the narrators who provide more illustrations and are the most enlightened are Simone Schwarz-Bart, because she narrates from the perspective of the mulatto, and Gioconda Belli, because her social horizon is the revolutionary one. The others are born within a romantic archaism allied to Neo-Positivism. In other words, with respect to the notion of property, they continue to sustain archaic patterns of thought.

The constitution of the revolutionary nation is born within two large epistemological determinants. First, nation appears as independence. That is why its gestation occupies a spatial location that I have distinguished here as the mountain in male literature, or the garden and the house in women's writing. Second, the literature of the revolutionary transition points to the primacy of international spheres. In the first and second transition, national liberation and economic development (= nature) have coupled, subordinating the cultural or quotidian. The relations of production (culture/the quotidian) are seen in the literature of the social sciences only as socializations of the economy and/or the political democratization (a blank space) of participation, or popular control.

Elite Women and Their Narratives of Transition: *Hacienda*/Garden/City

All the representations of gender in this study, without exception, are signed by one social class and, with only one exception, by the same ethnicity. What differentiates these narratives of transition, marking a break in the history of representation, is their moment of enunciation.

Insofar as nation is concerned I pay close attention to diverse moments of transition which, at the interior of the text, mark different rhythms. Writers from the islands return reiteratively and obsessively to the past century, to slavery and abolition, and to marooning. Writers from continental countries are worried about mixtures, peons, and masses. The combination of gender, ethnicity, and historical moment—abolition/emancipation, modernization/revolution—allows, in their heterogenous conjunctions, for the tentative tracings of the limits in the representation of ethnicity, gender, and nation influenced by master narratives.

None of the women writers studied enter the space of writing with a genuflection. All of them enter through the front door, through the door of having been educated abroad. All of them have been repositories of accumulated capital left by the liberal projects in the areas of education. All are women of good social standing, tied to *Independentista* families, the modernizing bourgeoisie, educated mulattas, who, in general, are daughters of merchants and landowners, members of the capitalist or semicapitalist class in the periphery who send their girls overseas to study foreign languages and to acquire table manners.

Between the novels of Teresa de la Parra (1926) and Gioconda Belli (1990), then, the graph of the development of the concept of transition in the nation-state of the central Caribbean region in this century can be traced as it was felt and perceived by elite women. The curve encompasses the years comprising the dates of publication of the first book by Teresa de la Parra, 1926, and the last of Belli's, 1990. Woman's writing reconstructs the past and writes the insertion of women within transitions.

In *Ifigenia,* but mainly in *Memorias de la mamá blanca,* Teresa de la Parra evokes a certain social-rural order, the *hacienda* system governed by the seigniorial, patriarchal oligarchy of *Independentista* leanings. This closed order is evoked backwards from what Raymond Williams calls the perspective of rural intellectual radicalism. In *Sofía de los presagios,* Gioconda Belli curiously rethinks the question of the rural order from the same perspective.

Both novelists are concerned with the countryside but also with the city, and both move within the sphere of the *hacienda,* of the plantation Great House, and the urban house. The formation of class generally occurs in the countryside, in the *hacienda,* or the productive place. Gender formation tends to take place in urban scenarios, spaces of development. The treatment of the peasant-rural space, the seat of the organized national agrarian economies, written in pastoral or semipastoral fashion, contrasts with the treatment of urban spaces, already transnationalized, where questions of the state and the spirit of the law define the place of women before the nation. In the rural order, women have more power, for they are seen as a class: under the patriarchal tutelage of the paterfamilias, yes, but like the rest of the family, on the back of the production of the labor of peons and servants or of the loyal salaried workers, well or badly paid. The prestige of serving those above, or fair wages, according to the social changes, legitimizes the new order in the novel. In the first case, lineage covers all house servants, and in the second a certain filtered socialist thought permits us to see the dreams of more just societies.

But the narrativization of countryside as such, of the rural order of the plantation, corresponds, rather, to Simone Schwarz-Bart, for Loynaz and Rhys, the other island novelists, construct an intermediate natural space and transform the countryside (hill, bush, forest, jungle, mountain) into *hortus conclusus,* Eden or garden. The distinction between country and city does not seem to be constituted in these nations or protonations, "negotiated republics" whose transnationalized economies from the very beginning had a different dynamism.

Essentially, the novelists here reproduce relations within their changing environments linked to these economies and to the social order created by the respective power groups, the sugar plantocracy. The three island novelists grapple with the transition from economies based centrally on slave labor to economies based centrally on wage slavery, and with the constitution of the nation-states. Semantic distinctions between the different meanings of nature establish the borders of the discursive fields between the masculine and feminine sensibilities. The territorial panorama, as much as the terms used to signify it, is a sign through which gender is visible.

The sensations of disorder and chaos, together with those of passage, essentially confirm the diverse sensibilities that come to play in the discursive transactions composing the respective works of these writers. Modernization and revolution are the two terms used here to demarcate the moments of transition and the social projects of modernization. The great narratives of the nation-state and their specific relation to what Vilas calls people-nation, which in feminine (and masculine) narratives are directly tied to the rural order, to the agrarian property and to ethno-nation, raise questions related to the concept of gender-nation in the constitution of a new social order.

PART II

Nation/Ethnicity/Gender/Genre

The Feminine

Hacienda/Nation—*Quid Pro Quo*

Transition/Tradition

When Teresa de la Parra decided to rename her novel from *Diario de una señorita que escribió porque se fastidia* (Diary of a Lady Who Wrote out of Boredom) to *Ifigenia* (1926), she was shrewdly constituting her protagonist against the symbolic shadow of Greek drama. Iphigenia, a figure dramatized by Aeschylus and Euripides, was, from the very beginning, an open semantic field. For Aeschylus the feminine is obedience and subserviency, for Euripides, an active subject. Because of this, his *Iphigenia in Aulis* has been considered a transitional piece, a bridge between classical tragedy and preclassical drama, portraying a shift as much as a step in the direction of that Modernity. In this way, the revised gender referent is positioned in a desideratum.

The fact that Euripides' figure is more appealing today must not confuse us. *Iphigenia* is not a feminist drama. Euripides' text displays kinship relations which found an actant in Helen. The terms of the discussion/dialogue between the two brothers Menelaus and Agamemnon, the ones who will decide the destiny of the feminine in *Iphigenia,* are political. To save her, they propose to trade her life for Calchas'. But the idea of deceiving Odysseus, commander of one of the most potent armies, deters them. Thus political pacts may not be altered and Iphigenia must be sacrificed.

To save the principle of male honor, Euripides makes her speak against herself. But her speech also makes it clear what she is dying for: to save Greek honor, the father's honor, the name of the clan. In order to ascend to the category of heroine, her monologue must be composed of signifiers that are gendered male, imitating those of the bravest men. Recognizing himself in her words, Achilles gives her his approval and she becomes his most precious object of desire. The solution to a political problem, predicated on the death of woman, is plotted within the dimension of morality. In the case of Greek drama, a treason is denounced. Helen's treason. Death is purification and the feminine thus passes into literary history as a quid pro quo.

This retrieved information expresses the same dilemma as de la Parra's protagonist María Eugenia Alonso. The feminine figure in de la Parra relives the drama of blood on a symbolic level. After a fierce war of words, in which Modernity struggles with tradition, this contemporary heroine ends up like her symbolic archetype, accepting the family voice, the voice of reason and of nation. *Iphigenia* brings to mind Jean Franco's observations on women and nations: to nations women are either mediums or traitors.

Gender/Genre: A Commercial Transaction

Ifigenia: Diario de una señorita que escribió porque se fastidia plots the story of María Eugenia Alonso, an impoverished woman of the oligarchy who has studied in Europe, and her vicissitudes on her return to her native land, Venezuela. European culture, habits, mores, and Modernization are contrasted with Venezuelan culture and civilization disfavorably. Venezuela's history and, in comparison with Paris and Spain, backwardness, serve to underscore María Eugenia's unhappiness. Contrast, then, shapes the mood of the narrative. First there is a geocultural contrast that emerges in a long letter from María Eugenia to her best friend Cristina and, subsequently, there is the contrast between men and women in the Venezuelan nation-state, portrayed in a private diary. Letters and diaries are the non-canonical genres consecrated in the novel, pre-texts that serve as a conduit for expressing women's ideas on nation, gender, and ethnicity. The letter functions as a report, the extensive debriefing of a Creole lady to her European friend on her un-national sentiments, her feelings about the *patria chica*, the petty conservatism of everyday life, the caricature of development that telephone lines and architectural design reveal, the insignificance of the railway and paved roads, flourishing export economy. Venezuela's landscape is, with the exception of its majestic mountains, a caricature.

The diary, on the other hand, is an internal acknowledgment of the oppression of women who have lost their fortune under the modern Venezuelan state. Money as capital and as rent, property as land, and capital accumulation are debated within the inner circle of patriarchal/patriotic families, inside the oligarchy's houses, decorated in the Orientalist style promoted by the aesthetics of *fin-de-siècle* Modernism, promoted by Rubén Darío.

What is debated in the living and dining rooms, on the galleries, and even in the kitchens and laundry rooms are marriages and the civil rights of women, how woman is legally constituted in the laws of the state. María Eugenia Alonso and Mercedes Galindo voice their disapproval and their unhappiness when their civil rights are curtailed. María Eugenia's grandmother, wiser in the ways and realities of the society and a politically conservative pragmatist, argues for accommodation, obedience, and subjection. Her daughter Clara is a clear victim of this position through which María Eugenia, under the guise of a marriage of convenience, is also victimized. In *Memorias de la mamá blanca,* Teresa de la Parra explicitly states her love for this old Mantuana lady, whom she venerates. But in *Ifigenia,* a more forceful dialogic narrative, de la Parra repudiates these women's positions, as they move to more modern circumstances.

To the debates on property and marriage, she adds observations on development and her position on mixed mestizo and mulatto republics. In María Eugenia's visit to La Pastora, the mulatta deserves utter contempt. Ugliness is the adjective used to qualify both mulatta and nation, or the nation as a mulatta, a geography populated and possibly governed, at least metaphorically and symbolically, by a mixture.

There is in the second volume of *Ifigenia* a lengthy discussion of romantic love. The discussion of romantic love begins in the first volume when, in the letter to Cristina, María Eugenia comments on fashion and make-up as related to the heroines of romance novels published in women's magazines like *La Mode Illustrée.* Kissing as a metonym for lovemaking and free lovemaking as a metonym for alternative models of coupling are touched on obtrusively. But the idea and influence of Romanticism in gender formation here is discussed in a way that is as enlightening as could be expected from women at the beginning of the century.

Ifigenia is, then, a transition. It is a road that begins in frivolity and ends in disenchantment. It is the route of sentimental education for women bound to the concept of money/rent. The possibility of having money establishes the difference between freedom and submission, between the independence of the "body and its acts" and the arbitration of the law, between one's own image as a *chien fuette* and a chic woman.

The discussion of these two planes of being revolves around a concrete sum of money: 20,000 francs (2,000 pesos, 8,000 bolivares). This money/rent/dowry is the origin of gaiety and the point of disillusion that frames the narrative. The amount reveals and hides the possibility of the blithe, frivolous, mundane, loose distinction between love and romantic sensibility, and subordinates this distinction to the mournful religious conservatism godfathered by the law of Venezuelan Modernity. In the possibility of expenditure, usufruct and its indiscriminate use, rests the transformation of the feminine principle: woman as a heroine of romance, a character of literature, a cover girl for a fashion magazine. Also there is the possibility of the realization of the feminine figure of Modernism, the polished hands of roses and white lilies, the fresh, smiling mouth of Darío's Countess Eulalia, "painted with lipstick by Guerlaine" (Parra, 1: 49).

Fashion and frivolity link two Modernist aesthetics: the Latin American and the European.[1] The personal sense of self, the constitution of the subject, is based on accessing, as well as using properly, fashion products that permit the transformation of appearances. Guerlaine nail polish, or the introduction of commercial advertising into the text as another voice, allows the articulation of these two types of Modernity. In fact, makeup and the perfect figure are understood as essential attributes of being a woman.

For this transaction, money is a necessity, but the concept of money itself is in question. For the second time, money becomes an issue in the text, discussed as land, as property, as the San Nicolas estate, as patrimony and heritage. A change of owners has taken place, and with it María Eugenia Alonso's own image vanishes. From totality to nothingness. The absence of money strips familiar knots—kinship, the severity of domestic law and matriarchal "protection," whose correlation is the spirit of socionational law, the empire of habit, patriarchal dominion—naked.

Without money, the future vanishes, for the absence of money is poverty, and poverty means "complete dependency" and "humiliation and pain." To be without money is to be unable to travel. It is to say farewell to "well-being," "success," "sumptuousness," "elegance," and the "good things" in life. It is to say farewell to Paris, to Europe, to international relationships. Happiness, freedom, and success are synonyms for money.

The discussion between uncles, nephews, granddaughters, and grandparents takes place precisely on this semantic plane. If money means property, property does not mean rent but productivity; and money means interests, percentages, and surplus value. The concept of money rests and oscillates again among these meanings: as expenditure and dissipation of the land rents, a conceptualization displaced by Modernity.

The dialoguing planes argue these positions in the inverse, for it is through the grandmother's mouth, in her monologue, that the voice of Latin American Modernity is placed; the grandmother contests and opposes the voice of European Modernism defended by the young María Eugenia as much as by her Uncle Pancho. The semantic levels invert their position; their positions invert the semantic planes. To the degree that the European Modernity of uncle and that of the niece coincide, it is associated with Venezuelan conservatism and projected onto two planes at the same time, moral and historical. The shift of property from María Eugenia to the uncle Eduardo, a shift occurring within the same family, is the passage from renter to producer, and from the conservative position to the Modern Latin American one. A pro-European Modernity is the obverse of a Latin American Modernity, as the pro-European Latin American sectors are conservative. For landless women, lacking a concept of productivity, Latin American Modernity signifies remaining at the discretion of kinship relations, in custody. The custodians are the owners of the *hacienda/latifundio*, those who couple the law of domestic habits and social law, a branch of the founding families that continues to exercise complete power over interpretation.[2] In her article on the avant-garde feminist novel, Francine Masiello argues that "the new perspective offered by women is not due to difference in social classes. . . . Rather the novelty is observed in the structure of their books, and the formal transgression of their literary work and their upsetting of the traditional frames" (808). And besides the exclusion from inheritance, "the novel obliges a reading on social marginality of woman who is excluded from the privileges of the civil code and the rights of the family code" (811).

The figure of the grandmother as a *Mantuana* matriarch occupies simultaneously positions of tradition and Modernity. She knows as much about interests as about percentages, and as much about labor as about history. She is the pivot upon which the semantic shift of meaning, which transition constitutes, turns. She is "of distinguished demeanor, and of easy and elegant word" (Parra, 1: 96), "has a gift for words" (1: 99), and "a convincing and magnetic tone" (1: 105). She is elegant, majestic, stately, soft, and loving. Her essential attribute is persuasion, occupying the masculine place of interpreter of politics and history. It is from her mouth that we become aware of the big and the small: we know, for instance, that interest rates could be between 9, 10, and 12 percent, and how much an investment of 2,000 pesos will yield.

But we know more. We know that Martín Alonso, the *Mantuano* grandfather, a man of "elegance," "distinction," "sumptuousness," "luxury," was one of the "first capitalists of Venezuela," that his "fortune" was in spices, "jewelry," "tapestries," "paintings," "rugs," "china" (1: 99), and that he went to Europe and "lost his judgment! That that went to his head! . . . [and] he never returned to Venezuela" (1: 100). The anti-emigrationist position, the turning of one's back on the land, the use and abuse of absentee administration, is kept to the fore, for fortunes dwindle with "very bad administration, revolutions, crises, price devaluations, etc."[3]—in some cases, from not taking into account the "use money must have" (1: 101). That's why Uncle Pancho's position is that "it is better to spend the money in having fun than to spend it in bad businesses, from which third parties assuredly benefit," while, for the grandmother, these are "corrupt doctrines" tantamount to drinking, shooting up morphine and snorting cocaine, scandals and duels (1: 94).

The terms of the discussion, then, can be seen as a series of aligned dichotomies: moral superiority, intelligence and religion, the past and outmoded habits, poverty, and Caracas (all components of Latin American Modernity, according to María Eugenia) versus the world, consumption, fun, travel, the present, wealth, and Paris—terms employed by the women discussants to signify real Modernity, European style. Or, indolence, laziness, overspending, squandering, dissipation, pleasures, obliviousness, luxury, rent, and bad education are counterposed to the intelligence and skill in the management of one's interests, the passion for agriculture, and the enthusiasm for industrial production that the grandmother espouses. Both the grandmother and the uncle want modernization without secularization, as Germani would have it.

The reordering of the family through concepts of national modernization, articulated in the terms indicated above, is debated through the conceptualization of the future of the protagonist. "Family" here refers to lineage, to the distinction between the major *Independentistas*, impoverished founding families, the rentists, and the "obscene oligarchy"—those who decided to invest their money to make capital. In lineage, the national history and its interpretation are put into play. As in Gallegos, the concept of history/war, of nation as geopolitics, is reordered on the terrain, as an economic geography and a legal space. The *hacienda* is always central to the discussion, but it is no longer visited *in situ;* its destiny is discussed in after-dinner conversation. In the rural estate converge the designs for new habits and the irrefutable word of the law. The grandmother's voice is the masculine voice in a woman's mouth.

That's why the new man, "old, avaricious, Jewish, thief, blackguard, kitsch. . . ." (1: 90), according to María Eugenia, the *homo economicus* according to the grandmother, is Uncle Eduardo, who:

> works assiduously without leaving the estate, almost without coming to Caracas; it could be said that there his children grew; as is natural he saved, and while your father spent without judgment, he was acquiring more and more. . . .
>
> He has raised an honorable family, has spent his life working, has never dragged himself into politics, . . . has never embarrassed his family by giving himself to drinking and gambling. (1: 103, 95)

Once the principle of money/capital has been established over the concept of money/rent, the sentimental formation of the formal young woman could begin distancing itself, as it is assumed, from the past, from the other history. This other history is the painful history of the Caracas aristocracy, of almost all those "Creoles" descending from the conquerors who called themselves "*Mantuanos*" under colonialism, who founded and governed cities, engraved their coat of arms on the doors of the old houses, built the independence of America with their own blood, who later decayed, oppressed under party persecutions and hatred,

> and whose granddaughters and great-granddaughters, today poor and obscure . . . without ever being ashamed of their poverty, wait with resignation the hour of marriage or the hour of death, making candy for parties or knitting wreaths of flowers for burials. (1: 107)

Body: Capital

Body is capital. The poor, declassé, disinherited, and dowryless woman must think in terms of the best use of that capital, must think of investing it properly. To invest in loans that yield dividends, small and constant, or to invest in *la toilette* are two possible alternatives, one relatively conservative, the other relatively radical. María Eugenia Alonso decides in favor of an audacious and expeditious investment: to invest in shaping her figure; to stop being "shy," "shabby," "ridiculous," "ashen," "*chien fuette*"—the image itself of orphanhood—"unfolding" into "a new personality." She decides to stop being such "a secondary character," to declare herself on strike against "shyness and humility," and to value herself "a million times more than the heroines of the novels" (1: 33).

Elegance, chic, is then a monetary risk. It is to place everything on a wager, that of simulating one's self, that of appearing as one's self, that of "interpreting oneself to oneself"; for the sake of marriage: Virginie from *Paul et Virginie*, a Watteau shepherdess, the girl from the Ross Pills poster, or the protagonist of a Romantic English novel.[4]

Something more is put into play in this choosing of investments for small capital. To choose means to "own her body and her acts." The possession of her body, the expropriation of her own body as personal capital, is independence and at the same time a consciousness of her value. Appreciation and value are correlative terms collected without appraisal. Value is in the first instance to make decisions and to change the looks, the design: "narrow the dress," "get a haircut," be a person "chic and *à la mode*" (1: 43). Take care of the exposed body parts: fingernails, hands, cheeks, mouth, eyes, the terms on which woman is appraised, for in a woman it "only counts to be beautiful" (1: 106), and because "a woman is never poor when she is . . . beautiful" (1: 126).

Value, price, and appraisals are debatable semantic fields, the intersections of points of view. Perhaps everyone in the family agrees with the idea that investments in physical appearance generate capital in the form of marriage, and that this is the seat of value.[5] But what *type* of value becomes a question, since, for María Eugenia Alonso in her first moment of struggle, marriage is to accept oneself as

> the most zero in the world, so that a man, seduced by my nullity, comes to give me the immense benefit of placing himself at my side, as if in the shape of figures, elevating me, thanks to his presence, to a round and respectable sum, thus acquiring certain and real value before society and the world. (1: 110)

Discussions of value make Uncle Pancho say to her: "you evaluate yourself very expensively," but he adds later that "consciousness of your own value [is] an indispensable condition for acquiring value" (1: 130). Aunt Clara, dissenting, places value and valuation in customs and character, a sign to her that María Eugenia Alonso is "conceited"; but Aunt Clara and Uncle Pancho are not in much disagreement about the value of a declassé woman. Disagreement, rather, rests in the nature of the wager, in the rise and fall of the *Mantuana* woman on the national stock market.

That her investments have yielded good dividends is demonstrated in the effect of her "travel dress . . . the most elegant and well-fashioned possible" (1: 143). Her manicured fingernails and her fresh mouth painted with Guerlaine lipstick have produced an effect in the Colombian poet wooing her. But the larger gamble is not international: the commodity circulates in the internal market and it is there that it must find its highest bidder. Uncle Pancho's proposal to risk her with Gabriel Olmedo—ambitious, intelligent, an oil investor, knowledgeable of agricultural prices in the world market—promises the highest return, and to this end larger investments—more expensive dresses and Mercedes' *savoir faire*—enter into play. Grandmother's proposal is Cesar Leal, "doctor of law, senator of the Republic, and present director of the Ministry of Public Works" (2: 98). To marry her off to the former, more capital is necessary; to marry her to the latter requires a change in habits: to be "irreproachable," "faultless." To leave the European world and to become Latin American is to depend, is "to stop owning her body and her acts," is to stop being, to reject the disguise, the mask of elegance and chic, and to become a worshipper of men, a devotee of domestic gods.

Social valuation, then, corresponds to complete personal devaluation, to abandon the idea that value is also "a gift for observation and a great facility for expression" (1: 34). Teresa de la Parra battles for her protagonist and espouses all of the liberal ideas of the rights of women learned from the Suffragette movements: "we women are no more than victims, pariahs, slaves, disinherited" (1: 136), to live under tutelage and to be good for nothing:

> You cannot go out alone because you do not know what you are exposing yourself to. . . . [E]ven though everybody speaks you shall not speak. . . . [T]hat comedy is admirable and very funny but you cannot even hold it in your hands. (1: 191)

The tutorial complies with the subordination of woman to patriarchy, which, according to Uncle Pancho, consists of women having two religions, the one they practice in church and the one they practice at home: two gods, one of them the man in the family, for it is "essential to feel a male superiority to whom [we] render blind tribute of obedience and servitude" (1: 128). Everything he does is well done and everything he says is law. And he has the right to get infuriated over the food or ironing and to censure failures in a "solemn and majestic" voice. Whether this is "oriental atavism" or "a simple economic problem," Uncle Pancho, the man of ideas, does not know (1: 129).

Society proposes submission to patriarchy, which is not only a domestic, house religion, but a national law. As doctor of law and senator, Cesar Leal will demonstrate later that "in life man must always conduct himself: as man! and woman: as woman!" (2: 93) and later still, that religion in a woman is completely indispensable and no woman has the right to say she does not believe . . . for what do they understand of metaphysics or biology or LaMark's theories. . . . I think, I have studied profoundly, I reflect, I have a certain mental capacity, I have my system, I have my special method, I have my etc. etc. . . . (2: 120)

It is this speech on knowledge delivered by Leal on several occasions that María Eugenia uses as the essence of value, as an evaluation of herself. It is on the basis of Senator Leal's criteria that Aunt Clara has called her arrogant, and grandmother has had her cloistered in San Nicolás. That's why Uncle Pancho ironically responds to the proposed equality of the sexes with the inequality of sexes as a natural law, since the former is "absurd," "contrary to the laws of nature which finds democracy detestable and finds justice abominable" (1: 128). Equality of the sexes is therefore a "puerile dream." Using mystical language Uncle Pancho exaggerates feminine devotion. Women are "dazzled by the idealist light of mysticism and virtue," he says; women "always run to offer themselves spontaneously in sacrifice" (1: 139). They love "the voluptuousness of submission," and exalt "love with self-flagellation" (ibid.). The feminine condition parodied by the enlightened man is one of asceticism and solitude, of self-sacrificing idealism, and of voluntary victimization by the executioner, of women who "ignore the demolishing force that their admirers exert" (ibid.).

María Eugenia responds with conclusive opinions.[6] Maleness is "never to learn . . . [to] have tact." It is to seem to know a lot and behave "as if they didn't know anything." It is to "ignore oneself." In her treatment of the masculine, de la Parra is far from indulgent. Irony permeates the text: for the characterization of the family and that of the suitors, and for the discussion of dowry and inheritance, estate productivity, or bad administration as well as (*pace* Jane Austin) the same seat of romantic love and marriage as the acquisition of capital, the open door to the outside world, she demonstrates no sympathy. Psychically and morally lacking, and even more so emotionally, they deserve a thorough critique. When they are not thieves they are arrogant, if not oblivious and disrespectful. In her system of values the masculine occupies the same place as the grotesque and the ugly—the opposite pole of elegance and chic—the place of *mestizaje* and *mulataje*, which she finds so repulsive. The masculine carries a negative value.

The only man who deserves some respect is María Eugenia's interlocutor, Uncle Pancho, iconoclast, anarchist, and cynic about the society in which he lives. He is a lover of modern women, Parisian luxuries, and dilettantism. He says to María Eugenia that the honor of man is "something indefinite, elastic, conventional" (1: 130), and it is to him that she confesses she would like to be a man: "if at least I had been born a man," because being a woman is

> the same as being a canary or a goldfinch. They lock you up in a cage, they take care of you, they feed you, and they don't let you out; while the rest go around merry and flying all over the place. What a horror it is to be a woman! What a horror! (1: 135)

Thus the debate on the formation of the gendered subject in Venezuela at the beginning of the century oscillates between marriage as value on one hand and independence and knowledge as value on the other. Of all the women under study in this text de la Parra is the foremother who exposes the constraints of the discussion of gender, who notices the connection between money and individual freedom, and the one who lobbies for the simple incorporation of women into the rights of citizens programmed by liberal revolutions and states.[7] In Christophine's mouth, Jean Rhys places the same advice for her pupil Antoinette, whose lackadaisical figure is one reason for suspecting her mulatticity, which devalues her in the eyes of her English husband.

Teresa de la Parra pronounces herself in favor of wisdom and knowledge for women and against innocence, about which she says:

> [T]he despotic urge to make us ignore in theory all those things that other people know or have known in practice, seems to me one of the major abuses that the strong have ever committed against the weak. . . . Sowing mysteries in life . . . disorients horribly . . . and I believe it to be in general a blindfold and a trap used by everyone to organize our lives more easily according to their whims. Innocence is a blind, a deaf, a paralytic woman whom human imbecility has crowned with roses. It is the most humiliating emblem of the submission and slavery in which almost all honest women live after they marry! (1: 190)

Irony and parody, ridicule and sarcasm prevail in the constitution of the relations of heterosexual couples. A complete rejection of such relations, properly understood only if negatively understood, is possible through literature that engenders resentment, through English novels like Jane Austin's, and also through an open discussion of taboos: divorce, or cohabitation without the mediation of the law.

To the degree that the narrative emphasizes gender, the emphasis on the economic nation dwindles, and vice versa. Nation passes from one stage to another, and consequently gender does the same. Nevertheless, Madame de la Parra's thesis, as with all the other women we will study, is simple: the new national projects do not necessarily imply a new subject-position for women. If the drama of Euripides' tragedy resides in the absence of free will and self-determination for women, for de la Parra in feminine narratives, the tragedy is identical.

Nation: Discursivity and Gender

For Teresa de la Parra, gender is a summation of historically and biographically related links; nation, a combination of natural and ethnographic landscapes; ethnicity, the nature and social typology of the work force.[8] The informative letter from María Eugenia Alonso to her friend Cristina addresses these three points of conflict on the agenda. They are also essential in her diary, where she writes them supposedly only for herself. The themes are also reiterated in *Las memorias de la mamá blanca* and in her public and private diaries and intimate and professional letters.

In her excellent study, *Las grietas de la ternura*, Elizabeth Garrels argues that Teresa de la Parra constructs her fantasies by ignoring the facts. She points out that a confrontation between historical discourse and her fiction shows a displacement, and this displacement is the site assigned to imagination. Garrels maintains that Teresa de la Parra is about seventy-five years behind her times; that she turns her back on or simply ignores contemporary historical facts. In Garrels' thesis we could situate an ideology, one which makes de la Parra one of the traditional epic historians of independence discussed by Gallegos, occupying a position signaled by Uslar Pietri when he historicizes Venezuelan society at the beginning of the century:

> [T]he so-called conservatives were, indeed, the rest of the *paecista* party, upholders of economic and political liberalism, respectful of the law and defenders of the institutions. The so-called liberals, and then federalists, were the militarists of the Reforms, the *anti-paecista,* those around Monagas, dictators in fact and egalitarians in principle, friends of armed revolt and of demagoguery. . . . There was no doctrine in the bands. . . . There were those who thought to divide [the nation-state] into two or three independent States, to distribute them among themselves, the irreconcilable local ones. . . . That was the time

of Guzman-Blanco. Against him, fearing the struggle, were the ancient conservatives, those whom he aggressively called the "obscene oligarchy." . . . [N]ot only these, but also other men somewhat marginal to the parties, anguished onlookers of a suicidal struggle, who see the nation decay and perish among the battles of its children blinded by hatred. There were those who believed that a civilized tradition had existed and was broken: who believed it possible to reestablish what Bolívar had called "the uses of civil society," who distrusted the warrior and violence, and believed in the efficacy of principles, of good, of justice. (1: 184–185)

Teresa de la Parra's inclination toward the impoverished oligarchy rather positions her as one of "the men somewhat marginal to the parties" whom Uslar Pietri describes. This position is notable in all her writings. That is why, rethinking Garrels' critique, I want to question the confrontation between Garrels' reading of history and de la Parra's fiction, and both with the quotidian which fiction and history supposedly represent: that is, the understanding of historical discourse as "truth" and "truth" as a textualization of the real in fiction; daily struggle to enforce the institutionalization of discourse, and how both discourse and its quotidian expressions are articulated within a concept of power relative to the nation-state. Fiction argues precisely the intradiscursive fissures, the rifts between the judicial and economic interpellations of behavior and the actual behaviors themselves. But in the case of de la Parra, she makes them more evident in *Ifigenia* than in *Las memorias de la mamá blanca,* this last book written, curiously, later. That is, in Teresa de la Parra there is a regression.

But it could also be argued that the discussion of discursive fissures in *Ifigenia* has its correlative in gendered perception and lineage. For the concept of the masculine sums up, in its attributes, the discourses of history and of "truth," institutionalized in a concept of power, which evokes the nation-state. In Gallegos, there is no doubt about this. In de la Parra, the masculine is found represented as a civil struggle in one text and as an intersectorial discussion within the constituted state in the other. The masculine suggests also the explanation of the concept of father (patriarchy), which in de la Parra evolves out of the elite lineage, out of the leaders of the Republic, as the proper place for the words *colony* and *independence,* adjacent to the word truth—as in her truth. Aristocracy is leisure or war (it is *Las memorias de la mamá blanca*): it is private writing (the mama's diary), or politics (the papa's military actions around the estate, in which the peons take part); it is liberal arts (still exclusively in male hands) or martial arts—in sum, the topoi of the masculine. The mama's private writing does not have the same status as the historical writing of María Eugenia's father, nor that of her grandfather Martín Alonso, much less that of the writing of the law argued at the close of the second volume through the mestizo Cesar Leal, or the economic discourse argued through the mestizo Gabriel Olmedo.

In contrast, the arguments over the feminine are remitted, pending judgement by the law: graceful and easy submission in one text, subordination and conclusive disputation in the other. In neither text is woman a subject of law. In both of them she is the object. As Masiello points out, the novel obliges a reading of woman as an object, determined by coordinates—sexual, emotional, educative. The fight against women here takes place in the professional and liberal arts, involving admittance to professions and public life. Participating in the liberal arts (to be a concert pianist, author, writer, to leave oral culture) not only means occupying a male universe (the masculinization of the feminine) but also means ceasing to compete in a diminished locale and opening the doors of the house to enter the public sphere and self-rule, becoming a subject, not simply an object, of law. The invocation of the Suffragettes in the text comes to legitimize the struggle of liberal women in the legal sphere and to distance the European nations from the Latin American ones. Yet sexuality, maternity, frivolity continue to be feminine weapons. Fashion is a weapon of seduction. With fashion women pretend to domesticate legality by marrying a convenient suitor,[9] to think of the transition toward a unified being, a sign that forces us to think of her within the problematics of Modernity.

But I want to make it clear that the argument against Positivism as devotion to work and the ethics of commercial utilitarianism, to what de la Parra calls materialism, is complex, for she is not against scientific and technical development, nor is she in favor of metaphysics and theology. Teresa de la Parra's positions are antireligious and pro-European. That means that Positivism is rejected only in one particular place: labor ethics. Neither Mercedes nor María Eugenia Alonso pronounce themselves against productivity; rather, they are against the time (their own) employed to generate it. It is not wealth nor what wealth buys. They refuse to become productive workers, to adopt the work ethic. And the change in the notion of the oligarchic social subject irks them.

Already in 1890, Manuel Vicente Romero García proposed in his *Peonía* that "everything must be changed, from family life to agricultural techniques and legislation" (1: 256–257). Like *Ifigenia,* that novel was a satire as much as a naive argument against backwardness, and the rural world was endowed with a fatal destructive power. Everything was going to end in tragedy. Idolatry, the experimental sciences, and the proscription of "metaphysics and theology and the explanation of man and life as phenomena of unending evolution" are proposed (Liscano 1969: 233).

Teresa de la Parra, like most Venezuelan writers, is within this tradition. Although remaining attached to a Romantic and idealistic conception of history, she reproduces Comte, Darwin, Spencer, Taine, Haeckel. Except for her position on the question of woman, her political conception, as Garrels insinuates, is antidemocratic and possibly authoritarian. With respect to Positivism itself, she belongs to the second generation, whose disheartened tone is more pessimistic.

The Country: A Discussion

For Teresa de la Parra, the country is also a discussion. Not Santos Luzardo's monologue but an argument between contending forces. Almost an altercation. The terms of the discussion are structures for examining a horizon within which opposing wisdoms converge. In this exchange of opinions the economic discussion is paramount, but it does not refer to agriculture exclusively. There are also mining interests, textile mills, cotton plantations, and oil wells. Neither is it solely economic. In the field of ideas, the position of women—their construction—is debated full force. In fact the change is discussed through the female body and its destiny. Articulated with property and the possession of money, ancient and modern ideas converge in the discussion of gender: a biography of the impoverished *Mantuanas* in one case, a deposition on elegance and the body in the other. The gendered nation does not disentangle itself from the economy or from history in this writing. Neither does it extricate itself from the horizon of Modernity. It debates the question of woman and of nation in the laws and in the extraction of petroleum, as much as in the formation of the new government. Gabriel Olmedo and Cesar Leal, both suitors of the impoverished *Mantuana,* come to mediate the dispute over the "indifference," "indolence," and "indulgence" defining the landowning class and the intellectual oligarchy of Parisian cut; the emerging bourgeoisie, utilitarian and mercantilist; and the black masses, ready to serve.

The discussion positions itself within elegance and chic, a knowledge of the European world. Frivolity delimits the fields. Frivolity is to speak well of oneself. With vanity. By using and adorning one's own body. As a sign of knowledge in woman. With cultivated arguments. In etiquette, the gift for words, quoting sources, evident in both Uncle Pancho and María Eugenia, the end of barbarism and the discourse of civilization becomes evident. And it is not on the plain, but in Caracas; not in the craft of the cowboy, in the exercise of strength and male dexterity, but in table conversation, in the capital, in places where good wine is abundant, food well-seasoned, that nation is also discussed.

We are among decent people, refined and discerning, who argue against mercantile utilitarianism, against bad taste. It is the worldly people, those who leave their own back yard, who can point their finger at the natives' "indolence." Located in the tone as much as in the arguments is, on the one hand, that which is called frivolous, and on the other, the seriousness of power and tradition. María Eugenia is frivolous. For her, her own good assessment and the cultivation of women's figures are capital whose power is relative. Uncle Pancho is frivolous. He knows the society from within and he knows himself to be a loser. The grandmother is serious. In her are united the strength of tradition and the strength of Modernity: the mother of the man who incarnates the most powerful economic forces, and who is a relative of all the *Mantuanos*.

Uncle Pancho's discourse as an employee of the Ministry of Foreign Relations, an ex-landowner and impoverished oligarch; the grandmother's discourse as a *Mantuana* matriarch, impoverished; and María Eugenia's revise the three basic positions of the national horizon. Discussions of the plain, cattle management, the ranch, and their productivity and legality present no problem. Uncle Eduardo, the rancher par excellence, has everything under control. Discussion takes place within the family, between the two branches of the Creole group: one spending, luxury-loving, and unproductive, and the other with productive and extractive projects. The marriage of María Eugenia to one of the modern ones comes to calm and postpone the discussion.

The decisive points are made in an ironic speech on civilization and barbarianism by Uncle Pancho, who argues his point backwards, for barbarianism against civilization—meaning by "civilization" contact with Europe, its culture, erudition, and technology—after the first encounter, after the formation of the Creole group and the oppression and exploitation of the indigenous peoples. The idealization and utopianization of this moment are described with feathers and hammocks and leisure. It is argumentation in favor of Europe—but against whom? Gobineau's position on races? At the center of the discussion is the mulatto. Or the mestizo:

The Venezuelan mestizo is the confluence of the three racial elements. Its sensibility is delicate and its gift for adaptation fast, his intelligence alive and light: charged by intuition, ambitious, egalitarian, devoted to magic, violent, generous, improvident, poor in popular art, sensitive to music, at odds with systematization, with order and hierarchy. . . . It is the mestizo soul which will give the nation its psychology and characterize its history. (Uslar Pietri, 17)

In the mulatta,

[O]ne could say that the profound race hatreds, which reconciled themselves for an instant to form it, continue struggling today in its features and spirit. And in that painful struggle, see if what triumphs is not the equivocation and the grotesque! . . . [I]t is true that there is in all of them something terribly unharmonious which is much worse than ugliness itself! Her spirit is the same, they do not have a defined personality and live in the middle of the most terrible disorientation. (Parra, 1: 121)

And last, already anticipating Modernity, there is Pancho's speech on absentee economic administration as an explanation of the loss of wealth. In this moment, his speech links up with the grandmother's, but the systems of values are diametrically opposed. What for Pancho is robbery, for the grandmother is labor.

A Sweet After-dinner Conversation

The Creole social hour begins at four or five o'clock in the afternoon and ends late at night, after the dinner conversation. At four, women gather in the boudoir, and when men arrive at twilight, cocktails are served on the gallery; after that they move on to the dining room. Between the boudoir, the gallery, and the dining room, social exchange transpires. Conversation is always pleasant and in good taste. This does not prevent polemics, exchanges of points of view, and traffic in ideas on politics, economy, and business, as well as on poetry and love. Within the boundaries of the most refined tropical courtesy, all themes of interest to the national culture are revised.

It is another world. At four o'clock in the afternoon, when María Eugenia Alonso passes through the majestic gates and sets foot on the "elegant gallery of Mercedes' house" (1: 199), she has left behind the grandmother's conflictive world, the other Venezuela, the Venezuela of the altercations over inheritance and land productivity, to be admitted into a deluxe Venezuela. Behind palm trees and orchids, behind one of the gallery doors, are the boudoir and the waiting room. It is Oriental sensualism, the apotheosis of comfort. There one finds "the Turkish incense burner, a leopard skin, and an ivory arch wrought in Japan" (1: 175)—the thousand and one nights! There are also silver and crystal, Chinese vases, Sévres and Sajonia porcelain, mirrors and tapestries. But that is somewhere else, in another room of the house. In the boudoir, "Mercedes has wished to Orientalize her Creole indolence," and has replaced the Havana-like palm trees and the hammocks with an immense Turkish divan. Among soft, fluffy pillows reposes the "very white" Mercedes Galindo. There, in that very place, she, the Creole, "white on all four sides," becomes Cleopatra, Semiramis.

This is the universe of feminine reflection. Her scenarios are replicas of Rubén Darío's Modernism. Mercedes' "indolence" is made up of readings, dreams, reflections, and rest. Mercedes, a tropical Semiramis, is surrounded by poetry: the Romantics, Musset, Chenier, Becquer, evoked from the Modernist props. But there is also Bernardin de St. Pierre and Watteau, whose landscapes serve as models for the constitution of Romantic love: *Paul et Virginie* or the shepherds and shepherdesses who embody the imaginary Creole simulacra. A fan of the eclogue.

The mundane and the Oriental are Paris: fashion, *toilette, Vogue*. The *seyant dress de crepe Georgette, de ourlet à jour,* with French small talk. In the boudoir the feminine universe is under discussion: the beauty of the body and manners, two of the components of "divine love," which, according to Gabriel Olmedo, are attributes of the ideal woman and an essential component of the "supreme trinity," of the "miraculous" trinity that, together with intelligence and money, constitutes the construction of happiness. Beauty and fashion sum up elegance, a transcendental signifier, as opposed to ugliness and the grotesque, to deformity and caricature. Elegance is discussed in French, in the boudoir, with *Vogue* magazine in hand while fixing the coiffure and speaking of fabrics, style, and clothes. Manners are also translated into French as *maladresse, gaffe, torte, brouille.*

Within the boudoir the fate of the rich woman without love is also spoken of. And therefore the duties of women, their obligations, and their role in the family are also a matter of conversation: to be "indispensable" to men, to be "compassionate," "unselfish," faithful to the "name" and "house," and "the alter ego." Even though women who agree to live that way know "all the repulsions of women who sell themselves in the street to the first passerby . . . these things no one knows, for they are concealed and silenced under conventionalisms and law" (1: 218). The delicate theme of divorce is broached. And later we discover that in Paris Mercedes Galindo is known to be very flirtatious with men, and to have lovers.

Women's discussions in the boudoir are a warm-up for the after-dinner conversation. For the *brouille, gaffe,* and *maladresse,* the conflict between grandmother and granddaughter, carried into the boudoir and rehearsed there, have been displaced from rent, money and surplus value, property rights, and inheritance to manners and *toilette.* This is one of the several instances in which biography is recapitulated in order to clarify the importance of certain items in the national agenda: labor, profit, inheritance, dilettante absenteeism and development, items which will be repeated in the sweet after-dinner conversation by Gabriel Olmedo, apparently the official voice of the government and the spokesman for the nationalist position of the times. His voice is identical to that of Santos Luzardo in what amounts to a call for national stability and the ideal government, which is one that "knows how to implant peace at all costs" (ibid.).

Once more the discussion is of the meaning of money for men and women, but mainly for women. It is a recapitulation of the devaluation that women undergo in the matrimonial market. It is a debate on poverty that places women at a disadvantage, susceptible to unfavorable and undesirable alliances. It is a forceful affirmation of the order of the new society. Social pacts and alliances are predicated on mixed ethnicity, on programs for "bettering" the race that are carried out from the nineteenth century on; on lineage mixed with intelligence and entrepreneurial mestizos; or on poor but ambitious and intelligent mestizos allied with wealthy mestizos already in the government, and such alliances are also the ruin, once and for all, of the sumptuary and the dilettantish branch of the *Mantuana* oligarchy. This explains why the poor white Creole (María Eugenia Alonso) does not have exchange value for the poor ambitious mestizo (Gabriel Olmedo), but why she does for the rich, intelligent progovernment mestizo (Cesar Leal). It also explains why the rich, white Creole (Uncle Eduardo) marries the virtuous mulatta (María Antonia), and why the rich, progovernment mestizo (Monasterios) establishes alliances with the poor, intelligent, ambitious mestizo through a marriage contract (María Monasterios and Gabriel Olmedo). Aunt Clara's spinsterhood is also introduced into the schema of whose fiancé married somebody else and who is used as a model for Olmedo's conduct. Uncle Pancho's bachelorhood and Mercedes' and Alberto's emigration to Europe are also explained according to the paradigm of poor/rich mestizo marriage contracts.

This ample traffic, a principle of the new social order, is established in the boudoir. Mediation by European culture and poetry, and Parisian culture in particular, by Mercedes' desire, and, for the most part, by the antimarriage and antiheterosexual thesis of de la Parra obscure in this moment the realist unraveling of plot, which will come to bear in the second volume of *Ifigenia,* when we pass from ideal candidate number one to ideal candidate number two, and the mediation of illustrated culture disappears.

There is a wager in favor of enlightened culture which is put into play in the boudoir, and that wager is on elegance and refined manners, on the beauty of the body in which the sumptuary oligarchy, Mercedes and Pancho, believe. Both speak of Gabriel Olmedo realistically. He has everything going for him. He has studied philosophy and political science in Europe. He has written books on sociology and American history. Although he does not "own his own fortune (a horrible deformity!)," Uncle Pancho says that he has "many influences in government thanks to which he will acquire a magnificent business which will make him very rich. He aspires to becoming a political figure" (1: 142). Mercedes adds that, in addition to being ambitious, he always wants more and more, that "he is involved in thousands of businesses and dreams of millions; in addition he has many political aspirations, and for that reason . . . fears marriage so much . . . the idea of any *entrave* which might impede his ascent scares him terribly" (1: 206). In other words, both *Mantuanos* bet on the *raffinée, gourmet, libre-penseur* face of the candidate to secure alliances. But they are very realistic and do not lose sight of the other aspect: oil extraction, government, what makes him in the last instance choose "a brownish girl, fat, small, who goes around all *fagotte,* the most common and vulgar in the world" (1: 208). But this is the theme of the sweet after-dinner conversation.

At twilight, cocktails are served. Women come out to the gallery. They exchange pleasantries. Afterwards, they go into the dining room. The couple presides over both ends of the table. Alberto Galindo is in a bad mood: he did not get the position he wanted in government. All his friends laugh about it. Pancho exaggerates and is ironic. Mercedes plays the second and disagrees. María Eugenia is silent. Gabriel Olmedo has the final word. Two interventions leave his position vis-à-vis Europe and money very clear. Against Uncle Pancho (and Mercedes and María Eugenia) he argues the national line. Against the *Mantuana* oligarchy that woos and promotes and wishes him on their side, the mestizo opposes the defense of Venezuela, a country where "there is organization . . . progress . . . peace"

(1: 227). The comparisons are discarded because in Europe traditions, the past, and "the firm traits of a race already made" are not tantamount to "the period of sociological gestation . . . of race fusion" that Venezuela is undergoing. In absolute agreement with Santos Luzardo, Olmedo also argues against the spirit of tyranny, a consequence of the "fusion of races," and of the "past triumphs and greatness" of the spirit of Independence. The thesis is rounded out by speaking of temperament, the "drive" of the Conquerors, of the pleasure in "squandering." We are, he says, "prodigal, generous, conceited, and ridiculous enough," upstart—

> a cocktail where all our psychological conditions are mixed with a little bit of bitterness . . . due to the immediate influence of this rich nature, leafy and luxuriant; it is the potent sap of the new land; it is the sun; it is the tropics! (1: 227)

Tropicalism is thus assigned as an explanation of the historical past, and a new Monetarist doctrine is restored as the ideology of the new nation-state. "Divine love" has its place in this ideology as a part of the "supreme trinity" of happiness; but to "divine love," which is a woman with a beautiful body and a select spirit, intelligence is added, "the subtle consciousness of things," and money, "without which the whole building will collapse" (1: 236). In this discussion of the trinity, all social groups take their place. To be a member of the new governing group, or of the nation-state, women must be beautiful and/or wealthy. Ethnic groups must have consciousness. And wealthy ones must know how to spend their money. Money is

> an always generous friend . . . a faithful and complacent servant. . . . [It] is not a despot or tyrant except with those who do not know how to treat it, like those imbecilic wealthy ones you [Pancho] speak about; but those who will know how to put it in its place and keep it there, those who will always have it at our feet, as those who dominate it without being dominated by it, let it come to us, with all its army of coins, and for that fight a servant or squire will accompany us and will help us to conquer life. (1: 236)

The theme of the loveless married woman as a prostitute, the discussion of divorce that it insinuates, the construction of the nation-state it proposes—everything is thrown together into a bottomless sack. On women's sacrifice and the prostitution of heterosexual love is predicated the destruction of the founding base of the mestizo republic, whose Monetarism, based on its ambition for money and governmental alliances, reeks.

Gender/Genre and Ethnicity

The white, oligarchic *Mantuana* nation is always the focus of discussion. The mulatta nation is an absurdity, a nightmare, the grotesque. The black nation, a "sympathetic" illiteracy. In the dialogic relationship between Gregoria and María Eugenia Alonso, Teresa de la Parra constructs a place for blacks. The illiterate maid,

> has epigrammatic gestures, falling eyelids that are parentheses, sudden silences that turn out to be very eloquent epilogues, and peals of laughter that describe in its notes . . . all feelings and passions that could stir in the human soul. (1: 165)

In this grammar, perfected by mimicry and seasoned with the sweetness of conversation in oral cultures, resides the secret of service. It is not washing and ironing, knowing how to cook, that is appreciated in this narrative, as it will be in Schwarz-Bart, but fidelity to the family, expressed as continuity, long years of service. Black nannies, wet nurses of the oligarchy, are repaid with favorable adjectives: "friends," "confidante," "mentor," "intelligent and wise," "a poet's soul," "disdainful of prejudice," "elegantly indifferent," and "sweetly pious," to give only a few examples.

Reading Jean Rhys, we will see that the debate over the representation of these women has stirred up trouble. Caribbean cultures have wanted to interpret them as signals of a world without representation but whose epistemologies exist and have contributed to the formation of mulatto countries. We will see how this criticism has tried to push the limits of the text by ascertaining on its margins the sense of these other oral cultures embodied in black women working as wet nurses.

The image of old servants as companions, the presence of these ancient guardians as historical continuity, is one of the architraves in the construction of both gender and nation—of gender, because physically and spiritually they support the white feminine protagonists; and of nation, because the representatives of ethnicity—the obscured faces of the Creole and of the mestizo—constitute the majority of the population and the majority of the labor force in their texts.

Servants are usually black or indigenous people. In Rhys, de la Parra, Loynaz, and Schwarz-Bart, they are black: Christophine, Gregoria, Laura and Télumée; in Belli, they are indigenous people. Their presence in the text is a citation, a phrase, a wordless existence, clear examples of subaltern cultures and repressed and marginalized epistemologies. Nevertheless, they are the historical deposits of the family. They know the historical truths of lineage and of patrilineal ascendance, of familial struggles and divisions; they are witnesses to the purity of blood, and possessors of very detailed information on dowries and financial credibility. Servants are relevant in moments of decay, loss of fortune, or psychic disorder and are therefore the chroniclers of old *Independentistas, Mantuana* families, the old planter class, the impoverished or revolutionary oligarchy. But their track is brief.

The briefest is Loynaz' "old maid, the fabulous maid" Laura, who becomes an archetype: "a figure dead in life," a zombi, but also "a figure wrought in quarried stone," like those supporting the architraves of the majestic gates. Laura is also "inquisitorial," "with a malignant and punishing expression." A woman who seems to "live in another world," gesticulating "as if arguing with some invisible being," pronouncing "half-enunciated words" between her teeth. A woman with "stony eyes, encrusted at the bottom of the corneas . . . fixed, immobile, as fallen," an ideological relative of Brontë's Bertha (Loynaz, 1: 102–103). On her lips this ancient woman, half dead, half blind, still a witch, stony sighted, still holds a curse—"You have the devil inside your body; you always had it . . . a hundred years since" (1: 103)—or an ominous piece of advice.

Against these masters and slaves who barely meet at the end of slavery, in the private spaces of the impoverished white oligarchic woman, we have the modern woman written by Schwarz-Bart, the ex-slave/servant, revolutionary mental subject, who now owns her own voice, or, written by de la Parra, for whom she is the servant of the *Mantuana* oligarchy but at the same time a point of reference for the ethno-nation, living in *La Pastora* and working in the fields of the estate.

Mulattoes and mestizos are not situated on the same signifying plane as blacks. They require a more complex interpretation and representation, not only because they embody an aspect of whites, but also because it is principally with them that the new social pact is being negotiated. Hence, their textual treatment serves as a conduit for doubting this "multi-colored mixture of races, where one could sense the white prevailing, but discredited as in the caricatures; the resemblance prevails in spite of the deformity" (Parra, 1: 122). This cacophony, this ugliness is the mulatta:

> a patient crucible where the heterogeneous elements of so many adventurous races fuse. . . . Enclosed in her are the causes of all our disquiet, of all our errors, our absurd democracy, our erring lack of stability. . . . [P]erhaps in her a new social type, exquisite, complex, which we do not still suspect, is being elaborated. (ibid.)

The blacks, as a function of their blackness, are always faithful and good servants. Gregoria is Christophine's alter ego, and her ideological function is to give us the other (the decaying) side of the family history. That is, in both cases, they are not only chroniclers and funds on deposit, but points of view, at times alternative to those expressed by a member of the family clan—the profile, hint, and blueprint of a possible revolutionary modern subjectivity and alternative epistemology. The writers in question make them a repository of truth as much as the representation of fidelity and devotion to the family.

In the case of Christophine, she and Antoinette are the only ones who know the true family history. Christophine is the one who advises Antoinette to renarrate, aloud, to her husband's face, her personal biography so that he knows the truth. In Teresa de la Parra, the structure is identical: María Eugenia Alonso, her grandmother, Uncle Pancho, and Gregoria are the ones who know the true biography of the clan of Alonso and Aguirre. But Gregoria and the grandmother sustain opposite points of view. As her mother's wet nurse, and because of the love she holds for María Eugenia, she renarrates the family's biography in such a way that María Eugenia finds it satisfactory.

The truths María Eugenia wishes to corroborate concern property ownership. The family is divided between the frivolous and supposedly disinterested—the grandfather, Enrique, María Eugenia's father—and the dishonest—Eduardo and his wife María Antonia, "a mulatta, whose parents were not married, loaded with evil and race-hatreds" (1: 188).

The View through the Binoculars

Textualizing nation has been one of the main obsessions of male writers. Textualizing social groups is a close second. These master narratives are so overwhelming that in plotting women and ethnicity the writer, and therefore the reader, feels very compelled, overdetermined. Nation is to gender and ethnicity what macronarratives are to micro- and what master genres are to subgenres.

In Teresa de la Parra, the concept of nation becomes evident in the contemplation of space, of signs that bring it together, as, for example, in the port of La Guayra and in Macuto beach—invoking comparisons between Europe and Venezuela. It is evident in signs delineating landscapes: the highway, for example; and in signs delineating sources of inspiration for poets and painters: for instance, the mountain. But it is also in neighborhoods like *La Pastora,* where nation is contemplated in terms of ethnicity; and in Mercedes' house, where the boudoir is a unique feminine space; and in the political discussions after dinner on the *hacienda* and in the house.

In de la Parra's *Ifigenia,* we can visualize the transition from one space to the other using the view through a pair of binoculars as a metaphor. Approaching land, peering through her binoculars, María Eugenia Alonso contemplates the nation from a ship. This distanced nation is at first de-scribed/felt in the language of Positivism. Nation is, therefore, what is visible: port and beach, export economy and tourist industry.

La Guayra/Macuto is the first dichotomy that the contemplating eye per-ceives—a dichotomy containing all the oppositions that such a perception represents: mestizo/white; poor/rich; work/recreation; ugliness/beauty. Nation is a bifurcated space. European harmony, fabricated through educa-tion, consumerism, and ethnic "homogeneity," disappears from the pano-rama but it remains a paradigmatic element of comparison.

Nation is dichotomy and contradiction but also physical landscape. It is a big mountain, with a group of tiny houses clinging to it like goats on a cliff, like a crèche. The train is very small and narrow, and the highway "more open but less daring." When, on top of the mountain, María Euge-nia turns her head to see what is behind her, she again sees La Guayra as a miniature: it looked "so little, so little," with all its houses, boats, ships—like "children's toys." A most diminutive world. Caracas is a city of compressed, one-story houses, oppressed by the roofs, gaudily painted.

As we can see, the clear distinction between the masculine space—ample, productive, wild—cannot but contrast with the smallness of this feminine space. Nation is, for the one, an epic, the place of his own action, the site where he becomes a man, and for the other, a poetic-pictorial object of contemplation. In man it is a vision *in situ,* in woman, a relative point of comparison. Santos left the plains of Arauco to go to Caracas to study, but María Eugenia Alonso lived as many years in Caracas as in Europe, and the years of absence erased the true dimensions of the country from her mem-ory. In comparison to Europe this is a minirepublic, the nation-country, a neoclassical and Romantic landscape: painting and poetry, the land more an object of contemplation than a political-productive organization.

The patriarchal *hacienda* is also more a point of reference than a meta-phor for the organization of the state. That is why the mountain, the Andes, the Avila, become vantage points from which the expatriate subject, colored by European schooling, contemplates a land "arrogant," "myste-rious," set "very high." Painters copy it with love, and with love all poets sing of it. This is the neoclassical country of Romantic Independence and *Independentistas,* not of Modern Neo-Positivism.

María Eugenia shuts her eyes to contemplate it with her inner vision or to eliminate it from her sight. The binoculars reversed makes things seem smaller. This is also the perspective of a Latin American subject educated abroad and recently returned. And the Modernity to which she clings is that of Modernism. It is an aesthetic, cosmopolitanized space: the trans-atlantic, Parisian fashion, education, and laissez-faire, although this last term invokes the frontier between genders. De la Parra's writings understand laissez-faire within the ideological terrain of everyday life and manners and customs; in Gallegos, as in the nation he ruled, it is strictly an economic term. In de la Parra, Gallegos' Modernity is underrated. In her narrative, the telephone cables that sag over the rooftops, and the telephone poles that stand impertinently with their arms open wide, like crosses, are deficiencies: they spoil. Dull and undeserving, they are like the cables and electric poles in Schwarz-Bart, except that they carry antithetical connotations.

Venezuela is thus first an unmediated mirror image. Later, upon acculturation, adjustment will come. Venezuela will come to mean productive policies, and then it will be discussed in terms of patriarchal symbolism. But in this moment, Venezuela's image is a bad copy, a reduction: Macuto, for instance, stands for Venezuela's Deauville or San Sebastian, just a caricature. One word captures it: ugly. As Gallegos' adjectives apply to both plain and woman, de la Parra's use of ugly and ugliness applies to Venezuela and mulattas, and consequently in both cases to nation: in Gallegos, a barbarian and untamed nation, and in de la Parra, an ugly one. Ugliness can only be circumvented by making the nation smaller, a miniature. In contrast to the conventions of current Primitivistic paintings, miniaturization and folklore—the picturesque—are the place of self-depreciation. María Eugenia asks Uncle Pancho to take her to see the ugliest, the poorest, the dirtiest, the saddest. Uncle Pancho, the civilized uncle with whom she allies herself, shows her the ugliness of her circumstances. On her visit to *La Pastora,* Caracas' poorest neighborhood, where she can see up close every detail of poverty, her vision of ethnicity, inspired by Gobineau, emerges full force. Nation there means dirt, badly paved streets, weeds, stones, a space inhabited by half-breeds.

Nation: A Polyphony

In the strictest Bakhtinian sense, *Ifigenia* is a polyphonic novel. The fierce battle waged over ideas includes all possible perspectives of the enlightened Modernist and Modernizing Venezuelan horizon, sprinkled with all the European knowledges available to its author.

It would be idle speculation to try to discern which of many voices is the voice of the author, since what can be touched is rather the problematization of the situation of the impoverished oligarchic woman within the national horizon of Modernization. What is obvious is the ridicule of the functional paradigms of gender assumed by Modernity. She conclusively demonstrates her belief in the civil rights of women, and therefore the conservatism implicit in the national projects.

That Madame de la Parra's sexual preference has, to a large extent, determined the terms of the discussion is undeniable; it is a matter of basic justice to acknowledge and communicate sexual preference within this or any text. But it is also her formal education that makes her accede to the limits of the liberal horizon and question the validity of the proposed emancipation. The concept of the subject she championed is clear through her diaries: a very well-articulated self and a total acceptance of her own value.[10] In several instances in this narrative, a comparison of her writings reveals an unequivocal narrative self. She has her own voice, mainly in her ideas on frivolity and elegance, in being an intelligent, attractive, reasonable person and an even better discussant, pleasant, entertaining.

Of her reading list there is little to be said. *Ifigenia* is written using the prestigious, enlightened European discourses: French, German, English, Italian, and Spanish literatures occupy a supple textual space. But the same arguments are borrowed in that other cultivated space to which she is opposed, at conferences, in *Las memorias de la mamá blanca*, in her letters and diaries, in her love for Venezuela, and in her family pride. For that reason, she does not let herself be swept up in sentimentalism, or in arguments and proposals from the bosom of the national *galleguista* oligarchy. Within the *hacienda*, she is barely interested in the house's outer shell. As in Belli's first novel, the San Nicolás estate is more a domestic unity, ornamentation and vines, than a productive dominion, even if property rights and inheritance form the larger structure of the text.

Nevertheless, in letting Gabriel Olmedo, Cesar Leal, the grandmother, Uncle Pancho, and Aunt Clara speak, she lets the voices be their own, and their positions are presented with all due respect to dialogism. I have underscored the most relevant questions of funding, as much the funding of the Republic as of the independence of gender, and I have detected a subterranean Monetarist, Neo-Positivist undercurrent in the midst of all the adherence to Rubén Darío and French Modernism. There is, no doubt, a profound understanding of the seriousness of the national debate together with a genuine respect for science and technology. There is also disrespect for the economic persona and a neglect of labor. Hers is therefore a European rather than a North American Neo-Positivism. Mr. Danger has no place in her novel, but neither does doña Bárbara.

If *mestizaje* perhaps concerns her, it concerns her as an already consolidated fact in civil society, in its meddling with family genes. But the national discussion she offers is very sophisticated, much more avant-garde than the one she recapitulates in her second book, where, as Garrels points out she definitely falls seventy-five years behind.

It is obvious that the discussion of gender parallels the formation of the modern nation-state. The larger the one the smaller the other. That is the condition of their relation: inverse and reverse, as can be appreciated very clearly in the second, much weaker, more obscure volume of her novel, which is more conformist and a clear example of a retreat from forms of social and political realism.

I have left aside a great deal of textual analysis—that which refers to the development of sentimental and Romantic sensibility in women (I believe de la Parra herself disqualifies it)—in order to fulfill my purpose, that of tying gender and nation; the juncture was financial sensibilities. Neither have I referred much to *Las memorias de la mamá blanca,* for substantially I subscribe to Garrels' critique. Furthermore, I believe that, in gender formation, María Eugenia Alonso is more substantive, and that, within herself, there is a variety of voices that run from simple ridicule to the most mediated parody, to irony and sarcasm. Heterosexual romance occupies, in the case of the Colombian poet, for instance, a very disqualified pole, but for all that no less telling, for the moment of physical contact, the moment of kissing, separates women and men in the three instances of heterosexuality. There are no caresses in this novel. Mercedes and Alberto barely speak to each other. Eduardo and María Antonia are a mutual aid society. And the rest are single: spinsters, widows, and bachelors. The discussion turns on other surroundings; although Romantic emotional masturbation occupies a great deal of textual space and deserves to be taken into consideration as the development of an alternative sensibility, it is not our purpose to examine it. To the degree that it touches on eroticism, and proposes divorces and other kinds of alternative couplings, it deserves our attention.

In closing I would like to underline the extraordinary characterization of two women at opposite ends of the spectrum: Mercedes Galindo and grandmother Eugenia. Narrated from within, both constitute, however, the European and Latin American side of the plot. The exquisite Mercedes, all propriety and all taste, as much as the no-less-distinguished grandmother, belong to a world already decayed, in which the spirit of both, conveyed by the protagonist, is crushed by the new utilitarian sensibility of Uncle Eduardo, Gabriel Olmedo, and Cesar Leal, the latter, like Santos Luzardo, sealing and ratifying the closure of the discussion, embodying the spirit of the law in the nation's Senate.

Garden/Nation—*Parva Domus: Magna Quies*

Old Houses/New Houses

On Havana's exquisite Línea Street, a few blocks from the splendour of Paseo Avenue, there is an old, great house surrounded by a lush garden. Propped up by a decaying cellar, probably conceived as a workplace, the first and only floor exposes the remnants of a delicately trellised gallery that hugs the house on all sides. The wooden frame is barely holding up. The carefully carved railings lining the balustrade are no longer standing. Through the red clay shingles of the peaked roofs, carefully decorated with gingerbread fretwork, grass grows, and old, braided twigs, vines, branches, and trunks of trees lean against the wall, obscuring the termite-eaten seals of the louvered windows. The shady arbor that once insulated the interior, keeping the tropical rooms cool, the plants growing through the lattice and the flowers blossoming on the terracota jars, once ballast on the cargo ships that transported meat and oil from the lesser Antilles are now gone. But the house is still white and seigneurial, and has not lost its aristocratic demeanor. At the beginning of the century this house must have been a strong beacon to its class; it was itself a class of house very different from the houses of Paseo Avenue, some of which were built around that period. The year Dulce María Loynaz won the National Poetry Award, I was told that that house was her patrimony, her father's house, the house of Enrique Loynaz del Castillo, a General of the Liberating Army.

It is not possible for me to read the novel *Jardín* (1935)[1] without thinking about that house, the house standing on Línea Street in Havana today. Several of the surrounding houses would have to be torn down to replant the trees described in the novel as stretching out to the sea. Cut off from the city and converted back into a country home, the great house on Línea

Street would have the same avenues as in *Jardín*, leading to the beach, reproducing and reconstituting scenarios in the novel.

This is one way of reintroducing what Edward Said calls worlding. But another way is to suggest an opposition between the two constructions, the old and the new, and to interpret this old agrarian house, a remnant of plantation architecture, as a historical utterance contrasting with other historical utterances. In this light, the old house on Línea Street, in relation to the new mansions of Paseo Avenue, will come to be less a house and more the re-presentation of a pavilion, the small pavilion in the middle of the lush garden where Loynaz' novel locates all the documents in which meaning gestates. *"Parva Domus, Magna Quies"*—"Small House, Great Quietude"—the inscription at the entrance of the pavilion—acquires symbolic implications through which I want to propose a metonymic reading of family and of nation.

The family here is not biological but social, the national family of the Cuban *Independentistas* that the novel describes—Gómez and the mulatto Maceo, under whose orders her father fought, but also Serafín Sánchez, and perhaps Quintín Banderas and Guillermo Moncada too, black men who led not on account of race but on the basis of military ability.[2] It would not be overstating the case to say that in writing Woman as frail, impoverished, and alone, then later having her marry a foreigner, Loynaz—like Teresa de la Parra and Jean Rhys—writes the biography of her own social group in the Other island after the abolition of slavery and the two wars, the small and the big, that culminated in independence under the Platt Amendment. Oligarchic women like Darío's princesses are alone (*Obras completas, passim*). And as in Raymond Williams' discussion of English country houses—which concentrates not on what they represent but on what they are, the result of opposing sociopolitical relations—Loynaz' house, the real as much as the imaginary, is empty. All the slaves are gone and only one remains in servitude, the old black nanny, Laura.

Dualism in the Garden

In *Jardín*, Dulce María Loynaz plots a woman, Bárbara, enclosed in a house and a garden. Within this garden she finds a pavilion, and inside the pavilion some love letters, and a dress belonging to another woman, possibly her great-grandmother, and a poster dated 184–. Before finding the pavilion, Bárbara wanders about in the garden, reflecting on the nature of the garden. And, in the house, she unravels her biography through her reading and interpretation of family photographs. Bárbara lives with Laura, a housemaid, a woman who, in contrast to Rhys' Christophine, is barely noticed and whose textual presence is limited to a very few, mostly negative, references in the text.

Reading the love letters, perhaps the most eventful and plot-oriented aspect of the text, Bárbara invents a romantic love which she wishes to recreate for herself. One day, ambling around the beach, she meets a foreigner, a nameless shipwrecked man who falls in love with her and proposes marriage. Like Rhys, Loynaz states that "the young seaman is only a complement in the book. That is why he is not named, not even with an initial letter" (P. Simón, 56). Bárbara accepts, and leaves her enchanted garden only to find Europe unbecoming. Civilization, technology, two children, and all the horrors of war are not enough to make her forget her enchanted house and garden. So then she decides to return. The immediate identification of her natural/social environment—beach, city, house, and garden— makes her leave the boat for the coast. When she finally reaches her house, the old structure, as if waiting for her return, collapses, killing her.

The novel could be divided into two parts, one developing the notions of house/garden/nation, and the other, woman's experience of cosmopolitan development. Thus, in the second part of the text, Bárbara wanders aimlessly in a European Neo-Positivistic landscape which only makes her more melancholy over the separation from her native milieu. The extremity with which the mechanization of time permeates everyday life disgusts her and makes her feel alienated. In fact, the whole second part of the novel is treated with such expediency as to give the impression of notes jotted down in a personal travel diary and then transferred to the novel. What is relevant throughout the narrative is the thorough solitude of Woman enclosed in a garden, and the irrelevance of coupling, marriage, and children.

Fina García Marruz has stated:

> If the historical context of the novel is taken into account (frustration of the republic, loss of foundational hope), [this historical context] becomes evident [in] the nexus between this closed-in, intimate atmosphere and the inescapable exterior surrounding [it]. (P. Simón, 549)

In fact, to construct a narrative about declassé nineteenth-century white women is not an easy task, and we must always surmise that it is done from what Jameson calls a melancholic perspective. In fact, according to its author, the novel was very problematic. That is the reason Loynaz withheld it for seventeen years and could have withheld it for still twenty more. What disturbs her is that *Jardín* has no genre, that it is not a novel, for it lacks "action," "plot," "time," and "space." If it has a plot, she says, it is weak and disconnected; and if it has action, it is loose and discontinuous. The story is thus without a spine, like an invertebrate, and the character barely flesh and bone, unreal. Because of its lack of normative narrative structures, it is impossible to make it fit the molds, tastes, manners, and beliefs of its times. And the text is thus declared ahead of its time by its author.

Textual doubts from women are not surprising. In fact one can argue they are a norm. They speak of women's social condition as much as of their consciousness of difference. In this case, however, Loynaz' doubts could be understood as reflections on pastiche.[3] For her narrative is made up of several narratives, in which the inquiring voice coordinates and relates all others. One of her main problems, she confesses, is the historical construction of gender, for woman has no history: woman is "less than the first woman, less than the first human being in the nebulous dawning of Creation" (105). "Her solitude . . . [is as] pure as [the] . . . chaos before the creation of the world" (108). Woman is an "intruder guest," an "unexpected newcomer," and this creates grave problems for her, mainly a lack of verisimilitude; she brings to Loynaz the ire of a lack of verisimilitude in an epoch that lives and dies for "realism."

It is difficult to determine the type of realism Loynaz is referring to, but in reading the text one is taken aback by an abrupt shift in meaning. It gives the impression that events have taken the author by surprise or that she has written the novel at two different moments. The protagonist follows two opposing constitutive principles, and her composition is double-edged. If the novel's premises were initially based on well-learned lessons of silence that make women remiss, quiet, conditioned to give up, to disappear, to be dispossessed of whatever is not strictly necessary and not to need too much, the second part of the text disavows these principles, and woman becomes a voracious consumer.

As we will examine later, the strong Modernist sensibility that informs the first woman does not cohere with the second, a woman constituted within the Neo-Positivistic discourse of progress, development, mechanization, and the productive use of time as money. This dislocation ties gender to nation and makes one represent the other. If, as Jean Franco has demonstrated, in male narratives of nation, Woman is its metaphor, in feminine narratives the pattern is inverted. Thus Loynaz, like Belli, Schwarz-Bart, Rhys, and de la Parra, not only inscribes a dislocated, disarticulated Woman in the history of the field, but also feminizes the concept of nation.

Considered from a feminist perspective, *Jardín* is a novel of ordeal.[4]

Woman wants to discover her own sense of self, deposited in the middle of the garden. Garden is then a laboratory, a cabinet, a world, and Woman an experimenter, an explorer, an interpreter. Endurance and wisdom are the narrative's intended products and that is why philosophical reflection overwhelms it. In passively looking for—or in accidentally finding—meaning, Woman begins to live her own history.

In this manner, I argue, *Jardín* plots stasis and duality, selects iconographic and symbolic representation, proposes the reading and writing of private letters as a historical record of gender construction, proposes imagination and dreams as a means through which to enter reality.[5] Thus we come across a third-person lyrical narrative of enclosure. Woman is silent because there is no one, except the old maid she dismisses, to have a dialogue with. Her speech act is babble, simple sentences cast to the winds: "This is the house," "This is the echo," "It is not raining anymore." And as we will see later, in the move from the first to the second letter of the alphabet, from A to B, she discovers passion along with identity.

Bárbara's enclosure in the garden is not at all surprising, for in Loynaz, as in Rhys, biography and literary invention are very close. In several interviews she has told the story of her secluded life:

> Our childhood and adolescense transpired in a secluded ambiance, surrounded by solicitous affection, by the excessive concern in which there was a kind of eagerness to preserve us from vague dangers, to keep us far from the ebb and flow of the world. (P. Simón, 70)

Gender/Genre in Transition

Such considerations of *Jardín*[6] allow us to illustrate the case of Woman's construction as a gender-in-transition which occurs with the closure of the *Independentista*'s project, in the transition from the nineteenth to the twentieth century, and in the new modernization projects in the Caribbean. Le Riverend tells us that by 1930 a new Cuban consciousness had emerged:

> [D]uring the years of Zayas' government [1921–1925], Cubans born between 1895 and 1902 reach maturity, that is, [they become] a new generation which is neither complicit with the growing deterioration that surrounds them [following] the intervention in the Republic, nor is it committed, as occurred with the mass of liberators, to follow certain warlords, commanders, or leaders whose actions after 1902 had been a flagrant negation of Martí's program. (198)

And Loló de la Torriente informs us that in the Feminine Club,

> passionate debates were raised on the rights of illegitimate children and the protection of the unwed mother, on women's suffrage and equality in wages, equal pay for equal work, for both sexes. (122)

In *Jardín,* therefore, I see the continuation of a concern with nation and modernization textualized earlier by Teresa de la Parra and later by Jean Rhys, notwithstanding Loynaz' assertion that "politics is a field she never *invades*" (P. Simón, 45; my emphasis). In my reading of this novel I want to uncover the existing dialogical relations between this text and the history of Latin American letters and national macronarratives, as well as to underscore what Loló de la Torriente asserts about Cuban women during this period:

> If, during the wars of '68 and '95, [women] had fearlessly put on the percale dress and the *yarey* hat to reach the *manigua,* and upon the inauguration of the Republic they were forgotten and their citizen's rights relegated [to oblivion], now, in the struggles of 1930, organizing and directing, suffering from ruthless attacks against their feelings and their patriotism, they were going to demonstrate that, steadfast before men's ingratitude, their quality continued to be fashioned of bronze. . . . She was not a romantic and poetic heroine. She was, indeed, a woman of flesh and bones. (215)

As we can clearly see, here discourses of both nation and gender intersect, but their images, mainly their representative metaphors, vary. They position themselves in oppositions determined by the author's gender. Where women are interested in placing the gendered subject at the center, men center nation. In this manner the reproductive-family pole and the productive-national one, the house and the nation, are defined as the primordial elements in the dialogue and the arenas in which discussions of meaning will be undertaken.[7]

Placing Loynaz' woman at the center, de la Parra and Rhys are comparative elements, in one case of a nationally constituted state, Venezuela, vis-à-vis a protostate (a primary definition of country, whose ordering elements are sentimental, religious, symbolic, and ritualistic), Jamaica, and in the other, a state in receivership, Cuba. The national discussion, therefore, will be written differently: in the first case, it is an internal national struggle amongst Venezuelan groups, with clear private-enterprise projects and an entrepreneurial group already constituted. In the second case, it is an international struggle between a state (England) and a protostate (Jamaica), with a ruined planter class and a recently emancipated black population still undifferentiated. And in the third, it is a transitional moment between the second and the first, a threatened state, whose socioethnic groups, through a common front, recently achieved their independence.

I do not want to suggest a reading on the preferential national axis and thus fall victim to hegemonic macronarrative guidelines. Used to reading along that axis, in reading characters, we generally read sectorial typologies and therefore we did macrological readings. I have proposed throughout this book, therefore, an inverse reading, considering as a central vector the intersection of ethnicity and gender, to see how national projects fare. Integral to such rereadings are considerations of the history of sensibility, the narrativizations of love and the prospects of coupling, where in fact the economic and social development projects document themselves through issues of gender.

Thinking from, towards, and on women, I must warn, is more advanced, that is, more complex in Venezuela—as much because of the historical moments de la Parra narrativizes in her novel *Ifigenia* as because of her life experience. Teresa de la Parra was educated in Europe and was a resident of France and Spain. In *Wide Sargasso Sea,* almost the opposite is true. In contrast, in *Jardín,* we find a worn-out sensibility, a disorientation and ambivalence similar to de la Parra's and Rhys', but whose narrativization is mixed, although the gendered subject continues to be constituted in solitude, imprisoned in its spaces—garden, attic, bedroom—or in history and the collective memory. In fact, while de la Parra was a widely traveled Venezuelan woman, Loynaz was a Cuban woman endowed with "a rare and fine temperament, sensitive to the mysterious and impenetrable and addicted to resignation" (Torriente, 153)—a temperament which was educated indoors, for she states:

> [O]ur elders were people of taste and cultivated knowledge. My mother had studied painting with a good professor and possessed a beautiful, dramatic voice. She used to sing professionally, accompanied by piano. That was the ambiance of our house. Everyone was pleased by the sensibility we were discovering. (P. Simón, 33)

All this during the years of "the great battles for citizenship," during "the best years of the formation of our civic criteria" (Torriente, 159).

There are nuances, however. If, according to de la Parra, the Venezuelan state discusses an intrasectorial and interethnic alliance, and recognizes that the entrepreneurial oligarchy has displaced the traditional one and that unproductive and luxurious spending must be replaced and reformulated—proposing a productive social subject who can establish relations with the external world and face Mr. Danger and doña Bárbara—it is logical that gender, as a productive national category, is going to be constituted with more elements and better judgment than in cases like Jamaica's. In Jamaica, the productive project has collapsed and a new one is not yet in place. The sugar oligarchy, the famous planter class, bases its sense of self as a social subject in its resemblances to the metropolis and in opposition to the local ethnic groups, not recognizing at the beginning the ethnic component as a priority for their social milieu (Ragatz, *passim*). Or there is the case of Cuba, a national state under the threat posed by the Platt Amendment: that is, a state threatened with extinction, with following the path of Puerto Rico. The emphasis on the nascent consciousness of and the struggle for the formation of civic criteria in 1930 underscore this predicament.

If, in the narrative extremes, we have Woman constructed first as a spokesperson for civil rights and as a legal subject, as a productive subject, that is, according to a liberal concept of Woman resembling the English Suffragette, and second as mentally disturbed, a woman who has lost all her parameters and whose place is in the asylum, then in the middle we have the constructions of transition. Corresponding to the Cuban awakening, Bárbara has one foot in enclosure, alienation, and decadence, and the other in modernization. In the first case, the project is national and in the second, international.

In *Jardín*, Loynaz' feminist social imaginary has embodied the image of a traditional woman and of a chic, elegant woman, the Object-Woman of fashion magazines, among them *La Mode Illustrée*, of which de la Parra's woman speaks so much. I see in this transformation a metaphor, that of an elaboration of the national project coming from destroyed sugar plantation economies setting out on the road of transnational economies, fundamentally related to European and U.S. markets.[8]

In the first instance, and in my opinion the best analyzed textually, the woman constructed as an image or metaphor of nation is elaborated following the tenets of a Modernist sensibility already outmoded. It is this Modernist sensibility that differentiates her from male modes of representation of the moment. Loynaz problematizes the idea of nation. Contrary to the image of the aggressive, barbarian, phallic women represented in the national narratives of land and forest, or the less aggressive but desensualized women who follow men to the plantation and end up somehow participating with them in production and therefore becoming productive and reproductive women simultaneously (I think here of the banana plantation texts), or simply hostages, as in *La Vorágine,* woman in this text is of a different nature.

Bárbara is in many ways a replica of the loved ones in Nervo, Silva, del Casal: pale, absent, airy, of nacre and ivory, delicate, insubstantial, woman fitting Pablo Neruda's dictum, "I like you when you are silent, because you seem absent." Woman in Loynaz is therefore solitude, color, pedigree, and marriage. Nacre, ivory, and pearl, let us not forget, are exotic Modernist import objects belonging to a Saidian Orientalist taste already *demodé* in 1935, the year *Jardín* was published. Woman is not a speaking subject; on the contrary, she is silent, absent, airy—all attributes of a recently constituted femininity already in the process of dissolution.[9]

Like Bárbara, the women central to de la Parra and Rhys are white; the three come from the social class exercising power and are therefore linked to the white women who populate Southern U.S. literatures.[10] In their whiteness, they contradict the original national paradigm of contemporaneous novels, in which textualized women already denote *mestizaje* and therefore the sectorial social pacts that define nation as multiethnic, political ideas that transcend their original discursive field and are later reproduced in literature.

To the degree that these women writers substitute one gendered subject for another, they also alter the national paradigm and introduce nuances into it, for it is on this whiteness that new types of alliances will be mapped. The marriage between Marisela and Santos Luzardo, for instance, permits the new ideas of capitalist property—fenced, productive, rational, and yielding—to succeed. In women the equivalent metaphors are enclosed, sensitive, and fecund. Thus is plotted the triumph of Modernization over backwardness, over unproductiveness. Doña Bárbara, a raped woman, responds to violation with a force that in a woman scares the spirit of public enterprise.[11]

In contrast to Gallegos' narrativization of gender, Teresa de la Parra presents a higher discursive level. She inverts the poles of meaning; her imaginary creature embodies in herself civilization. Barbarianism is assigned to men, mainly to suitors. Barbarianism is a male attribute, made evident in the movement away from finesse and into commercialism and monetarism, the spirit of free enterprise, the desire for a rationalization of the production of the countryside and of oil exploitation.

Feelings mediate solutions to national conflicts; they are also a metaphor for wealth and development. Textualized marriages lend themselves to a commercial reading. In *Doña Bárbara,* the pact between city and country people over property relations and forms of land tenure systems is a commercial transaction. The countryside and the port city come closer together in productive thought. In *Ifigenia* the opposite is true: the countryside and the pastoral *hacienda* are separated and counterposed to the city and productive values. That is why the developed *hacienda* pole wishes to neutralize the sector of the idle, consumption-oriented oligarchy, who are lazy, of *bolivariana* ancestry, which, in turn, fears its other self, the entrepreneurial sector associated with oil production.

The marital solutions—marriages as alliances and pacts—are in the case of women predicated on the bases of phenotype and skin color, which in Caribbean societies is synonymous with purity of blood. Purity of blood is in turn related to creolization processes and mixtures, and consequently with the battle to define nations as mestizo republics or to implant the idea of two de facto segregated republics. Blood ties with indigenous people are feared, but blood ties with blacks are feared even more. Nevertheless, in both cases, narrativization of the social pact indicates recognition, in the first case, of the multiethnic character of national space and, in the second, of the internal ruptures of the power elite.

In other instances, particularly those of the Caribbean islands, English or Spanish, white protagonists, Modernists of Tropical Gothicism, establish alliances at an international level. They are the ones who marry foreign suitors and who, in the English case, see in them the solution to the rights of primogeniture and the law of patriarchy, and who, in the Spanish case, see the opposite.[12] Contempt for local monetarism does not translate internationally.

To recapitulate, in the national macronarratives, logo- and phallocentric, gender appears as an object of exchange, as a means of establishing economic, political, or social transactions. Woman is already represented as an ethnically mixed subject. In the feminine narratives, on the contrary, she is still an object of exchange but her situation is not plotted as natural. On the contrary, the debate on marriage and its conceptualization troubles the narrative and calls into question fairness in the spirit of the law.

This can happen because the women represented belong to the same power group. And even if it is decadent power or the decadent side of power, they are repositories of lineage and tradition and are coveted as allies by the recently constituted power groups. They are dignified repositories, keepers, blood banks, and savings accounts for the entrepreneurial class. The transition between destitution and elegance, or between impoverished elegance and high fashion, is marked in their consumption as an investment in appearance. To dress Bárbara as a European is to make her follow the Eurocentric normative patterns.

But, whether woman is destitute and *declassé* or reclassified as a *Vogue* woman, male/female relations are characterized as dramatic due to the fact that white women are conscious of their sacrifice for the sake of a social pact, whereas for the mestiza the male author/narrator proposes miscegenation as a social privilege, as a means of ascending the social ladder, "improving the race," a move that brings her closer to power. If white women have to become Europeanized, mestizas have to be whitewashed.

These white women have a history. María Eugenia Alonso is related to Simón Bolívar's family. She is a *Mantuana* and as such she not only has a feeling of majesty and belonging but also rights granted by legal and educational privileges. She has studied in Europe. Loynaz' Bárbara is well read, very cultivated. But in both cases it is their historical ancestry which enables them to remain within a social circle to which they no longer belong economically. Aristocratic *Independentistas* as they are, even if they are totally dispossessed, impoverished, and indebted, their bodies are an asset, a kind of trust fund.

Woman has to utilize her family name and her sexual desirability as well as her ethnicity to keep a decorous economic place, and therefore she accepts her position as an object of exchange. She transforms herself into the chic woman of the avant-garde, into the object-woman of the republican Neo-Positivist program. This impoverished woman is heir to a past history she idealizes and glorifies, a history she knows only through the interpretation of written documents or the spoken word.

Their patrimonial social spaces have shrunk. Hence the signs of enclosure. Having enjoyed the ample geographical spaces of flourishing *haciendas* and prosperous plantations as their own spaces, white women are now circumscribed by their bedrooms. Their private rooms are safety-deposit boxes of virginity (purity of blood) but also, as Franco reminds us, prisons for virgins, places where nuns, celibate women, and rebels are situated in a state of siege. But these rooms are also privileged spaces for reproduction, a situation for women signifying the cost of social pacts and the laws obligating them. Bedrooms become combat zones.

Woman in de la Parra is educated. She partakes of all the frivolities and flirtatiousness of the new century; she is dressed by Parisian designers and is aware of the rights of women called for by the Suffragettes. She has to become familiar with the role assigned to Venezuelan women at the beginning of the century, and forced acceptance of prearranged marriages comes to be the only way of life available to her. Antoinette Cosway also resigns herself to leaving her native land, travels to England, and ends up locked in the attic of patriarchal mentality.

Being locked up in her house and forced to substitute a liberal, Neo-Positivist and Modern mentality for a conservative, oppressive, religious one, or else opt for madness, demonstrates that the only plan that Modern state programs have for women is that of domesticity. The national developmentist projects in Venezuela, Cuba, or Jamaica—the national definition of nation-state as oil or sugar-cane producers, the nation's entrance into Modernity and world markets—all continue to assign women to the reduced space of reproduction. It is on the basis of emotions, on the sensitivity assigned to women as their only patrimony, that gender discussion is limited to marriage, coupling, and heterosexual love, and it is against these delimiting aspects that de la Parra argues when speaking for her protagonist. In fact, as opposed to marriages of convenience and to marriage in general, she offers natural marriage, a free union that is declined by her character, who incorporates herself into the reproductive determinants assigned to her by the Modern state.

Whether she is locked up in her house, in the attic, or in the garden, the image of closure offered by these texts is very telling, but it is telling not only of heterosexual love and coupling but also of the larger project. To the exclusion of the image of woman in *Jardín*, in choosing marriage, the other two protagonists implode and die from a paucity of social life.

In *Jardín* the process is reversed. The narrative of enclosure precedes that of freedom, but freedom is understood as marriage. Closed up in a garden, a prisoner of luxurious foliage, disordered and threatening, alone in a house like the first woman of creation, Bárbara elaborates her own subject construction, and she does it by vehemently looking for and discovering, at the center of the garden, a pavilion which has for some hundred years stored some documents.

The idea of situating woman in a garden certainly brings to mind narratives which situate men in the bush, or on a sugar or banana plantation, and, as we have seen, these spaces as images of nation can easily be displaced by the image of house/garden as nation. The chaotic and disorderly garden, overgrown and unkept, can certainly be remetaphorized into nation, a nation recently having come out of an *Independentista* struggle whose canefields were burned, where disorder has ruled and where both export and subsistence economies have been leveled and reformulated.

It is enough to remember gender solitude and its identification with whiteness to extrapolate the concept of a Cuban nation that Loynaz proposes. In order to do that we simply collapse small house into big house and accept as a center of meaning the pavilion in the garden which she proposes and her character discovers. Inside the little house in the garden, Loynaz keeps the secrets of identities: the *Independentista* family history and her own. And the female protagonist, like Melquíades in Márquez' *One Hundred Years of Solitude,* comes to decode it. There are no clues given, and the only person who knows the secret and is in possession of the key code is the old black servant, Laura, who barely occupies textual space and who, for our purposes, serves only as negation. Laura, as much as Christophine in Rhys, acts as a repository of black ontologies and epistemologies—narrated by Schwarz-Bart—and turns her back. Gregoria, de la Parra's black nanny, could tell her everything, but the white lady doesn't want to hear it.

Bárbara must search, interpret, incorporate ciphered messages. In the reading and writing of documents, a handful of love letters, she finds registered the secular history of sensibility, delimited between 184– and 1910, dates framing national history. That women find their own history in love letters, that is, in the expression of sensibility, coupling, and marriage, is predictable. But that these findings are tied to an *Independentista* newspaper, *El Progreso,* framed between 184– and 1910, is not so ordinary. Putting on the dress of the person whom the letters address, possibly her great-grandmother, a dress that disintegrates and is gone with the wind, and reading the love letters written to this woman by a man as exalted as anonymous—all the while believing that they were addressed to her—Bárbara, the Modern woman, becomes aware simultaneously of gender and nation.

Antique objects—coffers, letters, daggers, whips, embalmed birds, red drapes, friezes with dragons, stained glass, gold, nacre, and jewels—are icons that speak of a past history reconstructed from the point of view of a decadent Modernist sensibility. José Martí, who influenced so much of Cuban history and culture, is naturally a hidden referent in this gendered narrative, though elsewhere she acknowledges it.

The idea of *hortus conclusus,* which remits garden to Eden and then Eden to classical macrologies, to the Bible, and to the first Woman and the first Man, is here reformulated. This Eve has two Adams, one writing himself and the other characterized for us. As in Rhys, both suitors lack proper names. From this *hortus conclusus,* women leave only if they marry and move from one house to another.

Curiously, this light woman, without family ties, to whom a gendered subject-position is assigned, discovers, in the history of an unfashionable sensibility she rejects, the expression of exalted love. . . , and after remaining in solitude—unless we consider emerging capital a companion—for more than half the text, as alone as the Latin American Republics must have been in their first moments of independence, magically finds Prince Charming. Blue are the eyes of the suitor who takes Bárbara away from barbarianism and dresses her according to European fashion, transforming her into a different woman. It is in this way that Bárbara the barbarian, the savage white, leaves her garden's natural state and becomes part of the international mercantile/emotional community.

From Micro- to Macronarratives

It is evident from my vocabulary that reading for the conceptualization of the national complicates gender analysis, but this has been my intention. I have left behind specificity to trace a strong line of gendered representations of ethnicity and nation. I have not mentioned the contracts binding speech that permit Caribbean protagonists to enter into dialogue with English and Spanish ones. Neither have I analyzed the rewriting of unauthorized behavior such as madness, eloping, and sexuality. Nor have I touched the textualization of fairy tales such as *Sleeping Beauty,* a story that comes to establish its ascendancy in the formations of a fantasy damaging to identity constitution in women.

The hundred years that Sleeping Beauty waits for her Prince Charming, the hundred years of solitude, and the histories of secular histories are the same hundred years Bárbara waits to reinterpret a family/national history that leads her, like a Sleeping Beauty, to love and happiness. Prince Charming is already coming from the Orient; he is the feminine mediator who in the history of meaning occupies the place of wisdom assigned to Melquíades the magician in male narratives. This is again the same hundred years of *Independentista* history that leads the Latin American republics to bargain their enchanted gardens, their forests, their plains, to enter the free market economies that, like the women in the novels, dress their power elites in European garb.

Golden dreams of development, mercantile utopias, transoceanic and transcontinental desires, took Latin America, as they took Bárbara, María Eugenia, and Antoinette, to visit all the cities in the world and to be present in all spaces, but, as in Loynaz' narrative, when they come back home, the old decrepit wall encircling the barbarian garden collapses, killing them.

Gathering these elements together—a small house inside a big house, inside an island, inside the world—enables us to translate these micronarratives into macronarratives and to extrapolate or read nation into garden and house, and history into family and into disorder, decay, political chaos, and disenchantment.

I have been arguing that although the novel intends to erase the world, the cities, and the people from the text, iconography, objects, things, letters, furniture, style, and decor bring it back. They connote epoch and history. The dialogue between mechanical invention and natural power dates the text and speaks of a preoccupation prevalent at the beginning of the century. It signals the entrance of Latin America into Modernity.

From here we can gather tropical madness, which, as in Rhys, is a historical madness, the madness of disorientation, the perennial loss of chronological parameters, simple anacrony. A centennial disorientation emerges in which age is displaced, where living foreign and alien lives is the norm, and where silence is a given. Like many future Latin American characters, Bárbara has forgotten her age; she does not remember who she is and finds her identity in old manuscripts.

The poetization of greenness and the struggle between green and stone, garden versus the world, can be read as the pictures of bush, mountain, and banana and sugar cane plantation, as places of inner being and combat zones of meaning. They equally represent national and international exploitation as well as independence and liberation. The bush in Rivera is a disturbed male space, a place of transnational exploitation where whites, Indians, and mestizos build export economies and wealth. The bush in the Caribbean has been a place of disorder, an area difficult to penetrate, where hiding is possible. "Mountain" operates as a generic term coined by testimonial literature as the place for guerrillas and the formation of the revolutionary state.

In like manner, garden is the geographical representation of feminine space. To the degree that national macronarratives do not give it a place, do not consider gender as part of their formative narratives, house/garden/ nation is the enclosed space where women vehemently look for meaning. That is why nature has not devoured everything yet. Devouring nature, a garden gone bush speaks eloquently of deterioration and decay, more of endings than of beginnings. Reflection on the inclement garden is overwhelming, and natural events—rain, wind, inanimate life—control the human lives subject to them.

For Loynaz' woman, garden is everything: "all of her country, all her space, all her world" (76). As an all-encompassing space limited only by ocean, garden is unquestionably as much a metaphor for country and for island as it is for house: "And the garden was already everything . . . it was the house, white garden, petrified. . . . The girl was garden. . . . Little garden, with entangled roots in the feet and shades of branches on the eyes" (65).

To oppose garden to bush, mountain, plain, as a locus of meaning and as a space for male/female interaction, supercedes representations of nature and natural exploitation as nation, and undertakes a new definition of national space as garden house, an enclosed feminine space and the place of reproduction. Fina García Marruz has called attention to this:

> One speaks of the "*selva*" by José Eustasio Rivera, of the "*pampa*" in Don Segundo Sombra, of the plains in *Doña Bárbara*, of the Great Savannah in Alejo Carpentier, but none of it is related to *Jardín* from our Dulce María Loynaz. And could it not be stated, from the very beginning, the common link of centering in a space, in nature—our American nature—the subsequent histories, not like a background scenario, but like a rooting theme? (549)

It is evident that Loynaz draws a transparent picture of national deterioration, and even when the texts supposedly occur during the 1930s, family history is traced back four generations. This way a woman named Bárbara, perhaps this Bárbara's great-grandmother, a maternal figure occupying the mother's space, since the real mother, like Antoinette's, went mad after the death of the male child, comes to position herself at the center of the quest.

This absent person, whose referent is Independence, an old story whose dust covers the family portraits, grants woman her subjective place in history. Newspapers, crucifix, words, and letters—mainly the letter A, which means *Apasionadamente, Apacentar, Apagar* (Passionately, Nourish, Stifle)—define the relations between two women and a young man, the young adolescent of the portrait who signs the pictures Alphonse, Armand, Albert, and Alfred, and the love letters: "luxurious and poetic, they rather resemble pagan psalms, canticles of a revivified Shulammite. Even the loved one is seen enveloped in a pink dawning fog. . ." (148). This male image symbolizes all the romantic images women fabricate of men: knight, first love, phantom, brother—images that seem to come from afar when we well know, she says, that they come from our own inner disquietude. From simple letters like A and B, she draws, then, ideas of passion, the name of the loved one, that of the women in the family. A and B are also men and women, love, coupling, elopement, world, and style.

At this interpretive moment a dialogue between fairy tales and the novel, plus the transposition of characters—Bárbara for Sleeping Beauty, takes place. Loynaz exposes the ideology of fantasy as a dangerous lie in gender formation. And in undressing the ideology of couples, love and passion, re-interpreted in the reading of documents, of private love letters that address the questions of unrealized love and passion, of eloping and prohibitions, as much as of foreign suitors, Loynaz calls into question the sanctity and veracity of heterosexual love.

And even high literature is deceptive in this narrative of enclosure. Reading literature is meaningless. Hagiographies, the classics of Homer and Shakespeare with their protagonists like Andromeda and Desdemona, the Bible and its Epistles, the European and Latin American Romantics (Goethe's Charlotte and Marguerite and Isaac's María), are of no use. Sleeping Beauty, on the contrary, has meaning. It is, then, not the canon but the objects of everyday life, the culture of the mundane, which lead to the inner world. Bárbara, as curious as Eve, as Lot's wife, like Alice in Wonderland, goes through a hole in the ground and discovers love.

Love: A Word to Feed the Worms

Modernism fashioned a woman-subject tied to feelings of love. This subject was constituted by definitions of the loved one as possession:

> Bárbara, she of the watery eyes. . . . Your name is mine. . . . Mine also are your eyes, through which I see your thoughts pass like red fishes in a golden aquarium. . . . And mine are your bluish lashes, and your perfumed braids, and the inclined lily of your neck! Mine is all of you—so white, so fine—mine all of you!" (143) [13]

This loved one, white, pale, gone as if in orgasm or in death, is also a docile child:

> Docile you look younger, more girlish, more mine perhaps. . . . Docile, and without thereby losing your usual seigneurial prestige, you are like a girl queen, like a tender little queen of Pragmatics, with shy eyes, with a profile drawing itself over a historicized drapery, with the candid hands collected over a golden sphere, as in pictures by Carolsfield." (163)

The idea of possessive love is conveyed through reproduction or inheritance, and that is why Bárbara takes possession of the great-grandmother, "still dormant within herself, remiss and languid as always" (144). Dualism between herself and the other, the same and distinct because all women are Woman:

> Ah? if she could have been the other one! . . . If she could push her, throw her behind the scene of time, supplant her in her own scenario. . . . Put on her eyes, her grace, her emotions, as she had put on her dress." (162)

In this artistic replica we find again the reproduction of a male sensibility through female writing, and the rendering of this fragmented sensibility as a thing of the past: love "the beautiful name . . . serves to fatten a worm's body" (161). What love means to men is written by a woman who in turn makes another woman interpret it. Loynaz appropriates the masculine voice and style to construct heterosexual love and to define what it means for him. In fact, the author has confessed that she borrowed from her husband's letters:

> I would hide you as one who commits a crime hides the crime; I would gather every trace of you, every lost thread leading to you; I would put all the energy, all the force, all the strain of remorse to push you to the bottom of my soul . . . for if death could hold you more than life, I would die this very moment so that my death would weigh on your life as a tombstone and you could no longer move anymore, nor smile to your doves, nor escape in the wings of your doves nor in the wings of a smile. . . . And you would remain with me forever. (167)

History thus recounted is told and lived twice. Symbolically the great-grandmother and the great-granddaughter fall in love with the same man and express affection similarly. Masculine writing imitated by a woman writer is one of Loynaz' achievements. Her contractual relation with Modernism makes it possible for the reader to forget her and to immerse herself in the construction of a male narrative of love. Transliteration of his expression and his feelings and her definite will to reproduce them verbatim, in such a way that heterosexual love succeeds, brings all the morbid reference points of Modernism to the fore in the text. His possessive appropriation and disintegrating desire for the loved one's body, all eyes and hands, earns this narrative entrance into the Modernization projects of state formation.

It is the male's appropriations of national resources and his projects of capitalist production that make him think of appropriating women by defining women as girls, conceding to men the custody of women. To have

Sleeping Beauty as a transcendental signifier is, then, a commentary on Modernist prose. The demanding and interpellating male voice of the narrator is also a transcendental signifier, for his voice trespasses chronology, and his desires still bear on women.

When Bárbara reads his letters, however, she does not completely fall for him or respond to the urgent needs expressed in his desperate voice. He is a man who, for all intents and purposes, we must be aware, occupies her great-grandfather's position. Incest, then, is the subtext of the love letters, and patriarchal government the ruler of subjective gender relations. This is so much so that in the end the utterance mistakes the two women, and the young man's voice interpellates young Bárbara across the centuries. He thus makes her occupy her great-grandmother's subject-position. Like Teresa de la Parra's protagonist, the Modern woman thus listens to the mandate of the old woman. Loynaz first silences both her protagonists and later collapses one into the other. The documented Bárbara and the protagonized Bárbara are identical, equally silent: the first Bárbara, because she only exists through personal objects or through the male voice that describes her physically and defines her emotionally. Thus constituted, when the second Bárbara reads the fragmented version of this construction she feels interpellated. The letters from the male subject explain her present condition: impoundment is a remnant of his morbid desires.

Closures, enclosures, and foreclosures. In land and in property. As in Gallegos' Bárbara, Modern ideas plot Woman as possession and as property, as slaves:

> I would like to begin taking hold of you in such a way that all-absorbed by me, all-drunk by me, there is not a single drop of you left to quench anyone's thirst . . . and I would like you [as] my slave, tied to me, in need of me with that necessity, that hunger, that misery with which I am in need of you. I would like you miserable and poor, dispossessed of everything meretritious and prestigious in you, so that you would have nothing, know or expect nothing more than me. (167)

The morbid aspects of documents need a more profound explanation. A hypothetical reading of his death wish does not speak optimistically of his new Modern economics, nor of his new gender construction. In this aspect, heterosexual love, as much as the Modern nation, is stillborn.

This petrified woman, catatonic, rendered illiterate, could on the other hand be interpreted as a woman marooned, seeking refuge in silence, looking for alliances with black women, with whom she willy-nilly shares the same enclosed spaces, with whom she bears ignorance and illiteracy, condemned to live in the oral world.

The ethnic pact that men propose in production, where fields must be cultivated by people of color, men or women or both, comes to mean in these feminine narratives of enclosure the same thing. Women keeping company with women, women advising women, and old black women advising young white women become expressions of the multiethnic pact at the level of gender. At bottom in her feminine social imagination, the white, feminine, literate oligarch has made black women the repositories of wisdom and endurance, endowing them with the power of the oral tradition. In the coming decades, it is their turn to speak.

Seigneurial houses, agrarian houses, ancient plantation houses, still standing in Caribbean cities, survive as living historical expressions of patriarchal structures of the *Independentista* epoch, where old black and white women, very much alone, totally impoverished, belonging to a world long gone, wait for their last days to come, tranquilly observing the results of a national pact begun in their youths.

4 / Jean Rhys

Island/Nation—*Hortus Conclusus*

Living Like a Ghost

Already in her old age, and after she had experienced many of life's troubles—exile, lack of love, abandonment, and poverty—Jean Rhys, like the airy protagonists of Loynaz we discussed earlier, finally came to know the glories of commercial success. She had spent most of her life in obscurity, pointed to as a phantom and an eccentric, known as an extremist, shy, though given to fits of violence, always complaining and unhappy, somewhat gloomy, her face fixed with bitterness, serious, but honest. These images are not meant to cast Jean Rhys as another romantic heroine, but rather are borrowed from real life. A glance at her letters from England reveals her perpetual dissatisfaction. Her critics have collected these letters and used them in their writing, fusing Rhys with her heroines in a sensibility born of postmortem respect in the midst of academic commercialization. The bio-bibliographical and psychological studies of Rhys not only make her a suitable object of study but also fatten academic curriculum vitae in England and the United States, and now ours as Caribbean scholars.

I am not going to treat here the themes already overelaborated by metropolitan criticism in English, but I want to point out that their common subtext is to establish Rhys' "Englishness": Jean Rhys, English narrator. They study four principal trends: the resemblance between the author and her protagonists, madness, Victorian Gothicism relating Rhys to Charlotte Brontë, and the nexus of mother/daughter relations.[1]

Caribbean critics, on the contrary, argue that Rhys' protagonists symbolize "the relationship between West Indian whites and England, and nature and consequences of their involvement with the world their ancestors came from" (Lai, 61). Themes of isolation, alienation, and the annihilation of desire are common to all the novels that deal with Europeans in the Caribbean (Ramchand 1969: *passim*). The situations of oppression, the crises of personal identity, and the harrowing malformations occurring in Rhys' novels are characteristic of situations produced by a history of colonialism.

I want to side here with these last critics to argue that Rhys' sensibility is an attribute of her national origins and recognize in Jean Rhys a Caribbean identity. I also want to examine the relationship between Bertha Mason/Antoinette Cosway and Christophine Dubois, which, together with the image of the wild garden as an island, represents nationalist sentiments, although these are more protonationalist sentiments, for the Jamaican nation-state is not yet constituted. But national feelings, or perhaps "place feelings," already exist. The organized power of the famous English estate—where the plantation is itself an economic and self-governing unit, with its administrative body of overseers and agents—has ceased to exist, and a more ample and Modern form of government must be installed in its place. Both sets of arguments presented by Rhys' critics are valid in this respect, but we must undertake a different reading to reveal their inner workings.[2]

A Litigated Writer

The world interrelationship between those islands considered nations, such as England, and those considered not-nations (territories, zones, colonies, protonations), as is the case of the geography textualized by Rhys (Jamaica, Martinique, Dominica, Barbados, Trinidad, and a Windward Island), socializes Rhys' text.

It is impossible to overlook the relationship between *Wide Sargasso Sea* (1966) and Brontë's canonical *Jane Eyre,* because Rhys has left it very well documented. But it is equally impossible to obviate the polemical nature of this relationship. That Jean Rhys wanted to contradict and contest Brontë's representation of the Creole Caribbean woman is also documented. The controversial arena for Rhys revolved around physical appearances and social behavior—ethnicity—together with the nature of heterosexual relationships between two social subjects coming from different cultural milieux. What is argued here is the textual re-writing not only of canonical literature, but also of the conceptions (epistemes) and narratives (ontologies) of place and people that both writers sustain, as well as the theoretical postulates of what makes a good heterosexual relationship work.

Literary critics from postmodern metropolitan societies—Gilbert and Gubar for instance—cannot deny the supporting base of Rhys' text. But they decide to read it in a different light. In their essays, they displace this base onto other areas of concern: madness, identity, mother/daughter, and woman/man relationships to which I alluded earlier. It is obvious that, in their cultural milieux, these matters are of utmost concern, perhaps because they have already solved primary, basic problems, such as those pointed out by Caribbean critics.[3] However, they cannot gloss over the fact that the origin of this textual dialogue is a fundamental disagreement between narratives and concepts, between English representations of the Caribbean islands and those of the inhabitants. In other words, even if sociopsychological matters—concerning the interrelationships of peoples among themselves or with other peoples—are very relevant (and they are), this fact does not displace discussions of primary issues, such as economics and politics.

The first conceptual divergence occurs, then, in Caribbean and metropolitan cultural readings of cultural conceptualizations of white, black, and mulatto ethnicities Rhys elaborates. In neglecting the underlying political relations expressed in ethno-national terms, metropolitan critics transform Antoinette into an ordinary white English woman whose only difference is to have been born overseas. Nevertheless, Brontë's originating text already interdicts this reading. Rochester's experience overseas, together with the metonymic description of the mad woman in the attic, facilitate misreadings and miswritings of ethnic vectors—whitewashing color (and with it, place) and slighting cultural differences in behavior, reading/writing the Creole woman as madness and bestiality.

Gayatri Spivak is right in calling attention to the representational relationship between ethnology, feminist liberal ideology, and the most prestigious English cultural investments (Spivak 1985: *passim*). The images of Caliban/cannibal, explored by Retamar, are also highlighted in her text. English canonical culture together with liberal feminist ideologies enter into an oppositional relationship with respect to colonial literatures within postcolonial studies. As Spivak demonstrates in her reading of Rhys' text, it is not Brontë's intention to have readers conceive Bertha/Antoinette as white but rather as Creole. The question of purity of blood is thus raised. Moving the arguments from the margins to the center, Antoinette Cosway/Bertha Mason (Rochester) could very well be considered the entrance of a metaphorical mulatta into an important English feminist canonical text. In this respect, Spivak's incisive reading of individualism into white liberal feminism is outstanding, and in coupling the darker sides of white liberal feminism with the most prestigious Shakespearean tradition of Prospero and Caliban, she, as usual, breaks new ground.

On the other hand, to write about mother/daughter relationships as the origins of madness, which is what all mulattoes (not only Daniel Cosway) do, is to confront tropical madness as evoked by the collapse of plantation economies. Madness is a historical topos in Caribbean literatures. It is a proper answer to historical situations. To disregard the historical origins of such madness is thus to gloss over the economic base underlined by the author and to leave up in the air the events behind the loss of reason and consciousness.[4] In the English critical texts, the origins of madness are not explored but offered as a point of departure. It is a genetic madness. It is the mother's madness, a blood-related disease, something inherited that makes Antoinette go mad and makes her lose her husband. We find ourselves again in the presence of a conceptual displacement from the collective to the individual, forgetting that Rhys does not constitute madness within her protagonist: she undergoes a geonational disorientation. The question as to where England is, whether or not there is such a place, or whether or not it had been invented, is a game in the text that metropolitan critics feel compelled to omit. Between the "imaginary" England— the iconographic England portrayed in Carolsfeld's or Miller's pictures— and the "real" England—the England of the enclosure in the attic, the patriarchal, punishing England—there is an abyss.

Two other variables can be introduced at this point. The first is the resemblances between author and protagonists, and the second is the other epistemologies that come to bear in the text. In the first case, to historicize Jean Rhys' biography through her protagonists not only means to establish the link between life and work, between the perpetual act of authorial self-representation through textuality, or the problems attached to Narcissism and self-vision and the erasure of the borders between private and public, but also to reformulate local and territorial identities, denationalization, and re-naturalization of a writer through protagonists. Hence the argument for Rhys' sympathies for stating the case of the underdog. This way of looking at her work simply discards questions of migrant cultures, deterritorialized or displaced cultures, conflictive assimilation and acculturation, questions which pervade so much of Rhys' private correspondence. In fact, the character of Aunt Cora, who is repatriated in the novel, is modeled after one of her beloved aunts from the Caribbean residing in England. Evoking climatic conditions, the vision of sunny atmospheres, warmth as a local referent, even a preference for bright colors (which I will expand upon later), are territorializing elements in her life and work.

In the second case, that of black (but predominantly mulatto) epistemologies and ontologies and their corollaries, the struggles between oral and written cultures, are questions that are not perceived, or are perceived only tangentially by these critics. In other words, once the geopolitical and economic readings are erased, the perception of difference within black and mulatto elements becomes muted. Slavery and the Emancipation Act, the primary signifiers informing the novel and the underlying national vision, become emptied of their meaning.

I bring these to the forefront to shed light on how zones, territories, and protonations are considered in both English and Caribbean texts. In the Spanish islands we will find protagonists very similar to Antoinette. But since they have been born in semiconstituted states, their destinies are different and their relationships with both the external world and heterosexual love, traveling, companionship, and enclosures are dealt with in other ways.

Garden as Representation of Nation

Wide Sargasso Sea is divided into three parts. The first tells the story of Annette, a ruined planter woman who lives with her two children, a boy and a girl—Antoinette—and her few remaining ex-slaves. She meets and marries a well-to-do suitor, who reconstructs the house and replants her garden. Part one ends, however, when the structure collapses during a black uprising. The second part tells Antoinette's story as a young lady, her education and forced marriage to an English man whom she first dauntlessly rejects, but subsequently accepts, accedes to marry, and finally falls madly in love with, just, in turn, to be belligerently rejected by him. On their honeymoon he becomes bewildered by the enchanted island and its radiant surroundings. In what for him is a wild and isolated site, bushland, he becomes deranged, and finds his way out through reading and writing. A letter from Antoinette's mulatto stepbrother, Daniel Cosway, explaining Annette and possibly Antoinette's misconduct, makes him decide to leave, after settling accounts with his black surroundings, threatening to imprison Antoinette's ex-nanny and friend Christophine, "making love" to the mulatto servant Amelié, and forcibly taking his legitimate wife to England. The third part narrates Antoinette's story in England, her confinement in the attic, and the novel closes with her burning of the house.

Wide Sargasso Sea is a brief novel addressing the important topics of slavery, West Indian society in the wake of Emancipation, the resiliency of black cultures, and the divergences between Victorian and Creole narratives. English men represent the nascent Modernizing plantocracy. Annette and Antoinette, as well as Amelié, are made indirectly to represent the problematics of the new mulatto societies in the West Indies. But it is around the characters of Christophine, Antoinette, and the English man "him" that questions of *arraigo* and nation-ness and nationhood, patrimony, inheritance, and landownership and rent, intertwined with coupling, love, and belonging are discussed.

In the first of the three parts into which *Wide Sargasso Sea* is divided, we find the textualization of homes—plantations or *haciendas*. As we saw in the case of Dulce María Loynaz from Spanish Cuba, the past is romanticized through reference to architecture: rooms, windows, *glacis*, servants, and planters' headquarters. The layout of the house, together with references to its deterioration or restoration, invoke social conflicts. As in many other representations of Caribbean houses, the image is of disorder: the garden has gone wild, the few servants are disobedient and unproductive, the distance between blacks and whites is dwindling.

A crucial shift has occurred between ex-planters and ex-slaves. There are no longer whips, orders, commands, and directions but dialogue in their place, signaling the entrance of reasonable negotiation into the discourses of power, as well as a contestation by the laborers. Friendship between a white and a black girl, competition, and sharing of clothing, are used to explore the theme of equality in the interpersonal relations of social subjects. In games and dialogues, in formal and informal education, intercultural symmetries that cut across race/class divisions point to the beginning of a new mentality. And the black and white images, one mirroring the other, the vanishing of English mediation (the icon of the Miller's *Daughter*), become integral to the formation of self. The image of the black self acts as a premonition and the substitution of the white self for the mulatto self in the mind of the white man, who puts together in his mind the half-caste Amelié and the white Creole Antoinette. The direct, specular self-reflection in childhood is replaced by a mental picture in youth, thus showing the tricky process of ideological formations. All this takes place at the end of the plantation economies, after the Emancipation Act in the middle of the nineteenth century, in more or less the same period that Dulce María Loynaz dates the documents found by her protagonist in the middle of a seemingly disordered and chaotic garden. National independentist history in one case and Emancipation in the other begin around 1838 or 1840.

For Caribbean readers textualization of history is nothing new. For whites the transition between slave and free labor economies was the beginning of chaos and solitude. For white people, company is predicated as white, and order is only understood as the exploitation of others. For blacks that was a possibility, the possibility of implementing reason and common sense into the world. Apropos of the death of Annette's only horse, Godfrey expresses his opinions: "I can't watch the horse day and night. I too old now. When old time go, let it go. No use grab at it" (Rhys 1985: 466).

The exchange of words between a white plantation owner and her subaltern, together with all such "dialogue" in the text, are the scale for measuring democracy, at least in its oral expression. To each interpellation there is a response, and the communication establishes open oppositional relations between two ontologies and two epistemologies. As a point of interest, Rhys has the two girls eat boiled plantain on a calabash dish with their hands, borrowing the scene from *Marly, or the Life of a Planter,* an anonymous nineteenth-century work that defines mulatto cultures on the basis of food and table manners. Eating with one's hands and without a plate bespeaks poor manners and bad taste for some, and economic necessity for others.

To this we must add that words denote the beginnings of a new sensibility together with a new conduct. Blacks call whites "white niggers," "white cockroaches," "colored," "the *sans culottes*," "the black English gentlemen." And when old servants are careless, planters commit suicide (Mr. Lutrell) or go crazy (Annette). No one wants to work anymore. Authority and cohesion are gone. The large property, the estate, Coulibri, the governing unit with its system of security and police, has stopped functioning, and new rules emerge that will come to form the new authority and state. Burning the plantation house (a house already gone to ruin and repaired), the rising up in arms of black servants and the surrounding population, and the liquidation of architecture as a standing symbol of power and authority are the erasure of a life-style that has come to an end. With the destruction of property and property rights and the onslaught of Annette's madness, the productive and reproductive proposals of that cultural horizon are foreclosed. The names of the places, the patronymics of estates, the allusions to privilege they denoted, like those that Fraginals transcribes in his poetic *El Ingenio,*[5] also indicate the other side of what blacks and mulattoes are fighting for. In Rhys, "Nelson's Rest," Mr. Lutrell's property, ceases forever to be a restful place.

It is for this reason that I see in the image of garden-gone-bush the seeds of the new nation, very similar to the metaphor of nation offered earlier by Loynaz in her book *Jardín*. The paths are covered by overgrown weeds. The smell of wilted flowers evokes death. Orchids have ceased to evoke ornamentation and have become threatening allegorical figures—snakes and tentacles. And the destroyed house, the glacis overlooking the oceans, and the death of the only son—heir and lord of the property and human chattel—are recipients of primogeniture, as much as marrying an English man symbolizes protonational transition: the end of plantation economies and supervised properties administered by foreign agents and overseers, with their vigilante system in place and the introduction of a free-labor economy which proposes importing laborers from the East Indies.

Negotiated here are power quotas, new labor forms and the new distribution of trades, together with the proposal of new relations between women and men. The empowered players are unquestionably the recently arrived white English lords and the new mulatto groups. Black rebels burn the plantation and the house, whatever was kept standing from the old slave world, but the beneficiaries are the half-castes, observant, peripheral to the text, educated, hidden. The marginal mulattoes are very much part of the negotiation.

Island as Representation of Nation

But it is only in the second part, the largest in the text, that we come to appreciate in depth the clear definition of territoriality on the side of the protagonist as much as the play in which all the social sectors take their part, and also the transnational interests intervening in the formation of the text. If in the first part of the novel white characters predominate, in the second, white characters, two of them, placed in the situation of an Edenic couple, are surrounded by blacks. This is aggravated by the fact that one of the white protagonists, the woman, has previously established an emotional pact with the place, the people, and their beliefs.

Here we must introduce into our study the discussion of Victorian Gothicism and translate it into Tropical Gothicism. If in Loynaz' novel a Modernist sensibility dominates and the world is described in the vocabulary coming from Latin American *Modernismo,* in Rhys' novel the English tradition comes to be a sign of cultural space. But as in the previous case, in which Modernism is yielding its hegemony bit by bit to a Neo-Positivist prose, in Rhys a Tropical Gothicism, or the tradition of magical realism, comes to fight in the arena, a discursive movement strong in Carpentier.

The incident of the burning parrot evokes the figure of Mackandal *sauvé* and the textual representation of the Haitian revolution in literature. But it is mainly in the grounding of plot in history that the instrumentalization of local style is most threatening.

The Victorian Gothic school presents itself not only in the dialogue between Jean Rhys and Charlotte Brontë, but also and most concretely in the tangle in which the main male character is involved. He invokes the lugubrious, oppressive and funereal through an alertness bordering on paranoia. Distrust is what the imperial subject feels. To his mentality can be attributed the transformation of open spaces into closed and the connotations that bright colors evoke in him.

It might seem odd that since Rhys deprived him of a patronymic and referred to him exclusively through the pronouns "him" or "he," criticism in English in postmodern societies insists on calling him by the name of Rochester. This is a way of making the English tradition of Brontë prevalent in the text. But, at the same time, such moves grant him the past that Rhys fabricates for him. This historical past refers to a wounded personality, yes, but also to an imperial subject disoriented by the tropical forest. Through reference to Victorian Gothicism we could push the arguments to their borders to make sense of the feeling of darkness and mystery akin to this sensibility, the representation of imperial fear in the colonies. This hypothesis would also account for the Romanticism invoked by the volume of Byron's poetry on the shelves of a house hidden in the countryside of a God-forsaken geography.

If instead of invoking Gothic stylistics we take a circuitous route and call this historical situation by a less poetic and more political noun—marooning—we will be following more local and less English determinants of the text. It is in this situation that Annette, Mr. Lutrell, and whites in Jamaica in general see themselves at Coulibri, a situation analogous to Tarzan's, Robinson Crusoe's, the Lord of the Flies', or Hasenfus'. What Annette feels, her premonition, is her awareness of the hegemony that black cultures are acquiring on the terrain: to be marooned is a synonym for being surrounded, in a state of siege. The territory is being defined as Other, numerically: by a simple majority of voices heard the place is becoming black. Had Rhys historicized a different historical moment, her imaginary creature, Antoinette, could have followed Christophine's advice and opted for divorce and economic independence, in such a way that the third part, instead of enclosure and foreclosure, would have proffered solitude.

In the second part, textual space becomes a prison for him. He is totally surrounded and he is in the hands of black people. He doesn't know the place—exits or entrances. Most of the time he feels lost—generic mango trees make it impossible for him to distinguish one spot from the other. He does not speak the language and he does not know the cultural habits and manners which he finds odd and suspicious. No wonder his obsession is with finding the way out, with how these places are connected by mail.

The place to which they arrive for their honeymoon, this generic, un-named Windward island, is the end or the beginning of the world, a para-dise lost or found that plays with the biblical macronarratives. For the mentality of the protagonist and her author that island is definitively the garden of Eden. Massacre, the name of the localized space, however, from the very first moment, establishes an opposition and a contrast between the attractively intoxicating beauty of nature and the history it evokes. Who was massacred here, he wonders. Blacks? By the use of this particular noun we can gather that the massacred ones were whites, for when blacks are killed the act invokes the name of the law and it is called justice.

The openness of the island naturally evokes the closedness of the cities he is accustomed to. Too much is what he predicates. Too much what? Too much blue, too much purple, too much green. Criticism in English system-atically and persistently quotes these claustrophobic feelings in the presence of brightness. I presume the phrase touches some nerve in a culture that prefers pastel colors to vivid ones. Rhys, on the contrary, remarks favor-ably on these luminous colors that she seems to adore—violets, greens, yellows—the colors of tropical birds.

Disorientation also reigns in Loynaz' garden. However, losing parame-ters is only true here for the English male protagonist. All others know the area well and are familiar with each and every one of its roads and paths. Nature talks to them in the form of signs, smells, and colors: clove, cin-namon, roses, and oranges. That is why synesthesia, corporeal sensibility, sensuality—characteristics of magical realism as opposed to Victorian Gothicism—scare the English mind accustomed to thinking, to reasoning, to using one's head to the detriment of all other body organs.

The distinction between him and her, the space of the much problema-tized ethnicity, comes to play an important role in thought. Her ethnicity locks up the plot. Helped by a Gothic sensibility and immersed in a tropical *real maravilloso* (or, looking at the twentieth century from the nineteenth: in one moment, the former, an exacerbated nationalism and a struggle for national frontiers and self determination; in the other, the latter, a moment of national reformulation), Brontë's nineteenth-century protagonist says: "Creole of pure English descent she may be, but they are not English or European either" (496). He had not seen her so clearly in Spanish Town because there are other white people in the city, but here, in the country-side, all mediations gone in the open mountain, and surrounded by blacks, the resemblances between her and the half-caste Amelié become manifest.

What is curious in this national-cultural disorientation is that everyone is trying to give him the clues but he refuses to understand. Nobody wants to keep any secrets, not even Christophine, the strongest representative of black ethnicity and the incontestable center of the narrative. But he has no eyes to see, nor ears to hear. The overwhelming reality of Caribbean nations is totally alien to him and that is why he is disturbed. But as disoriented as he is, he doesn't forget who he is or what he wants. First is to get out of there. Second, to find any way out. And third, to leave his male, imperial imprint by kidnaping the white, and sexually abusing the mulatta.

This is what Christophine knows. She knows white behavior, their fear and contempt, their ignorance of place, and their underwriting of white des-potism. And that is why she knows that her wisdom and obeah, grounded in the narratives and conceptualizations of ancestor worship, do not reach them. Ellipsis in this text is, then, a sign of white misunderstanding of black knowledge.

He responds not to orality, not to signs, gestures, or use of the body. What reaches him is writing, the printed word, and that is why Daniel Cosway vitally interferes in the text: not only because Daniel is mulatto and as a mulatto he is the perfect mediator, the one who can understand both codes and translate them, but also because in his own person he in-carnates one possibility for a nation combining the two histories. Because he is a mulatto he understands white and black epistemologies. He knows how to reach him by increasing his inner doubts, doubts in reference to a bewitched space, his wife's mental sanity, her sexuality, and her ethnicity.

Mulattoes confabulated against whites and the ex-house slaves and allied themselves with the new group of white metropolitans who came to refor-mulate the economy. Daniel Cosway shows him an island mentality and in this sense Daniel is Ariel, the colonized intellectual who understands the language and wants to benefit from it. Amelié, the half-caste, Antoinette's Other, is his counterpart.

The Birth of Mulatto Countries

Long before the Emancipation Act, the Haitian Revolution, and the *Inde-pendentista* wars, Caribbean societies were mulatto. Acculturation began at the moment of encounter and was propitiated through a long and ir-reversible cohabitation. In the daily linguistic misunderstanding and the abuse of the black body, mestizo cultures began. Between the English and the African, and between the French, the Spanish, and the African, the patois. A new language and a new syntax express the form of interdependence and the undifferentiated in the white/black relationship: cultural entanglements. The new language is also systematically inscribed along the length of the abused social body. Beliefs and visions branded in the flesh. Lies and truths, confused, pulse in the same body.

In *Wide Sargasso Sea,* the constitution of the novel's structure through reiteration is a product of blood and biography, and each one of the social subjects represented wants to tell the truth: Daniel, the mulatto, sees himself compelled by truth; Antoinette, the white, wants to deny Daniel's truths; Christophine, the black, says the mulatto Daniel lies.

Since the speaking "I" occupies several positions at the same time, relativism installs itself in the narrative. Daniel, for instance, occupies the place of the masculine, the mulatto, and the religious. In this sense, his truth is multidimensional. Truth, as a space for the disentanglement of gender relations, of ethnic relations, is placed in a moral dimension. Antoinette and Christophine attempt to clarify the same points. Truth is situated in a biological fact: in the body, inside it, and in the purity of blood. English tradition invokes in this respect the Spanish tradition. Purity of blood always refers to ethnicity: a phenotype added to beliefs and manners. Daniel Cosway situates himself in the position of judge and inquisitor. Man to man, he is going to tell the truth and thus establish a socio-cultural/financial pact.

This truth as morality unearths a secret, that of woman's surrender: the behavior of Annette, Antoinette's mother; the behavior of Daniel's mother. Under segregated maternity there is justice as much as social injustice. In Annette, deviant conduct, her frivolity, her black hair, her dancing skills, the fact that she laughs, makes her suspicious. Her madness is tied to this suspicion. Bad blood, then, is an ambiguous expression. It refers to both mixed blood and madness. Daniel's mother is a "sly-boots," lewd and slippery: therefore, in Daniel, the old Cosway disavows his paternity. In both cases the origin of the biological formation of the mulatto is put into question and is subject to doubt.

Lies and deception cordon off more specifically the spheres of good and evil. The deliberate act of lying is a sociobiological effect. Lineage must be clear and patrilineality must be established by means of the uncontested purity of the white woman's body. White women and black women both are each the producer and reproducer of their respective cultural identities. They are in charge of reproducing the two republics, and of violating the bipolarity and the beginning of *mestizaje* as a fact of blood.

That is why stories of lineage are told, retold, and revised. The first part of the novel tells the world the history of social bloodlines. The second part informs the English character. It clarifies for him which lines are direct and which are mixed. Antoinette relates them to him twice, first to impart general information, a briefing, and later, to clarify formally, first in writing and then orally. Conversation is a means of affective reconciliation. Daniel tells it twice, once in writing and once orally, both tellings directed to the same interlocutor and with the intention of being funded. Daniel wants to be paid to tell the truth, and for keeping the secret. Christophine repeats it again to obtain retribution, either in the form of affection for Antoinette or in the form of her financial freedom.

Despite the retelling of biography in fiction, letters, and dialogues, attempts at clarification prove impossible. Whites, blacks, and mulattoes espouse contradictory truths. The pyramidic hegemonic structure of discourse invokes patriarchy, Christianity, and colonialism as master narratives, molds and models of social articulation. Sandra Drake points out, for reasons similar to mine, that "this level of literary intertextual referentiality invokes and is paralleled by the extratextual referentiality to Europe's historical narrative" (99).

The scaffold supports the obvious: the impurity of blood in mulatto societies as they pass into statehood. They are argued in terms of the impossible: the purity of blood of mestizo societies. Charlotte Brontë is certain of the mixtures. For European societies there is no doubt that those who leave their territory convert themselves into *indianos*. Colonial societies can never be or resemble European societies. The feminine in the colonial territories is not the same as the feminine in the metropole. Nineteenth-century Caribbean colonial wealth had already vilified men, and therefore the social pact between the metropolis and the colony registers a reformulation: no to the alliances between poor metropolitan men and wealthy colonial women, yes to an alliance between the man newly enriched in the colonies and the poor, semiprofessional woman. Charlotte Brontë is interested in cementing the construction of her protagonist and has her succeed in this new type of morality: a driven woman, a professional. Gayatri Spivak sees this very well: a liberal pact between women. It is not altogether wrong to read *Jane Eyre* as a defense of the formation of the professional middle class, masculine and feminine, on the basis of the economic and now cultural exploitation of overseas territories: the Indies—East and West.

Jean Rhys, Creole, situated on the other side, can respond. Her sensibility permits her to discern the innuendos. At the allegorical representational level, Antoinette runs the same fate as sugar: highly praised and valued, protected during mercantilism prior to the Emancipation Act and totally devalued in the transition toward laissez-faire. In eliminating all mercantile protection and other kinds of favored status, in conceding to the island all the freedom to negotiate, East/West competition brings their decay. The historians Edward Long and Bryan Edwards, both sugar planters, narrate this transition and establish narratives for sugar similar to those that Rhys constructs for the young Creole.

Sugar as regional representation, the product as island, is the seat of value of this social group; it is what makes white white, what makes the *indiano* European; it is the object of exchange that sustains lineage, ethnic biography, blood, and the tenor of the metaphor that enters into crisis precisely at the moment of transition between mercantilism and laissez-faire, a transition rearranging the social composition and the manner of seeing, perceiving, and writing the social groups and their pacts.

Truth and lies are not, then as now, terms localizable only within the religious discourse of preachers (as is the case of Daniel), but can be found in the economic debates over mercantile protectionism. The planter class calls the Abolitionist lobby within the English Parliament deceptive, treacherous. The lobbies for the planter class no longer have any effect; on the contrary, the abolitionist societies achieve the hegemonic voice in Parliament. This shift in the notions of wealth and lineage has placed the wealthy heirs of plantation economies in an arena of unequal competition. The mestizo character of the zone comes to occupy its place within marginality, in madness, in the attic, in mulatticity. Doubt has no place in the space of the formation of malformations. "At issue is the abolition of European plantation slavery and the transition—or failed transition—to some other set of social relations that would constitute a viable Caribbean identity," says Drake (97). "Malformation" is the nature of residual forms of discarded power.

To the degree that the text argues the articulation of this particular moment (Independence) through another (Emancipation), it repeats the reiterative structures that indicate that the question is not yet resolved, since it remains a matter of debate. Jean Rhys is irritated by the legislation of English law over the Caribbean feminine written in English Letters, and decides to give an explanation. She decides to rewrite the past at the moment in which the nature and composition of the Commonwealth is under discussion. She reconstructs the moment of free trade at the moment of political emancipation. And she discovers, naturally, the other protagonists invisible to Brontë. For she narrates from the other side, from the side of a constituted nation-state, or a nation-state wishing to be constituted, after Bustamante and Norman Manley—that is, a nation whose national and self-serving international pacts were already made, and in which the West Indies had a place assigned as and within marginality; a space within which the feminine was mulatticity. For if woman is the symbol of nation, historically the functional metaphor, the vehicle of country, then Creole madness reproduces denationalization.

For Jean Rhys the question involves other parameters. What to do with discarded societies, with those productive geographies that have now reverted to jungle—garden gone bush. The first task is to remetaphorize them. Uncultivated barbarian nature is the ideal place to retire in the second part of the book. In the book's first part, social disorder is a save-yourself-if-you-can situation. It is the defeat of labor ethics and of the social organization of labor, but also the insinuation that the new order is based on wage labor, cheap labor, the incorporation of new ethnic groups, and the reinforcement of cultural syncretism. In the second part, the principle of order disappears and an alleged ethnic harmony prevails in the absence of labor. There are only servants and domestic economies. He wonders how this area communicates with the rest of the world, how mail travels, but he does not inquire as to how the bottles of rum are purchased and who produces food. On the margins of this "harmony" lives Christophine. Her son Jo-Jo is the only one working. We assume this because he holds a basket on his head, suggesting some type of productive relation, a market perhaps. But structured social relations exist. It is evidenced through the master/bosses/servants, mail, and preachers. There is, then, a movement toward statehood and the creation of the mestizo republics.

In this "harmonious" society, the ordering principle is submission and hiding the fact that wealth is based on the violent extraction of labor. The natural protection of human communities, the type of natural societies conceptualized in the Enlightenment, seats of utopian thinking, is belied in practice. The principle of disorder appears in ideation. Truths and lies as ideas and ideologies are debated through the woman's body, as we said at the beginning. Annette is in this sense the central locus of meaning, not very different from the structuring function that doña Bárbara serves in Gallegos, insofar as the formation of the nation-state is concerned.

But in addition, a generational horizon marks the second and third epistemological erasures. Tia, Myra, Amelié, Hilda, and Antoinette all belong to the same generation. When Antoinette leaves the island, textual space is left to them. But that is another story.

Thus, the national question is posed from two perspectives: that of black epistemologies, and that of the nation as a literary trope—Eden, Garden, El Dorado. The arguments of two feminist critics, one from the East Indies and the other from South Africa, are very pertinent: the first, Gayatri Spivak, reading the myths of Narcissus and Oedipus, and the second, Benita Perry, opposing Spivak on the question of black epistemologies and the textual space granted to them.

We have already mentioned Spivak's arguments on the individualism of white feminism, and her reference to cultural funds, to Narcissus and Oedipus, and to trace distinctions. Spivak asserts that Christophine marks the limits of Rhys' discourse, while Perry asserts that Spivak's reading is myopic because she cannot see the traces of radical subalternity, proposing Christophine as a radical alterity powerfully displacing Rhys' racism. She wants to see in Christophine a radical alternative to European paradigms.

I believe that each argues one side of an important recognition, that in a sense both are right. If we compare Christophine's textual space with the space of Schwarz-Bart's Queen without a Name, Spivak is right. Christophine's voice is important as counterweight and counterpoint, a hue, the tip of the iceberg. And in this Perry argues correctly for the alternative paradigm. But given that mulatto as an ethnic social category is absent from racial identity in hegemonic U.S. society, the figure and image of the mulatto is not foregrounded in their debate. It seems to me that these two critics do not concede to the mulatto (a) due importance in the space of the text and (b) the importance of writing in oral cultures. And that is why Perry argues for Christophine and not for Cosway.

Oral versus Written Cultures

Let us keep the figure of Daniel for later and remember that the knowledge of the Caribbean that Rhys displays in the text is framed by the texts inscribed in the novel. I am referring to the exchange of letters between the central male protagonist ("him") and the rest: the private correspondence between him and his father; him and Mr. Fraser, the established representation of the law; and Daniel Cosway's letters to him. Of a different, although equally important, nature are the texts (1) *The Glittering Coronet of Isles*, in which he learns one definition, fundamental for him, of the text and the culture it represents: zombi—white obeah transforms his wife into a metropolitan zombi; (2) an Orientalist book, Thomas De Quincey's *Confessions of an Opium Eater;* and (3) an incomplete text, *Life and Letters of . . .* (Rhys, 522).

Written culture is the real and decisive counterweight to oral cultures, understood here as black cultures. Christophine advises Antoinette to tell him the truth but her oral story cannot untell Cosway's written text. To understand the island, he does not mind what he sees and hears but rather what he reads, that is, the interpretation of writing, and that is why the definition of the zombi calls his attention. Zombi means either him or her. And all threads intertwine in the letter of the law in the form of a political file on the black woman. Her name is Josephine or Christophine Dubois, a servant of the Cosways, proprietress of a plot of land in Granbois. If she persists in her behavior, Mr. Fraser will send the police to fetch her.

The black woman's name denotes where she is from as much as a sense of nationality. Garden gone bush—or ambushed—responds to origins in the sense of being from or coming from: Granbois, the Big Forest. Christophine's family name is Dubois—"of the forest." And in this sense it is the blacks who fight over territory. Mulattoes and whites have decided to come to reside there anew. Thus stated, in Christophine as actant lies the clue to understanding a narrative for black people enunciative of their citizenship. Since the arguments belong within the polemics of nationalism and globalism, writing nation within cultural readings is important. El Dorado, Miller's *Daughter*'s icon, is, in this case, a reflection on place, or site as a country, as a field. Being and place work in conjunction indistinctly and simultaneously. In my reading, site/place/nation is what signifies naming Christophine "Dubois" and making her a proprietress in "Granbois."

There is another loose thread, that of the individual "I" in relation to place, being a nation that, in a sense, Rhys discusses through her protagonist's nation as well as her own. Being and "I" work jointly. Place and nation are prescribed in both the English and the Caribbean texts, and both discuss not only territoriality but identity as well. That identity, written in English Literature, is what Rhys counterposes.[6]

And it is precisely at this juncture that the struggle between English and Caribbean peoples is most intense, and where feminist criticism becomes avant-garde. The idea of counterposing Jane Eyre to Antoinette Cosway, of making one into the image of the other, is what is put into play. But in this game the rules concern what I call mulatto republics as well as black epistemologies. Antoinette/Bertha becomes the 'inner soul' of the English feminine "I," but that feminine "I" is obscure and animal, represented in the image of a Caribbean Creole woman.

In Gilbert and Gubar's arguments on the relation of both protagonists, there is no doubt that gender studies in postmodern societies see in the image of the West Indian woman only a metaphor for their Woman's inner self, in this case, Jane Eyre's, and the alter ego that a woman has to overcome in order to constitute herself as a subject. But, curiously, it is a Caribbean Creole of mixed kinship whose two names, Antoinette Cosway and Bertha Mason, constitute the poetic feminine figure which serves as a referent for the metaphor "The Mad Woman in the Attic," which, according to these two critics, represents the most common situation of the woman writer and is, therefore, a metaphor for their own self-representation.

Which of the multiple personae the North American critics have in mind in making this construct of the Creole self the repressed self in their readings of Englishness is important, since the double representation of this character, Antoinette, the Creole-woman construct of the Creole Jean Rhys, and Bertha, the Creole construct of a Creole woman of the disinherited white man (a construct of the English man made by two women, Rhys and Brontë) is the mirror in which the multiple identities of otherness—race, class, gender, and islands that are not nations—are seen and lost at the same time, but which simultaneously serves as an introduction to the image and a comparison for the woman without a mirror, the construct without history of the woman constructed by Dulce María Loynaz in *Jardín*.

The thesis embodied in the figure of otherness as mediation between being and soul, of the woman writer in England, and the different visions of self of *Jane Eyre*—orphaned, trapped, imprisoned—has little if anything to do with the images of her own alterity that Rhys constructs in Antoinette which are hued by a change in ethnic conceptions: what Antoinette is for Jane Eyre, her dark side (in the literal as well as the metaphorical sense), Tia and Amelié principally are for Antoinette. And in both cases what mediates is an ethnic conception tangential to the national conception. The text Brontë and Gilbert and Gubar build to imprison them is that of "a huge woman, in stature almost equal to her husband," with an enormous "virile force," a "criminal" being imprisoned in the attic with "a ja, ja low and slow." Bertha is a "rich, big, florid, sensual and extravagant woman" (Gilbert and Gubar, 360–361).

Cora Kaplan argues that Freud's explication of fantasy in looking for the "true story of the history of the individual subject," and his own need for a

> theory, and his literal embodiment in notions of the "primitive" and the "archaic" as a set of social practices suggests the way in which primal fantasy remains morally and ethically ambiguous. . . . (1986: 132)

126 / *The Feminine*

Kaplan writes that he enters the discussions of fantasy of colonial discourse of "otherness," in which a degraded subject executes the forbidden scenarios of European cultures. The moral sublimation of the different levels of fantasy via invocations of the racial hierarchy is directly expressed in Freud's discussion of the hybrid nature of fantasy as conscious and unconscious forms and façades in dreams:

> In 'The Unconscious' (1915) Freud uses the example of individuals of "mixed race" to illustrate the ways in which primal fantasy both hides and reveals its origins when it is embedded in an apparently coherent, sophisticated fantasy narrative. . . . We may compare them with individuals of mixed race, who, taken all around, resemble white men, but who betray their color descent by some striking feature or other, and on that account are excluded from society and enjoy none of the privileges of white people. (1986: 132–133)

In this light we are invited to see Bertha Mason as a historical link between English metropolitan literatures and colonial literatures, as the textualization of women in general and as the textualization of ethnic women in particular, but mainly we are to remember that in mulatto nations, as Rhys says in a letter: "All creoles are not negros. On the contrary" (Wyndham, 152).

National Literatures

It is from the standpoint of nation, of "national" literatures and their own self representation, that madness and ethnicity—with all the confusing and dialogic identities implicit therein—come to constitute the backbone of a structured poetics that involves such complex questions as global relations during the collapse of slave-bound economies. Madness in both protagonist and antagonist (versus the representation of sanity as ethnically bound to blacks) is very much in question.

To a specialist in Caribbean literatures, however, there is a missing link in the interpretation. To a specialist, the figure of Daniel Cosway is fundamental. His double patronymic, Cosway/Boyd, proclaims his mixed identity. And the fact that he is instrumental in rupturing the relation between Him and Her (Adam and Eve as paradisiacal erotic relations, in which Narcissistic images involve two sexes and two persons but supposedly only one ethnicity) is merely predictable.

The nation that materializes as a coalition of whites and mulattoes is a well-documented historical struggle. The two-faced, two-sided mulatto, who for Caribbean letters displays functions similar to the alleged homogeneity of continental blood, is an embattled field of interpretation. Placed over against his two component ethnicities, in this particular text he betrays both, and in so doing he props up the power of the English nation, marginalizes black power, and himself falls victim to the Oedipus complex—the savage as the child of a white father. For the motives behind his betrayal, like the motives behind the Englishman's marriage, reside equally in the desire to reject the father: money, given to the white woman in Daniel's case and to the firstborn in the Englishman's, functions as remedy, a remedy of historical dues. The fact that biblical scripture—the sacred, as written text, and the written law—is the main instrument of their— Daniel and "his"—strategy homogenizes the sacred law of patrilineal inheritance through the English law of endowment, by means of which one (the English son) surrenders self, and the other (the Caribbean son) independent nationhood.

Madness, then, is indeed the most important all-encompassing metaphor, since it stands for loss of self, loss of identity, loss of nation, and loss of property, as much as for male/female, white/black/mulatto/Creole, and colony/metropolis relationships. That is why black epistemologies stand out as knowledge bound inextricably to the oral.

This is perhaps why Rhys establishes a fundamental difference between beliefs and knowledge: "We believe what we have been told, the theory. What we know, we know" (*My day*, n.p.).

> "England," said Christophine, who was watching me. "You think there is such a place?"
> "How can you ask that? You know there is."
> "I never see the damn place, how I know?"
> "You do not believe that there is a country called England?"
> She blinked and answered quickly, "I don't say I don't believe, I say I don't know. I know what I see with my eyes and I never see it. Besides I ask myself is this place like they tell us? Some say one thing, some different, I hear it cold to freeze your bones and they thief your money, clever like the devil." (525)

Knowledge is empirical, for theories are distrusted. Theories are the site of lies. Pragmatism versus theoreticism is one of the many ongoing debates it takes to figure out interethnic encounters. For white practices interdict and negate white theories. Fanon has much to say on the subject. It should not be surprising then that French Creole terms, introduced as scarecrows in the language, create such noise, or that the profile, the bare sketch of a character, exercises such a powerful influence in the composition of a text, as if to say that the fictionalized, the portrayed and represented, world belongs to her: hers is the site; hers is the atmosphere; hers is the country. For Christophine is made to appear as the center of the novel, what gives credence, credentials, credit to Rhys and Rhys' Antoinette.

Maintenance and support are two words that describe the nature of Christophine's assistance to white/Creole epistemologies, both terms understood as collateral, capital in both economic and psychic terms. If not, observe how the third and slimmest portion of the novel, the section where Brontë/Rhys come to agree, and from which Christophine is absent, where her body is totally removed, is the place in textuality where the Creole self as character crumbles. Very much like reality in general, the reality of plantation economies, whose collapse the novel also textualizes, goes under when black labor—more so than mulatto—stops. That is why Coulibri, as a site of plantation government, is garden gone bush. The image of a garden (Eden/El Dorado) gone wild, or of Eden gone Mountain, or of plantation gone bush, parallels the disordered state of Creole consciousness (and of perturbed white English subjectivities). But here we must add that when garden goes wild, bush, this image as representation of white psychic disorder also stands for maroonage, for guerrilla warfare under colonialism, and therefore as metaphor for liberation, self-determination, and national formation.

Mind you, when the white Creole Antoinette is made to feel at ease with both black people and the site of maroonage, white English Caribbean literature is enriched, and thus national sentiments are textualized—nation as country and country as in countryside, the most elemental, pre-State (but post-plantocracy) social organization—as a

> proto-nationalism of the people, patriotic feelings based often, as in Ireland and Poland, on religion, or on symbols and rituals, or on the consciousness of belonging to "a lasting political entity." (Hobsbawm, 24)

When the representation of the Creole in English literatures is rescripted, a national literature emerges. When madness is renegotiated and shown to be reciprocal, site/self and self/site are underscored as one and the same. Atmosphere is what counts in *Wide Sargasso Sea*, it is argued by renowned Caribbean (and English) writers. Is it in vain that Rhys makes Antoinette quest for identity? Note:

That's what they call all of us who were here before their own people in Africa sold them to the slave traders. And I've heard English women call us white niggers. So between you I often wonder who I am and where is my country and where do I belong and why was I ever born at all. Will you go now please. I must dress like Christophine said. (519)

Black epistemologies do not necessarily dismiss white ones. On the contrary, they acknowledge their power as much as they assert they cannot intersect. Although there is reluctance among blacks to engage in conversation, they are ready to negotiate. A little bit of love and a little bit of understanding is all that is asked from a young and already very hardened white Englishman, although this begging is the position of the Creole. In raising the issues of love and sharing the inheritance with him, and in advising separation to her, Christophine is plotting the two alternatives— simultaneously for women and for nation—for a politics of a common front in which both contribute. Her strongest advice is to separate, to let go. Her advice is self-determination, independence: "Get up, girl, and dress yourself. Woman must have spunk to live in this wicked world" (518)— advice for women and for colonial peoples alike?

If not, then there is retreat, maroonage. For to remain is to change identities, to lose oneself, to go mad. Antoinette is not Bertha, neither is she Jane. Nor is Jane Charlotte or Antoinette, nor Tia Amelié or Hilda. The dilemma of a white Creole is all of them. The dilemma of Christophine is none. And in the whole novel only two black children, one boy, one girl, cry at separation. Baptiste and Christophine both turn their backs.

Orality as silence and as a way of keeping knowledge a socially private mistrust, sensuality as rejected knowledge and discretion, and paranoia as forms of interethnic encounters also deserve comment. Read across one vector, the second part of the novel displays a peculiarly English male cultural paranoia, a mild sort of madness that comes as a result of his misreading, his lack of a proper language, his neglect of the function of orality in understanding and communication. Intuition supplants reason, and knowledge comes through the pores of the body, through smell and scents, through vision, through personal contact and sight: body knowledge. He is overwhelmed by the lushness, the luxuriousness, and sensuality of the place, which, for a Victorian Englishman, must have been a sin— sensual pleasure, a breaking of the strongest cultural taboo, that which separates them from us. Pleasure might have been understood as the path to savagery, and sexual intercourse the beginning of mixed blood.

He then defends himself by means of translation. Vision, smell, and sounds are translated into racist and colonialist English cultural tropes. It is not only in the cultural construction, as we see it written in the book, of *The Glittering Coronet of Isles,* but also in the process of interpretation and translation, the concrete management of words, that power (or endurance) originates. It is through books that he comes to live reality, through Daniel's letter to him, through his letter to his father, through Mr. Fraser's letter about Christophine, and through this book that interprets and explains to him the power of black epistemologies—and this makes him understand zombiism: "A zombi is a dead person who seems to be alive or a living person who is dead" (522). In other words, it makes it possible to understand what Antoinette means when she says: "Say die and I will die. You don't believe me? Then try, try, say die and watch me die" (513), and it is what makes him understand the power of words well managed, hence naming her Bertha, Marionette—white obeah.

Fearing the white English manipulation of knowledge, blacks and Creoles alike try to teach him slowly, but when they see him refuse, they stop. The text is filled with silences. Silence, where the spoken word stops, signals the clear and conscious limit of an epistemology, of black epistemologies which see bush as a site of emancipation, and misunderstanding as a site of power and of negotiations possible in the establishing of common fronts. White Creole representation implodes in Caribbean letters, but a complicity of silence remains. In several instances when she is directly addressed, she skews knowledge—"nothing," "everything," "some things," and "nobody" are all expressions that bring Antoinette and her author close to English Caribbean letters.

Christophine is disturbing because he makes us see her as disturbing. To understand this, we must just try to compare the first depiction of Christophine, given by Antoinette, plus all her cultural explanations that fall into the void, with the second depiction, of which he is in charge. The image is so aggrandized in his imagination as to reproduce the picture of Brontë's mad woman in the attic. That is, Rhys has the particular boundaries she needs to read into the English male and female elaboration of blackness; and blackness, Negritude, is what is in question here, blackness as the province of blacks and of colonial subjects—both West Indian and African. Ethnic ambiguity is one of the main bones of contention in the dialogue between Rhys and Brontë, not to mention Creole as essence, a vision of cultural miscegenation (a kind of nationalism?) made by Caribbean cultures themselves (Brathwaite and W. Harris, *passim*).

Perhaps, in line with these facts, we can see the usefulness of Spivak's reading of the Oedipus myth into the text. For me, the presence of patrilineal inheritance, the rights of primogeniture, is a travesty of patriarchy and therefore of nation and, moreover, of government. In reading Oedipus into the relations between the male protagonist and his father, questions of law—of the father and of empire—are foregrounded, and the principles of national formation for the colonies overridden in the book. However, we must keep in mind that the only person who refers to the island as country is Christophine, in her most quoted line, referring precisely to the enforcement of law: "No police here. . . . No chain gang, no tread machine, no dark jail either. This is free country and I am free woman" (557). Everybody else calls it place. Dominica—and by extension Jamaica, Trinidad, Martinique, all the "God-forsaken islands" (556) mentioned in the book— is thus viewed and textualized, left registered as nature, as garden, a garden where native (and nonnative) whites enjoy or go mad. And as nature, that is, property (English property), it behooves English laws (state and government/nation) to rule. The question is thus complex, but all the terms of the debate are on the floor and therefore both critics, Spivak and Perry, prove their points.

The idea of nature, both as women and as property, and the metaphor of garden, as site/place, then, stand here for (1) self—in the sense of autonomy, of Narcissus who sees his own reflection, of women who expropriate their own metaphorization of nation and replot it (Franco, *passim*), and (2) nation, in the macro sense of self that it incorporates, that is, social identity and the construction of the social text. When she, the Creole, loses control and is abducted—as slaves were—forcibly carried to England, Creoles and women lose out and leave English subjects and their law face to face with black ethnicity. When the woman loses out, when she surrenders to passion (love or hate), Law—as government and as nation—is kept in the service and control of the father, and thus, in literature as in society, patriarchy is reestablished. Poetic tropes—women as colonial subjects and men as metropolitan subjects, or third- and first-rate citizenships—are, like the literary figures of Brontë, strongly pre-scribed. That is why Rhys moves away from her, very much disliking the image of the lunatic as a "paper tiger," her character "withered," "loathsome." Bertha Mason had to be reconstructed as Antoinette: "then, the Creole I will live!"

5 / Simone Schwarz-Bart

Provision Grounds/Nation—*Et in Arcadia Ego*

The Minination: A Stranded Island

From the opening moments of her two texts, *The Bridge of Beyond* (1972) and *Ti Jean L'Horizon* (1979), Simone Schwarz-Bart establishes a certain territoriality. She uses the distinctions between language and speech, center and margins, above and below, to map out borders. Beginning from a circumscribed space, ethnicity, origins, histories, and lineages are constituted, within an affective geography we can call "country" so as to distinguish it from "nation" and from "the national state." The most representative sign of this progress is in the metaphor "The Bridge of Beyond," or "Between Two Worlds," the titles that accompany her two novels *Pluie et vent sur Télumée miracle* and *Ti Jean L'Horizon* in the English translations.

The most damning qualities of this "country" are its tininess and irrelevance, damning because they cannot guarantee visibility either in history or in geography books. In fact, "specialists have determined once and for all that the country is insignificant" (*TJ*, 9). Seen as nature, Karukera, the indigenous name for the "island of beautiful waters," is at best a watercolor, a "land of no importance." Assimilated into the feminine in its invisibility and irrelevance, in its history and its microspatial geography, having arisen like the woman "who comes from nothing, to be nothing, hardly even stray shadows," the purpose of this text is the constitution of this "country's" past through speech and orality and the writing of history by literary means, letteristic genuflection to cultures of "sand and wind, that are born and die with words . . . and somehow manage to reinvent themselves day by day" (*TJ*, 11).

In *Between Two Worlds,* or *Ti Jean L'Horizon,* a novel of national quest, an enormous beast has blocked out the sun and submerged the land in eternal darkness. The hero must solve the riddle concerning the nature of the phenomenon and eventually overcome it. Ti Jean is the legendary hero, son of Wademba, an indomitable African maroon forest recluse, and his daughter Ma Eloise. Ti Jean begins his journey by walking inside the beast and traveling in its insides until he finds himself in Africa. Beginning to map out a territoriality of ancestry, in Africa Ti Jean is guided by Maïari, a young child, to the land of his ancestors. Fond-Zombi (Guadeloupe) and the land of the Zonanke (Africa) are thus connected. However, throughout his journey Ti Jean realizes he is a stranger. He then begins asking for home and initiates his journey back. With the help of an older, phantasmagorical and mythical woman, who tries and examines his feelings and affects, his sensuality, he finally finds his way out of Africa and passes into France, to wander around in what is also a foreign land, this time guided by Old Eusebius. Eventually Ti Jean comes back to Guadeloupe, conquers the beast, and brings the sun back to his native land.

Pluie et vent sur Télumée miracle or *Bridge of Beyond* is more of a woman's book. It is the story of the Lugandor family and its ancestry, and is more focused on family than it is on nation. The central figures are the grandmother, Queen without a Name, and her granddaughter Télumée. The novel tells the story of the undaunted, enduring, and resilient love the old woman feels for her entire family, symbolized in the young Télumée she helps raise, and of the bereavements of poor black Guadaloupan people as they go through life. Feelings of love and endearment exist side by side with feelings of hatred and resentment: there is the battering of women by men as much as tender feelings of men toward women. Télumée is thus loved and hated, the object of caresses and pampering and of rejection and pain. In the end, the encouragement and support of women deliver her through life, and at the novel's close we can see how young Télumée has come to occupy her grandmother's position.

Both novels honor the struggles of black people and both constitute a strong support for feelings of confidence, stressing the positive in heritage under unfavorable conditions. Nation is tiny and insignificant, but affect soars high, never waning. Both narratives then enhance what is bravest in the human condition and project their enduring wisdom and comfort far beyond the garden house circumscribing their minuscule ethnic nation.

The discursive contracts of this narrative revolve on axes of oppositions and antinomies. In this cultural milieu we can distinguish the oppositions of language and speech, structures of reference and transitory expression.

The narrative of Simone Schwarz-Bart situates itself in the intersection. In the historical/written expression, the narrative inscribes the historical/geographic constitution of black oral/written cultures. The power that writing holds over the word, its weight upon the oral cultures, is acknowledged tangentially in the brief but sharp allusions to school and scholarship, where textbooks portray blacks as monkeys.

Geography and blood, space and family, are constitutive elements of explanations of origins. There is no doubt that the construction of history is predicated on the basis of the formation of the social family. And in each case it is tied to origin and lineage. In *Ti Jean,* much as in *testimonio,* lineage is also a historical construction, passing through the heroic spirit, through the desire and the will to forge this otherness.

In the narratives of de la Parra and Loynaz, lineage refers to the Founding Families and Wars of Independence. In the case of Belli and Schwarz-Bart, it is a lineage of popular resistance. As in the masculine narratives, the heroic crosses the geographic. In agrarian societies, or in agrarian moments in a society, in the geography—plain, mountain, forest, thicket—the First Family is forged, the businessman, the worker, the maroon, the new man. That's why in *Ti Jean* the road leading to the mountain is closed, accessible only to the chosen by way of the myth of rebirth through the return of origins. The high place is impenetrable, a savage landscape, unstripped; the high plateau in *Ti Jean,* like El Chipote in the culture of wartime Nicaragua, is the habitat of rebels, the manufacturing center of alternate significations, the point from which alterity is transmitted and transacted, through the oral agents of the word and histories as the repository of value.

As with the opposing categories that signal the subject positions within her circumstance, Schwarz-Bart fences off the territory on which the various discourses are situated. And as in Rhys, space is defined more in geographic than in political terms: the island, whose essential peculiarity is its tininess. The tiny, the microspace, the French district in the colony, completes the polarization of the established categories whose explicit antinomy is the macrospace: the national French State, France, the Republic. As in *Wide Sargasso Sea,* European nations are invented spaces. Here France is the dream of Elie, from which all that survives are "confused visions, a few pictures of snow and strange leafless trees in a book, a map of France, and some illustrations representing the seasons. . ." (*BB,* 54).

The representation of the country as island, as nature, and as geography contrasts, then, with the representation of France as illustration, as much in the pictorial as in the conceptual sense. France is a longing—a desire to be a "great researcher," "a customs officer," or to own "a convertible," "a suit," "a brocade dress"—or France is a school. The description of the white people's house and its economy completes the image of the nation, since both nation and house occupy the places of the macronarratives, the macrospaces, the center. It remains to be seen how these binary realities are articulated, concentrating primarily on four key moments: territorialization, the white people's house, the multiple meanings of invisibility, and the reconstruction of Africa, because in these moments we can see most clearly the convergence and divergence of these binary tensions.

Territorialization

By "territorialization" I mean the expression of a textual desire to bind one's self to the land, to point out each place that the narrated social subject occupies and to assign them a particular sensibility in such a way that the physical geography, the topography of the terrain, manages to reconcile subject and country, ethnicity and place, masculine and feminine.

The landscape is thus in agreement with the social topography: Guadeloupe is divided into thirty-two communities of which the text is concerned with a third: acting as a backdrop for L'Abondonnée and La Folie, they are: La Rame, Valbadiane, La Ronciere, Dara, Le Corbet, Mount Balata, and the center, where the lives represented come together and disperse, Fond-Zombi.

Fond-Zombi, the very name of which confronts a double darkness, territorial extremes, is obscure structures and subjective obscurities, invisibilities; it is an object of passion in both texts, the difference being that *The Bridge of Beyond* is a border while *Ti Jean* is a port of entry. *The Bridge of Beyond* is the representation of the soul, of the black community, of blackness and its ethico-tragic sense, of its sententiousness and resistance, an inferior fatherland. In *Ti Jean* it is the "lowlands" ("En-bas"), the limit between the "Frenchified" and the "chameleons," "macaques," the Westernized blacks, and the others, those who remained in the caves, removed from market economies and French schools, abandoned to highlands, sites, places where they lived and continue to live like maroons, preserving their African traditions, reproducing in that foreign place the memorized and oral culture that has earned them the name of "the Inscrutables."

I want to argue that to territorialize is to draw ethnic borders, to fence off, to privatize and establish certain fields, to delimit. The paths that lead through the bamboo and the banana fields, to the left and to the right, are borders, signs of confrontation between two ways of living: the factory and engines on one hand, and the forest of valuable woods on the other. The latter is a confrontational space, a rearguard that has begun to dwindle, withdrawing and receding: the precious woods, used as firewood for the sugar cane engines, or as boards for the huts, leave their stumps, marks of their amputation. And so deforestation takes place. And beyond the obviously economic, toward which Fraginals gestures in the case of Cuba, deforestation is also a political event. Far away, mentioned only in passing as inhospitable places, the two seats of central administrative power of the French nation, Basse-Terre and Pointe-à-Pitre, are presided over by the garrisons of the militias.

The play between margins and centers, then, is many-sided, as are the references to "the center" in the French Caribbean territories. Their points of return, naturally, are France and Africa. Country, fatherland, and nation are in no way synonymous, nor do they exist nominated as such, as interchangeable referents, in continuous alterations and displacements. They signal instead the terms of the slippery map, an intimate geography relative to the subject position. But it is suggested that nation has at least two meanings: (1) the territory, related to the nation-building novel, to the masculine novels of Gallegos and Rivera in the Caribbean, and (2) the origin, in the sense of sources, of birth, of descendence. To be black in terms of nation is here to have been born in Africa.

In *Ti Jean*, Africa is the transcendental signifier, the center. But Africa is a historicized centrality. In the literature of 1979 it is already passé. Much like the characters of Carpentier, whose parameters for "here" and "there" take on globality itself, the hero of this text comes and goes, returns, and longs, from the African "there" to the "here" of Guadeloupe. The reconstruction of the African chronotrope is no longer symbolic, but rather metasymbolic: it is the historicization or the reflection of the symbol, which we will explore shortly.

Let us say in passing that this involves discerning a reconstituted and revised Negritude, one that approaches "Africa" in a different way. We are not concerned with discarding but rather decentering the discourse of identity, since this former Africa, the imagined Africa of post-emancipation scholarship, can no longer gauge the emigrated meleé culture, the mixed and creolized version of that continent that the new intellectual cadres have experienced, some of whom have by now lived in modern Africa and live within a modernization of the society portrayed at the end of *Bridge of Beyond:* power lines, paved streets, electricity, and the new water well of the rural workers' huts. For this new intellectual sector, educated in France, language, in the first instance, and the school and the church in the second—the two institutions interpellated by Schwarz-Bart, with the seat of control in Rame and branches in Basse-Terre and Pointe-á-Pitre—is French.

From the initial moment of the texts, the debate is dated. The polemic refers to at least two different concepts of Negritude: (1) as an ideology that forms around the constitution of place and being, and (2) as the interpellated collective ethnic subject. Just as for Maryse Conde in *Season in Rhiata,* political ideology aside, Africa seems foreign precisely because of the very same character of Antillean miscegenation. The same antinomies that open the narrative denote France, Western culture, in different theoretical moments, and the historicity of its analytical categories. For this reason the ideas of the "bridge" and the "beyond" constitute the principal metaphors of the cultural crosshatching of the open character whom we can read in the "beyond." My thesis, therefore, is that Negritude, as a literary discourse, is the subjectivity constituted from the position of the mulatto subject, as frail as the bridge that leads to the beyond, like the passage of the slave ships across the Atlantic, like the structures of the house of L'Abandonée, all of them its metonyms.

Territorialization: The Emotive Fact

Earlier I held that territorialization as geography is also the construction of an emotive map. The sites, the places, and the municipalities are named following heartfelt mandates. Or, to say it in another way, they are enclosed within the relations between couples and within the constitution of emotivity and family. Behind *Ti Jean*'s L'Abandonée, for instance, there is a sentimental history, the history of miscegenation, of mixture, of the formation of *mestizaje,* to which the mulatta narrator hardly refers at all. In the protagonist Regina, Télumée's half-sister in *Bridge of Beyond,* we can perhaps see allusions to this mulatticity in a Frenchification that has something to do with ethnicity. Hubert, her father from Desirade, occupies a blank space. He is the unwritten, the erased. If the subaltern is the unsaid, the unrepresented, in the writing of the inversion of codes, exemplified here, this man (because he is a white man who disobeys the rules of whiteness) is situated in the position of the subaltern. Regina "sleeping in a bed, eating apples from France, wearing a dress with puffed sleeves and going to school," is signaled as nonblack, as mulatta (*BB,* 40).

However it is at *Ti Jean*'s L'Abandonée that the true history of the biologic-emotive crossroads of the races is narrated. The house is named after its builder, the white Creole Colbert Lanony, the only white man with a name in a text in which names signal magic, almost destiny, history, identity. Naming him singles him out as he singled himself out from his ethnicity when he went to live over at L'Abandonée with a black woman, "far from the eyes that looked askance at his love" (*TJ*, 12), severed from the society that had declared their affinity profane. Now the house is abandoned, but the structure of the house is still solid, and therefore cannot help but signify, especially in a text where housing is the marked representation of the ethno-social. L'Abandonée represents "an outlawed white man's fancy for a negress" (*TJ*, 13).

Interethnic relationships are thus constituted outside of the spirit of established law and order. And so it remains outside official state history and is written as a detour, probably within criminal records. The hero becomes a madman: if white, eccentric; if black, bewildered—he who has lost his reason and is rendered illegible in the codes of the nation, since his decentralization has conjured up the crisis of metropolitan identity.

L'Abandonée takes us, in one sense, to the place of *mestizaje,* as well as of love and desertion; in another sense, to one of the attributes of pain, the place of Negritude. Love/pain is the overriding antinomy of the text. That explains why the residual structure of the exchange that takes the form of the house evinces simultaneously devastation and solidity. The same is true for La Folie, as we will see further on. Desertion and madness are two emotions feminizing the territorialization and "geographication" of the country, and both are fundamentally tied to the changes suffered by the gendered and the ethnic subject.

Territorialization: The Economic Fact

Another trajectory of this territorialization is marked by the coexistence of two economies: the agro-export (sugar cane and bananas), and the subsistence. In fact there is a third economy, that of hunting, fishing, and food gathering, but it is rather minuscule, although important, as we will see shortly. The majority of the land on this small island belongs to agro-export economies: sugar cane and bananas. The roads lined on both sides by cultivated fields signify borders. The subsistence economy is restricted to that which in Caribbean culture has come to be known as a provision ground: a small plot of land to cultivate in order to eat, sell, or exchange—

sweet potatoes, fruits, bananas—reminiscent of the slave plantation. The primitive economy of the Inscrutables (hunting, fishing, food gathering) is not textualized in detail in *Ti Jean*. Those from the Hermandad de los Desplazados, "those who hate money and will throw it away if it is given to them," stick to this economy nevertheless—the primitive economy of "I'll give you this, you give me that," where only part of the exchange is through money.

In Old Abel's barshop, in Monsieur Tertullien's, in the timber and fishing industries, or in the sowing of the gardens—masculine activities, just as making manioc crackers out of coconut milk and processed sugar are feminine activities—there is money involved. But money as capital is only produced in sugar and bananas, economies that include the participation of both men and women. Money is the dividing agent between slave and master.

The economy of subsistence and exchange clearly charts the social map, populating these districts with artisans, fishermen, producers of oil, and distributors of rum, some of whom now "play the role of aristocrats." But in its poverty, with its small and bereft houses, the largest of which has four rooms, everyday life tends fundamentally toward slavery. While the still social landscape reflects insignificance and tininess, nature is repossessed generically, reminding us, in its nominalization and its sense of protecting darkness, of that naturalization of politics and the constitution of the new national state that abounds in guerrilla testimonials. *Ti Jean* and Central American guerrilla testimonials are, in fact, contemporaneous.

Territorialization, seen in these economic terms, is expressed in subsistence economies, in the tendency towards miniaturization that in Fond-Zombi corresponds to the landscape. Miniaturization is indeed uttered within a semantic universe quite different from Teresa de la Parra's. One can well argue that what is established in the differentiation between the two poetics is the narrative persona of the text that places the subject in a different position, but there is also the inclusion of the category of work as a discursive agent. Miniaturization in Schwarz-Bart expresses the real shrinking of vital space in subsistence economies. While in de la Parra objects are seen from a distance, like picturesque figures of aesthetic contemplation, in Schwarz-Bart objects are the reconstitution and recuperation of space and the subject of polemics.

The social landscape in Schwarz-Bart, then, is not only poetry and lyricism; neither does it project an aesthetic of entertainment. The discursive contracts in fact negotiate lyricism with magical realism, with allegory and

the everyday language of sociology and of domestic economies, assessing
for us the valuables: a small room with an iron bed, perhaps

> covered with the poor man's sheet—four flour bags with the print still
> showing despite much washing. The bed alone took up half the avail-
> able space. The other half contained a table, two chairs, and a rocker
> of plain unvarnished wood. (*BB*, 28)

The precariousness of the furniture matches the rest of the household
items: the heating stove made of stone, the pallet on the floor. And there is
an uncertainty, a fragility in the face of nature, due to the possibility of the
destruction of the house by a cyclone, uprooting the entire household: "the
men and women of Fond-Zombi . . . lived exposed to the sun, rain, and
wind; they could howl, they could die, they existed in total uncertainty"
(*BB*, 44). The other houses in the text, Ma Cia's, Télumée's, are all varia-
tions on the same theme, when no longer bereft of the essentials. They are
unequivocal signs of the homogeneous poverty of subsistence economies
living side by side with the agro-export economies in agrarian societies.
And discord is established with the solidity of a single object in the white
people's house: "in the dining room full of solid mahogany furniture an-
chored, heavily, immutable, to the floor" (*BB*, 60). Adjectives used in the
space of whites refer to objects. The same adjectives, used in the space of
blacks, refer to subjects.

Territorialization: The Spirit of the Law

In this sociotextualization, the region's underdevelopment is unimportant:
nature as nature, in its potential, never appears disentangled from the
national state, from the spirit of the law. Testimonial literature chooses the
mountain, the jungle, the hillside, the swamp, as referent, symbol, and sign
of the construction of the new nation, and supposedly tries to describe it in
its putative simplistic sparseness, to narrativize it less poetically and more
realistically, rhetorically finding itself faced with the problem that nature,
in the first place, was already a besieged and threatened place, attenuated,
as nature never was at the beginning of this century, by forces of order and
by the concept of law.

At the same time, nature could not but be represented by a master metaphor, that of the matrix, the uterus, the mother who gestates only sons, the
masculine of the new nation. The shock in Gallegos' *Doña Bárbara* is that
suddenly the flatlands gestate a woman, a mestiza of mixed lineage. But

thus conceived, the metaphor of the mother earth and the "mother father-land" was a concept rendered fragile, feminized; it was a transfixable and vulnerable uterus: the abortable maternity, since the fatherland is threatened, militarized, and militarizable. Where the economic concept of the productive land was not, as it was in the nation-building novel, appropriate for ruling and government, for controlling and determining the lives of the men, as in the writings from plantation economies—from Quintana, Duncan, and Gutiérrez, to the trilogy of Miguel Angel Asturias in Central America—the army has needed to be overwritten, illustrated, visualized.

In the case of Schwarz-Bart, as in the testimonials, the separation between flat, unadorned nature and the other nature, the economic, that which denotes ports and agro-exports as much as that of the cultivated gardens/provision grounds that bifurcate reality, is a sharp incision, a national wound that divides cultures, reason, mentalities, and sensibilities, and which shows the multinationality of the national states as well as the gravitation of the ethno-nation, in the same way and with the same force that language is distinguished from the word, from the voice, from speech, in the case of some and not in the case of others.

Perhaps it would be more apropos to name some territories, zones, places, spaces, and other like national states, and thus speak of zonifications or territorialization, as we did in considering writings by men, in the middle of which emerge the signs of power as in, let's say, the white's house as a governed and governing space, in the former a signified and in the latter a signifier, depending on whether it represents the government of the territory, or the governed territory.

As Homi Bhabha has argued, this ambivalence in cultural signs and their metaphorized representations of power is a characteristic of all colonial realities. An external colonization established the borders between republics in the cases of Colombia, Venezuela, and Brazil. In the two masculine Caribbean nation-building narratives, the references to the central government, to the law and its transgressions, to the consulates as seats and representations of the nation in the international terrain, contrast zones and territories like La Maporita, Casanaré, the flatlands, Apure, El Miedo, and Altamira. In Schwarz-Bart the references to Central government contrast citizenships within a colonialist relationship between France and Guadeloupe: France is more the law than the law itself.

On the site of the plantation, located in the geographic region or territory where the rubber plant is exploited, the leaders and administrators exercise the functions of the state and the army, as administrators of land

and goods, and establish the norms and regulations of the economic behavior of the social subjects. In this way we can observe the intervention of the law in *The Bridge of Beyond*. The colonial administration acts as a presence in respectable institutions such as the school and the church.

In the masculine narrative, economic comportment is hegemonic, leading the other components of subjectivity and of the personality, which are subordinated to it. In the case of *La Vorágine,* it is the search for the woman, the child, and the emotive and ethical values that have deferred to the family that place this institution in a secondary space with respect to the economy. Nothing like this happens in the intersections of productivity/emotivity/nationality in Schwarz-Bart, a scathing difference between gendered orientations toward writing.

France in both cases occupies the place of the sign. In the case of the Modernist sensibility that still informs *La Vorágine,* the French language comes to represent, within the category of the citizen of France, the authority of a humanist culture preoccupied with the well-being of the rubber workers, personified in the old man Silva. In other words, civilization, predictably, perishes in the hands of a modernized barbarianism. In the case of Schwarz-Bart, more entrenched in the Francophone tradition, France signifies its symbols: the flag, magnitude, majesty, and glory, reproduced within this signifying world in the school, in the rudiments of literacy, even if the beneficent influence of civilization over barbarianism remains counterindicated, for sarcasm critiques the theory of evolution that identifies black with animal, black with cannibal. Social Darwinism and the counterposition of the land itself, with its trees, rivers, water currents, sun, and torrential rains that flood the text, flank the concept of schooling on both sides.

Letters, words, speech, and writing, in their most comprehensive and global aspects—those that construct subjects under French citizenship and those that by way of repetition and the memorization of lessons reproduce ideologies—comply with a dictum: while French men were already citizens, Africans were still "monkeys with their tails cut off," "wild savages now running through the bush, dancing naked, and eating people stewed in pots" (*BB,* 52, 61).

Territorialization: The Ideological Fact

In *Ti Jean,* the textualization of Africa is also a quest. Geography aside, the areas scrutinized represent history in search of its territorialization. The search for identity is, in a certain sense, the transliteration of the obsession with origins. It is not surprising that the search, as well as the orientation, involves the concepts of country, gender, and ethnicity, since the narrator is a woman and a mulatta. Momentarily bracketing the fact that references to the land are linked to the metaphor of motherhood, textualized desires unravel longings for fatherland, country, and place through the mediation of woman. Desire for the fatherland and the libido converge in magic, myth, and bewitchment, as revealed in Ti Jean's encounter with the Queen of the Large Breasts.

As a symbol, Africa naturally is a preoccupation for the localization, in both senses, of geography, territory, and history. In the fourth section of *Ti Jean*, three moments explicitly address this question. In the third and last, Ti Jean "asks himself in what epoch he had fallen, after he walked into the open jaws, into the heart of the Creature: in what Africa?" (138)— for which there are two responses: one geographic—the place is situated "between the Seetnae and the great mouth of the Niger river" (*TJ,* 139)— and the other historical, tied to lineage, when Ti Jean repeats his grandfather's words:

> If some day you show up over there, in my village Obanishe, over the delta of the Niger, you or your children or your grandchildren or any of your distant descendants, even the thousandth generation, all you will have to say is that your ancestor was called Wademba, to be welcomed as brothers and sisters. (*TJ,* 148)

This relative in Niger, Nigeria, land of the slave-trading coast, is the local for whom Ti Jean asks around. He wants to find out when the whites proclaimed themselves King of Dahomey. Maïari, a child who has escaped from the coast, tells him a story with a clue. Maïari's narrative of slavery includes his description of a character named Bernus. In Bernus, history then makes sense, for his story converges with a narrative recorded by an old man who wandered about Fond-Zombi, and who claimed to have participated in the conquest of Africa, a black man in the splendor of his twenty years, "decked out in the same outrageous uniform that the escaped slave described" (164).

Tying together the two histories—which are in fact the same history narrated in two different geographies by two autonomous narrators—is that which pursues and signals the narrative of the myth of the reencounter, since, as much in the similarity of landscapes as in their dissimilarity, in the dialogues between the ten-year-old African Maïari and an intemperate Ti

Jean, in the encounter with the Sonanques, these two histories are rearticu-
lated in their moment of fission and explain something that, fundamentally,
one comes to read as the meaning of the word nation, of territorial identity, and of history in blackness that represents Ti Jean, inserted within
a geopolitics dominated by France. In this sense we may distinguish the
meanings of the word nation in the two cultures.

But what is curious about this unfolding of the new Negritude and its
vision of Africa is that what is remarked in the meetings are the fare-
wells. The foreignness and alterity of Ti Jean is stated by itself, first, in his
having the political impression of "being an exile in his own land" (*TJ*,
127) and, then, in his rage, when he shouts: "I come from my country and
from my country I come, under my own roof . . . I am not a foreigner,
not a foreigner. . . . You people sold me . . . to the white people from the
coast" (*TJ*, 146). In spite of this a group of three Africans insists: "Who
are you and what do you plan to find among us?" (*TJ*, 149). To respond
with a recitation of lineage would be useless. Simone Schwarz-Bart knows
it, and she insists in having the Africans order him: "Go back to where you
came from. . . . How many children sprung from nothingness will be born
among us, blinded by the desire to confuse their blood with ours" (ibid.).
This seals the dialogue as a metahistorical confrontation between black
Guadeloupans and Africans.

Discrepancies and deafness aside, their common origin cannot help but
announce itself in the comparisons of landscapes, flavors, and costumes;
nor can otherness help but triumph, as seen so clearly in the words, examples, and narratives, but above all in the exchange that makes them
possible. And that is why they say:

> the arrow that killed Wademba was cast before the day of his birth . . .
> at the beginning of the beginning, when the egg from which the Sonan-
> ques would be born was still dormant in the heart of the earth. (*TJ*, 136)

The ten-year-old African boy who introduces the foreigner to the African world teaches him, as his first lesson, that the word black "doesn't
belong to our language, is not from here" (*TJ*, 139) and, second, that the
word "brother" is odd to him. When the boy wants to show him affection
he calls him "cousin." In this dialogic series, Ti Jean always stands out as
ignorant, unaware of the physical and social territory where he must learn
to integrate himself, and the history of a rejection is registered. The cultural
traits he doesn't know are underscored.

The distances between blacks, being second class among Africans, is
marked by the entry of whites in the African continent, by the diaspora

and breach occasioned by the slave trade. We have already pointed out that Ti Jean appears in Africa just at the moment at which the slave contract is carried out with the collaboration of the other African tribes. It coincides with the beginning of colonialism, for whites come to realize that they can control the territory politically and instill in it the spirit of their laws.

Under slavery, whites are the borders dividing blacks from blacks, the mediation between them in slavery's heyday and its aftermath. The Sonanques refuse to accept anyone who has been a slave into their group, for in the past the maximum punishment for treason was to sell the subjects into slavery and condemn them up to the last generation. Blacks from Guadeloupe who want to find their roots on this continent are punished people, and some centuries later are rejected as foreigners, since they are descendants of those who have been condemned. The mediation of whites has transformed them into cultures tied to slavery, and therefore miscegenized. For this reason I argued earlier that this 1979 Africa is an Africa mediated by *mestizaje* and modernization, and influenced by the direct contract islanders have with their social organization. Africa is no longer, at the beginning of the century, what the myth of Negritude thought it was, "this prodigious land where gods chose their dwelling places" (*TJ*, 135).

In the first encounter of the two worlds, there is nevertheless a recognition, a resemblance, an ancestry in common, an understanding of language, or at least a having-been-here-in-a-dream. If not, as Maïari says, how is it that they can communicate? Being part of the two social spaces is decisive of this ambiguity. In the village the drums announce Ti Jean as a "friend," but later he is treated as "a foreigner with the face of Wademba." That is, with the face of his ancestors—a nonwhite. And the character is situated "on horseback between two equally impossible worlds" (*TJ*, 134).

The myth of territoriality is constructed as a circle in which, in a sort of reciprocal history, Maïari remembers that other ten-year-old boy who was called Wademba when they expelled him from the community. Maïari knows Ti Jean's ancestral history since his respective tribes have been at war. War, arms, and the truth learned from "the tip of the spear" (*TJ*, 132) make the forces of war intervene within the constitution of the history of migrations and the populational and ethnic encounters. The history of the ancestors is a political history. Gaor, his grandfather/great-grandfather, is the one who achieved peace between the Sonanques and the Ba'Sonanques tribes, "without a word of peace being pronounced" (*TJ*, 143), taking on his own shoulders the hatred of his tribe, which was internally a slave tribe and which took part in the traffic in blacks for the whites.

One can almost hear behind the words of Maïari the echo of a historic discussion carried out in the sixties throughout the transmigrated black diaspora. It is a valid assumption that in this conflict both sides (the African and the Caribbean) lost. The resettling of diasporan blacks back in Africa was a post-abolition nineteenth-century project that never took place, but as a project it left its mark in the social imagination of transmigrated black cultures. In the dialogue between black cultures, slavery continued to be a bone of contention. The contempt that continental Africans feel toward the islander has its origins there. The longing of the islander to transcend slavery without achieving it began then. But for Simone Schwarz-Bart the controversy is a family quarrel and is spoken of in poetic rather than political terms. In her texts, lyricism is a means of displacing the conflicts from the political arena.

Territorialization as the Site of Patriarchy

To identify the center with patriarchy and patronage, with the metropolis, and with domination and power is commonplace enough. In the Caribbean literatures that plot Africa, geopolitical concerns are preponderant, to the detriment of gender considerations, reconstructing a nationality or a patriarchy that leaves woman unnamed as a social subject. It is important, then, to inquire as to how ethnicity, nation, and gender are interwoven in feminine narratives.

The discourses of traditional ethnography and literary history have colluded in a construction of an Africa whose culture is read in terms of these disciplines. There is a general ignorance of the African landscape, generically referred to as hills and grasslands, landscapes rooted in and nurtured by traditional anthropology and travel narratives.[1] The inclusion of the discourse of these disciplines softens the image of a contemporary Africa, historically represented in its rawness by distanced white women authors like Isak Dinesen, Nadine Gordimer, and even Doris Lessing, or black separatists like Ama Ata Aidoo. The contemporary social conflicts of this continent are, in this text, extrapolated from the past and placed in symbolic lines of poetic prose.

The literary reconstitution of social spaces supported in ethnography represents today a homogenizing vision of the African continent. The repetition of cultural landscapes, naturally, returns to these older narratives, now in question. The new cultural studies has polemically denounced the criteria that these disciplines use to reconstruct different types of societies, à la V. S. Reid's *The Leopard,* where Africa is a vast Eden. The net result is what, following Said, I have called worlding and alterizing, dual processes that nevertheless make the continent reappear as acceptable in the social imaginary of the centers of colonial power. This is an undifferentiated, denationalized, tribalized Africa, represented as a series of primitive communities that are evaluated with standard parameters. The composition of patriarchy and polygamy would be two polemical topoi from which to organize the spatial dispositions of everyday life: the hierarchies and ascendencies within the sociohistorical subjects and their configurations, and the division of labor. The total structure is presented as a severely policed area of harmonic composition which it is forbidden to analyze, since patriarchy and polygamy constitute interior narratives, high-security areas of ethnicity, the place from which Eurocentric distances or racist First Worldisms are exorcised.

So Africa becomes a holy, untouchable place. It is an immutable social area, a chronotrope, and not, as is assumed, a social geography. But in this pocket of immutability, the "effect of residual presence" as much as "the function of information retrieval" coincide. It is an extrapolation of the quest for a personal/social history that leads to an imposed transplanting and uprooting. And from there issue the urgencies of the return. The myth of the return of the kingdom of shadows, as a metaphor for slavery, is also carried out through Western cultural signs, like the myth of Plato's cave and Dante's voyage to the kingdom of the dead. Lycanthropy is an African contribution, a natural erasure that is a sign of power.

Naturally the subject is put in the place of origin in the moment of scission, "the epoch in which the deepest of their blood ran" (*TJ*, 186). But it is also localized in "the midst of past heroes." The patrician black African from whom the hero is descended is mythic. His government is nonetheless patriarchal. Since incest is the condition of both his birth and of the retention of power within the clan, Gaor/Wademba, father/grandfather of Ti Jean, presides over the structure of a governmental postulation of the masculine.

Nevertheless, there are distinctions between him and his ancestors, shifts in perspectives owing to changes in place, to changes in the centrality of signification that in those years was displaced from Africa to Guadeloupe. Oddly enough there is a reradicalization of black agendas insofar as the black intelligentsia decides upon a return to the natal country and their incorporation into the neocolonial governments, as is the case with Césaire, Senghor, and Eric Williams, but there are also the writers who choose to situate themselves territorially in the country of their birth.

Decentering Africa in the black intellectual conscience/consciousness is a result of the uneasiness over the meaning of Africa's previous centralization. This is Ti Jean's question. He wants to dislocate the response, wrenching it from a dream or utopic place. This is also the question to which the text responds. Insofar as the text raises and answers the questions simultaneously, the larger question is of interest to the island intelligentsia, to the intellectual group that formulates it, to the literary institution that writes it.

The question the text answers refers concretely to ancestry and utopias. In these formulations the signs of transition between Negritude and its intellectual successor are also overt, evidence of the transition to modernity, a modernization the text reiterates insistently, like the attention paid to the introduction of electricity. Artificial illumination—electricity—makes Guadeloupe simulate France.

Insofar as the transition to modernity implies a radical break with the ancestors, their retextualization is a farewell. To be sure, this is also the case of the retextualization of the Founding Families in Loynaz, de la Parra, Belli, and Rhys. The historic ancestors textualized or evoked—Bolívar, Martí, Maceo, Sandino—as much as those who are mythically constructed—Gaor/Wademba and the lesser goddess Christophine—are ancient figures whose epoch is mythic, of millenniums. In the case of Schwarz-Bart, they are dated at the beginning of slavery and tribal Africa. The ancestors are, for blacks, those who have survived the flow of capital and have chosen to live in the subsistence economies of hunting, fishing, and food gathering. In this respect their economic practices are identical to the African tribal practices of the text, whose economic references are clouded over by the hegemony of the discourse of the warrior, but money as labor (Modernity's signifier par excellance) is not mentioned even once in this reconstituted Africa.

The ancestors have already become rhetorical figures, the past, history, tradition, poetry. That is, they are the lyrical reconstruction of ethnicity, represented in the ideal of independence. The textualization of the historical figures, their metamorphosis into figures (in Auerbach's sense of the term), syncretizes epochs and allows for their circumscription qua epochs. They are people cordoned off, museum pieces imprisoned in the pantheon of the illustrious ones. In *Ti Jean L'Horizon,* two women, Ma Vitaline and Ma Eloise, occupy the place of the ancestors, and in fact all of the elders act as such in the text. However, the two sovereign figures are Wademba and Eusebio, in whose duality and intimate symbiotic relationship we see the masculine blueprints that couple war (history) and wisdom (tradition) orally bequeathed to Ti Jean.

As a personification of masculine power and of the patriarchal government, they are the ones who choose the successor protagonist and bequeath the inheritance of wisdom and power, together with their martial arts. Eusebio, the master, calls him "my little boy." And like a good teacher, he interpellates him, he listens to him, he interprets, and he guides him. The formation of the narrative persona, who must cross the two central circles of fire, the African space and the French space, is chaperoned by Eusebio, who, in cases of extreme indecision, vocalizes the sentences of survival: you prevail "if you impose silence on your innards" (*TJ,* 236). The only cord by which you may suspend yourself is in your own spirit. Advice is understood not as repression or individualism, but rather as the strength of self-knowledge, tolerance, patience, fortitude, of virtues that have already been indicated by the feminine principles of inner power, the emotive, represented by the Queen of the Large Breasts.

However, unlike Ti Jean's encounter with the feminine, the masculine principle (wisdom but also war) is not tied to danger, not located in the innards of the earth, although both refer to the principles of life and death, Eros and Thanatos. In the exchange with the father, the little boy can allow himself the expression of fragility; the little boy can be just that, because in the interaction with him, what the father assures him of is the transference of power, his inheritance: the right to political primogeniture. In this case primogeniture is palpable in the father's choice and in his care. For woman, on the other hand, father equals rape, incest, power. In Wademba, Ma Eloise faces these three practices of the masculine. For the woman the father is, in this text, the sign of repression, violence, and irrationality. Father is negation.

The dream, the fancy, is placed, in this case, in a slippery terrain between history as a political economy, as slavery, and history as utopia, as reconstruction, as a place of masculine desire for the masculine, which in the case of Ti Jean is related to his discoveries in Africa. In this desire, as in the masculine desire for the feminine, magic intervenes as a medium and an agent. The thousand and one tests that the hero must undergo to constitute himself as an ethnic, historic, national, and masculine subject are administered through magic, and negotiate their expression within the discourses of magical realism and ethnology.

The new subject oscillates and is constituted between the boundaries of Africa and Guadeloupe. Ti Jean doesn't reject the geographic trek which is his to make, and undertakes it as much for the world of the living (today) as for the dead (yesterday), but not for one moment does he cease to think of the return. One can argue that going back to the sources is then the fundamental ideological agenda of the new blackness, the nucleus of its signification. And in fact, the tension in "here/in your house" that the child Maïari points out to him is, for him, the question of geographic-cultural similarities, as much as the unveiling of the myths. To discover the "dream" of Wademba, to defalsify the facts of the highest semantic charge, is a goal: that of revealing that it was the same ancestral tribes who sold the blacks to the whites and who linked slavery to punishment, a kind of martial breach that resolves intertribal affairs; and these very ancestral tribes are the ones who treat as taboo the reincorporation of anyone who had been a slave. As I argued earlier, slavery is the beginning of African exile and *mestizaje*.

The relationship of the narrator to the institution of slavery produces a double rejection, that of feeling exiled within oneself and that of being called a foreigner in the same house as one's parents. To this scathing wound we attribute the scission between the first and second Negritude, a Negritude more antillean, which is the more realistic, considering present political agendas, an ideological fact that is felt in the incorporation of the Western tradition into the literary discursive contracts. No one who has been educated in the West can help but recognize the master narratives that structure *Ti Jean L'Horizon*. This simply means that Ti Jean's doubts about nationality and identity, and his situation between two worlds, have their correlatives in writing, which reconstructs them, gathering a tradition that expresses the search for an identity in a language and in a manner of speaking that must necessarily be its negation.

The Feminine as Territorialization of Desire

Everything seems to indicate that the locus of the feminine in both texts is magic, witchery. Woman imagines that man imagines her power rests in enchantment. Woman's power resides in transmutation, appearing and disappearing, knowing the secrets of nature, being old and young at the same time. Power in woman and fear in man occupy the same place and relate to each other through desire, the irresistible desire of man for woman; lust transcends and disassociates itself from reproduction: it is the space in which man waves his white flag and becomes conscious of his impotence. Empowerment and disempowerment occur simultaneously at the moment in which desire appears.

Since, for the most part, woman's emotions and sexuality are unknown elements for man, he locates them in the dimension of enchantment and interprets them as a supernatural presence. And in order to subordinate and control them he must word them in myth. In *Bridge of Beyond*, it is the myth of the guiablesse. In this figure, "the most wicked of the spirits, the woman with the cloven hoof who feeds exclusively on your desire to live, and whose charms drive you sooner or later to suicide," he predicates a negative invisibility for man that radicalizes the power his desire concedes to woman. The fear of sharing power is localized in the body of woman, in her physical geography, in her anatomy "in the hollow of her thighs" (*BB*, 5).

Outside this anatomic localization of masculine desire and its representation in the invisible, the feminine occupies other important places, especially as related to sensibility and feeling, that are invisible to men. That's why Elie mistreats Télumée, telling her, "I'm going to teach you the meaning of the word woman . . . a black maroon with no woods to run to," or, "Man has strength, woman has cunning, but however cunning she might be, her womb is there to betray her. It's her ruin" (*BB*, 45). And, on the contrary, when a woman recovers and gets back on her feet, she affirms the existence of her breasts and legs.

The feminine also adheres to food, to the knowledge woman has of the brews that cause misfortune, among them the loss of will which can be read not only as the loss of power over one's self, but as emasculation, insofar as it induces unmanly, or feminine behavior. Desire can therefore change the sign of man to non-man, that is, to woman or to something in between, the status of gayness, for instance, a man/woman. Tenderness, feelings, and respect feminize the masculine. That's why the "*docteur-feuilles*," the brewers, are imagined as old women, beyond the age of an active libido, beyond the age at which their bodies are considered sexually desirable. Old women cannot occupy the place of woman that is referred to in the sentence, "man must see woman and pay attention to her, if not he will lose his two eyes" (*BB*, 40). Ma Cia, Ma Eloise, and Télumée are witch-women who can no longer bewitch, and they are women in which the signs of mysticism, the power of the priestess, the serenity and the tranquility of the soul, coincide. They are all centered women.

The struggle for gender definitions is therefore located in the attempt to separate biology from reproduction, from man's desire for woman, in old age, and the constitution of the woman subject as a subject on which equality and power are predicated, that is, as incorporating the masculine.

This change of signs is undesirable. The man/woman relationship, as a biological or emotive fact/fear, has a crude, animal dimension in these texts, related to the culturally relative sexual postures, and ravishings without carnal contact but with masculine intervention. Biological reproduction, in other words, is imagined and represented as rape. In *Ti Jean L'Horizon*, Wademba, the father of the clan of the Inscrutables, grabs

> a papaya stalk . . . he greases . . . with a drop of carapato oil, he puts it into the interior of the little girl's cavern, he stretches her over the bed: he sweetly inserts a strip of papaya within the most intimate depths of her nature. He seemed satisfied to see that she has been opened by the malice of his age. (*TJ*, 19–20)

And when Awa finds Jean L'Horizon, "she lifts up her skirt and opens her legs toward the sky, expertly opening with her fingers the pearled borders of her lips" (*TJ*, 21). Later, when their child, Ti Jean, forms a clan with Onjalí in Africa, we can see anew how the surprise emerges:

> Until then, without being really frugal with her body, the young wife gave nothing other than the traditional position of the Ba'Sonanques, a position that was so common that the people of Fond-Zombi regarded it with disdain, as a pure and simple waste of time. And later, announcing her pregnancy, she manifested her gratitude acrobatically, standing on one leg with the other audaciously slung over Ti Jean's shoulder. (*TJ*, 173–174)

It is not this interaction, then, which signifies woman in the text. This is simply the natural dimension of the feminine, the species. The man/woman relationship is made more explicit elsewhere. It is introduced through myth and attached to it, above all, the myth of the return, the encounter, the orientation, the earth.

The Kingdom of the Shades as Territory of Gender and Desire

Gender differentiation resorts to Plato's androgyny to explain the separation between the sexes. Equality is thus a dysfunctional biological unity (a concept in which homophobia resides), because genders have different agendas, perhaps: "Man to the right, woman to the left . . . everyone in his or her own house, doing his or her own thing" (*TJ*, 201). The Christian principle of gender differentiation as punishment, incorporated into this explanation, is tied to the spirit of the law of patriarchy. Punishment is the same as contradicting patriarchal desire. Punishment is the outcome of threatening the hegemony of masculine power. For this reason it is written as respect for the spirit of the law.

The myth of punishment and example, as a dynamic of patriarchal hegemony, is transmitted by woman. Woman is bearer and reproducer of obedience to men, and the transmitter of the taboo of the androgyne. But the ideological reproduction of masculinity radiates the obscuring of desire, the blurring of desire for sexual differentiation. One can argue that to know the masculine and the feminine and to accede to them both is the quintessence of the hidden desire of writing.

Like Gallegos' doña Bárbara, the Queen of the Large Breasts embodies the principle of the grotesque feminine. She is the devourer of men, who uses her attributes as traps. In her, it is not *mestizaje* and property disputes that are called into question but rather the postulate of gender differentiation. To arrive at its presence is not the equivalent of initiating a dispute or of winning a settlement, but rather of reconciliation: it is to imply what it is that one wants from life, since she knows all the roads. The feminine in the feminine narrative is the principle of harmony. Nevertheless, the enigmatic construction of the feminine resorts to commonplaces, to grotesque representations and uterovaginal symbologies. The feminine compass is a vagina, a cavern that narrows, until it becomes a passageway like a throat, leading to an expansive uterine chamber where she resides.

The textual symbology betrays a Freudian unconscious in which the discourse of desire is entangled, making the vagina the place of its satisfaction and remembering simultaneously that the exit is the entrance to the uterus, where life gestates. The sexual act is thus coupled with a birth that can turn man into child and woman into mother, satisfying the Oedipus complex but acceding to incest. In the vagina, Eros and Thanatos occupy the same space.

Constructed as darkness, humidity, narrowness, and prison, the site becomes a metaphor for domesticity and lends an exchange of disquietudes in the form of an oracle. Between the feminine and the masculine, direct discourse is nowhere possible. The planes of the man/woman exchange of gender differentiation are symbolic. The symbols outline desire, a mobile that takes the subject to penetrate the chamber of the den from which one cannot leave. The visualization of the feminine principle as something materialized in oldness, flaccidness, dirtiness, an old woman whose "breasts hang to below her belly, like dried tobacco leaves" (*TJ*, 108), transforms the woman into a mother, a transformation that is very revealing of the fear that man feels in the face of the other. In this instance, the grotesque is a formation defacing the subject to disqualify it.

Here as well, we find the case of the dialectical construction of desire as its negation. That which is undesirable is in the first place feminine, but that which is desirable is also feminine. The feminine is a double bind, a trap, a loss of liberty and mobility, but it is primarily and above all an enigma, a play of appearances and essences, a tongue twister. The text demands of man the capacity to see beyond the physical, to explore the field of tenderness. The dialogue between Ti Jean and The Queen of the Large Breasts manifests the feminine desire, and assumes a knowledge of masculine fear in its articulation.

Of the two teachings and of the two roads in Ti Jean's search, one concerns power and patriarchal wisdom, a fund of accumulated value that in turn articulates power, the war, the whites, while the other concerns interior knowledge, the internal stare, emotive development. Both are expressions of desire, but, in the second case, desire is unlocalizable, an interrogative. Desire is that which is unplaceable, unnameable. Their interior territorialization, their inner geographies, in which woman occupies a central space, the place of desire, woman with productive principle and the reproducer of desire, as mediator between the interior and exterior, in Ti Jean's case of the intimate knowledge of himself and his nation, is, riddle of riddles, only a means of expressing obscurity. Desire is in this sense a secret tie to sexuality presented as difference, and to identity postulated as androgyny, a sexuality mediated by culture and ideology. The man/woman relationship presupposes this symbiosis as a condition of liberation. Whereas man possesses knowledge of the quotidian control of power and its exercise and resistance (war), woman possesses the knowledge of desire and identity (peace). On the symbolic plane of language in this narrative, both are carried to the encounter with themselves and with the nation, expressing the strong Positivist ties of self and politics.

In the feminine narrative of the quest for nationality, the masculine and the feminine are united in the desire of man for woman and in the capacity of the woman to utilize the desire instructively. The conjunction of the masculine and the feminine in both is found on the lost road toward a double territorial localization, one that has as much to do with the interior fatherland and the geographic nation as with the phenomena of modernization, namely the electrification of the workers' huts, the incorporation of the intelligentsia into their native country, and the recognition of *melée*, mulatto culture, and *mestizaje*. This is a moment in which the utopic construction of the nation is transacted and the active incorporation of the native intelligentsia, as a living force in their country, is realized.

Belle-Feuille: The House of the Whites

All of the feminine narratives in this study speak of lived-in, livable houses. None quite like *Jardín,* a lyric novel of which Pedro Simón has said that the house seems to be the main character—the house and its natural lawn/ garden. *Los últimos días de una casa* (The Latter Days of a House), is the suggestive title of a long poem by Loynaz. Houses abound in the contemporary books by Loynaz, and in René Méndez Capote's *Memorias de una cubanita nació con el siglo* (Memories of a Cuban Girl Born with the Century), a text which evokes Alejo Carpentier's *El siglo de las luces* and suggests that the house is from that moment already a metaphor for nation. The house is a representation of a patrician nation, especially the house of the patrician nationalists. Loynaz and Méndez Capote are also contemporaries of Teresa de la Parra and are her interlocutors, and all of them speak of the house as a place of the birth of ancestry, lineage. The *Independentista,* the Founding Families, the house/*hacienda,* the house of the patron, the Great House. Gioconda Belli tries a sign shift and substitutes the revolutionary nation for the founding fatherland, but in her text the latter has not disappeared. On the contrary, it is the counterpoint that calls for the structuring of the new national habitat.

Belle-Feuille is such a representation. It is the invocation of this privileged space, Schwarz-Bart's *Desaragnes*—that of the spiders. The name evokes the well-being all the other houses convey, but especially de la Parra's *Memorias de la mamá blanca.* Belle-Feuille's social organization, however, differs, since it deals here with the French tradition, signified by the *Béchamel* sauce that is so appreciated in the text. But *Belle-Feuille* contrasts in its name with *L'Abandoneé,* the site in which Queen without a Name, the protagonist's grandmother protagonist, on confronting the death of her daughter by fire, will seek refuge.

L'Abandonée is the place of repose where the zombi family finds refuge when Queen loses speech. Belle-Feuille is also a place counterpoised to Fond-Zombie, the essential territoriality of the blacks, their fatherland, their place, their space, where there seem to be no whites, except as a historic reference, as a tale or a legend, even if they are to be found only around the bend in the road, on the path to the canefields and from there to the meadow, the English garden reminiscent of country houses.

The geography described is interesting as, when the road that leads to the school makes a sharp turn, the discourse becomes entirely economic:

> a road that ran between nothing but canefields, without a cabin, without a tree in sight, without anything to arrest the eye. It was the time of year when the whites set fire to their land and black stumps stretched out endlessly with a bitter reek of nature smoked and cured. (*BB*, 58)

Looking for shade, for rest, burned by the high sun, the protagonist says:

> I came to a long, silky green path all shiny with rich grass and shaded by clumps of white, pink, and red hibiscus. Just behind me the road between the canes went on still, but already I felt as if I were in another world. (ibid.)

The lordly house, with its columns, bougainvilleas, stone steps, porch, picture windows, silence, and fresh air, is not, as in the case of Loynaz, uninhabited, or inhabited by a single woman with a single servant. It isn't surrounded by peasants, or by serfs—half servants and half workers—as in de la Parra. On the contrary, Belle-Feuille is a house whose space is clearly separated from that other space, from the area of domesticity and from the area of productivity. It is a modern space, where the division of labor remains clearly established: the owner of the means of production, the wage workers, and the subsistence communities from which the domestic and field wage workers come.

This is nonetheless the compass of the women of porcelain, who in *mestizaje* command more attention than in these islands where apartheid rules. The descendent of "the White of the Whites" is thin, with the air of an old maid, with white-yellowish hair, with painted toenails, sandals, and intense blue eyes: in short, a painting by Carolsfeld in Loynaz; Miller's *Daughter* in Jean Rhys; and the young girl in the vaporous dress reclining in the pasture who says, "the world was mine and everything in it belonged to me," as with Gioconda Belli's protagonist and de la Parra's Virginia of Saint Pierre.

As much in its spaces, measured in square meters, as in its organization, that is, in its furnishings and the food and the wardrobes, unsurpassable barriers are established between these two human groups who inhabit the place and whose values, everyday habits, beings, and appearances form two republics, two ontologies and two epistemologies at least, that are mutually interpellatable.

The scarcity of furniture, to which the writing demands we pay attention, to the point of telling us who has and who hasn't a bed, what type of mattress is used and is "real" and "authentic," how many glasses and bowls each house has; the punctiliously detailed description of the inhabited space, the type of roof that covers the protecting windows; the foodstuffs, what is eaten and the style in which it is cooked, and the amount of oil splashed over the vegetables—all manifest once again the desire to differentiate between groups. But the fundamental issue perceptible behind the writing is a rescue, a valorization, of the black world and of its moral and physical beauty. Here, the confrontation between voice and language among blacks with which we began this section has, as one of its strongest expressions, the ability to undermine the certitude with which Schwarz-Bart qualifies her characters.

So let us say, then, that the house of the whites obeys the sectional division and the textual imprisonment that white ethnicity is subjected to in this text. Both the house in this text and the France of *Ti Jean L'Horizon* are encircled so as to delimit them. The personified white person is totally pigeonholed and circumscribed. Their reduction to a domestic habitus does not, nevertheless, invalidate their social ubiquity, as is seen in the circumscription of the domestic economies by the sugar and banana fields. Both are damned spheres with edges that cut, borders shielded by authority and power that, to be transacted, must show safe conduct.

Outside the inhabited house, the mansion, the stately country house, whites are represented metonymically. Their bodies, habits, customs, and everyday lives are only textualized within their houses. Outside they are agents of production, of oppression and the harshness of work. Outside the house it is only the white person who is pitied by the blacks, despite the rags that cover the blacks as they cultivate the sugarcane. But inside his house the white person is something else, and for that reason the house of the white person is important as a socioeconomic site.

The house of the whites is also the center of whiteness, "the whiteness of the whites," an expression that corresponds to Negritude in this narrative of antinomic transactions. There is no doubt that cruelty is a metonym for whiteness. The white person is the bonebreaker, "who limped, who could lift a horse, whose hair gleamed like the midday sun, who'd squeeze a little negro in his arms until he died" just to "relieve his own bad temper" (*BB,* 57).

But white is not only a hyperbole. It is, above all, a social structure, the border where imprisonment ends and comfort begins—"Culture," since blacks have been enslaved up to this point, "the poultry in the cages, tied up, [with] terror in his eyes," and the master is at the "*Desaragnes* house at *Belle-Feuille*" (37). Whiteness (Blanquitude) and blackness (Negritude) are thus mutually spoken. Both are the subject of the utterance, and both are reproduced by means of the voice even if both are notarized in the text. But it is in the reproduction and representation of speech, in the voice, where both constructions are expressed. And it is within the house and the hut that this becomes evident.

Not only, then, is it the wealth and the grandeur, the splendor and the self-sufficiency, that signal the macrostructure of the Great House, but it is also the visible contrast, the locus of the antinomy between the two cultures. The house of the "whiteness of the whites" is the factory where signification and "culture" are produced. And it is curiously produced by way of woman's voice. It is not only the graphemization, the inscription, which incises the formation of the black's blackness.

Scholasticism is scarce, but the black accedes to the voice of the white. It is there that these distinctions are so important, and in order to understand them we must make long Derridean and Saussurian excursions and see, before entering the domestic *habitus* proper, how the conceptions of country, land, and nationality are articulated.

While Ti Jean takes refuge and cover in the sentence that separates language and speech, and can from that point reconstruct the account of the culture and the traditions transmitted by the ancestors, *Bridge of Beyond* articulates these accounts through subsistence economies, encrusted in the plantation economies of the postslavery period and the relations between subsistence and export economies. In the first case, the fundamental sign is emigration, the survival of the Atlantic crossing, the slave owner's middle passage, a bridge toward Antillian *mestizaje,* the passage from one continent to another and therefore the construction of "Africa" as a transcendental signifier interweaving three concepts of nation: nation in the sense of being a black African; nation in the sense of having been born in Africa or being a first generation Guadeloupan, a founder; and nation in the Western sense of the formation of the national state, of Guadeloupe as a French province. In the second case, the subsistence and plantation economies are tied to the hegemonic cultural *habitus* of blacks and whites respectively, represented in their houses, and also to states within states, marginal cultures within colonial cultures, subordinated to autonomous national states as in the case of Guadeloupe's relation to France.

Voice, speech, words, as black attributes, or as reflections on black culture, are polysemic, at times contradictory, revealing diverse points of view, heteroglossia, the insidious intersections of the historic voices of the whites, spoken by the characters according to their circumstances. In this sense, as we have said, the Inscrutables use *simio* and *macaco* as expressions of mimesis to refer to the cultured and to the mixed. But the reflections on speech, on words, well define the position of the ethnic subject, in this case black. In the more general sense, the disarticulation of speech is invoked in the silence of those who speak and are neither seen nor heard, in the words that do not signify, since in the absence of the interlocutor they are only wind, air, nature. While for whites black speech signifies a physical fact, an emission of air, language remains intact and circulates by word of mouth within the community of the speakers of the group, silhouettes of orality, the tales without which there is no life: "Understand, my good old man" says one of the woman guides to Ti Jean, "that, unlike that which happens in our lives, all our tales have happy endings: if not, why tell them?" (*TJ*, 205). Speech is also articulated with invisibility, with the nonbeing of black ethnicity in France or the being of gender despite hatred, and with the reconstitution of Africa as a fountain of identity.

That's why Victory, Télumée's mother, reflects on words and silences. She doesn't speak, but sings. She doesn't speak, doesn't reflect, doesn't give her opinion; she repeats the generic, the clichéd, that which is already established in the words of the song which is not of her creation, because "certain words were null and empty; it's nice to hear them but better to forget them" (*BB*, 52). For Ellie, for example, "the very word cane drove him wild, filled him with incomprehensible fury" (54). And that's why Télumée, in the house of the white man, says she "sang every part, every cry, possession, submission, domination, despair, scorn, and the longing to throw [herself] off the top of the mountain" (63).

The sententious style, with signifiers tacitly understood by the community of speakers, whose semantic charges are contained within the colonialist and postemancipation economies with interethnic cultural negotiations, is made clearer when Schwarz-Bart allows other voices to enter, the true, hegemonic voices, that define "the whiteness of the whites," the cruelty expressed in this text as grotesque, as a formulation of the social imaginary that outdates the sign, while simultaneously exaggerating the referent.

The Woman of Porcelain Constitutes Ethnicity

There are words that must be heard and later forgotten, advises Victory, Télumée's mother. The words that comprise the voice of Madame

Dasargnes are found within this classification. As in Rigoberta Menchú's testimonial, the encounter between mistress and servant is a combat zone in which the mistress has all the weapons, the most important of which is language, which, in the case of the exchange, is the language of commerce and economy, the language of transaction.

In the first instance, there is the attempt to establish the hegemony of command and to point out the source of its power: employment or unemployment and, ergo, pay. The interrogation on aptitudes and skills—washing, ironing, cooking—is doubly sloped. It means knowing how to perform the various chores, how to be officious, having technical know-how, or not. Substitution is the space within which ethnicity is constituted, in the counterpositions of ironing and cooking, for example: "iron, don't just beat old rags," or "cook, don't just throw bread crumbs in a frying pan with hot water." The counterposition between mine, defined as a seat of value, and yours, as a seat of valuelessness, is the beginning of an exchange that tends toward sexuality—"this is a respectable house"—ethnicity, and, by means of a logical leap, physical beauty and the phenotype.

In counterposition to the complete superiority of the white over the indigenous population in the case of Rigoberta, and of the "effect of the real" that the testimonial genre achieves, narrative fiction in the novel allows itself poetic justice when it introduces a servant whose negotiation with the mistress occurs at the same level of utterance, with a lexicon that would be the pride of the academy: "Yes, I know. [Ironing is] placing a shiny surface over poplin shirts with winged collars," Télumée answers. And unlike the loquaciousness of Gregoria in Teresa de la Parra, the old servant woman who recites a memorial of the family with names, titles, birth dates, and ideological and moral filiations, the beautiful Télumée, being interpellated, continues starching the shirt in silence when the old housewife comes to supervise—and establishes, under official pretext of supervising the chores, her tendency to banter. "I was already used to these tricks, this humbug. I took the words and sat on them with all my sturdy weight—white man's words, that's all" (*BB*, 61).

The harshest attacks are the constant blasts of gratuitous criticisms: if she sings because she sings, if she's lovely because she's lovely, if she does things well because she does them well. The unrelenting struggle develops in the search for perfection in these occupations as much as in finding just the right weapon. For the white mistress, black maternity, for example, means a mortgaged uterus. And so words are liquid like water, and Télumée slides between them so as to let them pass her by. But not all of them do and Schwarz-Bart accommodates the doubt that takes the protagonist by surprise when she affirms: "It wasn't my fault he'd [God] given me a blue-black skin and a face not overflowing with beauty" (76). And when Télumée looks at herself in the mirror, she says, "a fear would come over me, a disagreeable sensation, the thought that I was still the same black girl with stormy tresses, with sooty skin and roving eyes, who had hired herself out at Belle-Feuille and would not escape heaven's vengeance." That is, there is no concept of norm or moral law nor of family possibilities. In this last instance, the text agrees with the white woman. We will know later that "God is white and pink, and where there is a white man is where there is light," while blackness "is a well of sins, a demonic creature" (*TJ*, 149).

Ethnicity is constituted in these voices as a negation of the positive, as physical and moral inspection, the questioning of occupations that implies doubt concerning the ability to carry them out. Blacks are only acceptable when they see themselves as the blackest of blacks "that is constituted by the whitest of the whites," and this is articulated in the example of Amboise, of the black from Paris, "one who earned his living 'being' a Negro in a cage, yelling and throwing himself about like a lunatic, which according to Amboise was just what the whites liked to see" (*BB*, 149).

Against this ethnicity, constituted inside the space protected by the house of the plantation owners and now reduced to a domestic sphere, the author's narrative strategy of political consciousness that articulates and contradicts who blacks are is displayed as a narrative strategy. It is here that we find the sententious character of the narrative, which not only imitates and reproduces an orality, but also utilizes maxims and proverbs to oraculize being. "Those who," "no one who," "A woman/a little girl," and "He who" are expressions that refer to all blacks. The description of Queen without a Name as "not a princess," "not a cannibal" alludes to this ideology. The adjectives employed to describe beauty—"brilliant," "clear mahogany," "satin," "iridescence," "hollyhock"—are other ways of opposing the positive to the negative. But it is at the end of the text that Télumée tells us that she has finally understood what it is to be black:

> wind and sail at the same time, at once drummer and dancer, a first-class sham, trying to collect by the basketful the sweetness that falls scattered from above, and inventing sweetness when it doesn't fall on him, and at least he has that if nothing else. (*BB*, 137)

Or worse, to be black is to be "like a gun loaded with blanks, while the wickedness of life is a gun loaded with bullets that pierce and kill you" (161).

In this way, there are word-bullets that must be emptied, deactivated, but there are others that must be heard because "with a word you can prevent a man from destroying himself" (*BB*, 53). As in the former case, in which Victoria remains silent under the weight of words, in this instance the unnamed Queen speaks. The reflection on the value of the word refers to her power. There are words which, like seeds, are not wise to spread to the whole world. "There are many things, in fact, of which one shouldn't speak" (87). To curse an unfortunate person, for example, is to give him the coup de grace, and "certain words, certain descriptions, should suck up people's soul and poison them" (149).

The Meanings of Invisibility

The first sense of invisibility is linked to the size of the nation. Invisibility means not appearing on maps or in history. In *Ti Jean L'Horizon,* when the man is looking for his land and finds a woman to help him, he identifies himself as Guadeloupan and says "my country is so small that no one knows it, and my nation is so small that it hardly believes in its own existence" (209).

Lineage is intimately connected as well to territorialization and therefore simultaneously to invisibility and to the social family. Clearly territorialized between L'Abandonée and La Folie, two geographies, the history of a lineage transpires. Between "En-haut" (the highlands) and "En-bas" (the lowlands) it is the same. In L'Abandonée, lineage is established from fathers to sons, supporting itself on the moral qualities of blackness, in its collective aspect. We have already pointed out the abundance of sententious phrases about who black people are and how they live. But L'Abandonée is also the place of happiness, where the black couple can carry out a relationship of affective normality and sufficient productivity. This is not the case in La Folie. As its name indicates, this is the place of misfortune and it is situated next to the canefield, in a self-named collective called the Brotherhood of the Displaced, where the Wanderers live.

Historic visibility lives in the myth of invisibility, in the lineage of the Inscrutable and their descendants, in their symbolic territory. Visibility and invisibility interrelate through the lived experiences of blacks from all latitudes, as Ralph Ellison demonstrates in his metaphor of the invisible man. Invisibility is a black attribute that materializes in a special way in man, for example in Amboise in his years in France. Ti Jean walks "the streets of a deserted city, the snout of death close on his heels . . . and he ran from house to house, screaming 'It's Ti Jean! Why won't you let me in?' But the doors remained stubbornly closed" (240). "Invisibility," then, is a socio-political concept. It is white people's negation of black people. But it also manifests itself in regards to woman. In her case it is related to the lack of affection and the hardness and abuse of man. The disaffection of Elie, for example, causes Télumée to enclose herself in a total sadness that makes her seem like a spirit, that is, dead, a zombi.

But in woman, the loss of affection is the cause of invisibility, a state of death-in-life that in *Bridge of Beyond* has its economic correlatives and articulates invisibility through adversity, through the absence of a family structure and a negation of lineage, and through work in the canefields. Invisibility also means social withdrawal, to go where one will not be seen. La Folie is such a place. La Folie is the place of the unloved, the aban-doned. In this sense La Folie is like an outdoor sanitarium, a psychiatric hospital, a clinic, where the displaced, the rejected, go. In this sense it is interesting to see how Schwarz-Bart tries to interlink the map of mental perturbation with that of production, and cane work with withdrawal. In some ways it is the lovesickness that we see working in *La Vorágine*, the disaffection that takes man toward the rubber plantations. Work as pun-ishment has its biblical origins but also its well-demarcated references in economic history.

La Folie as a representation of withdrawal is a kind of geography of the invisible. It is where those who have come from the thirty-two communi-ties live, "exempt from all rules and all memory, surprise, or fear" (128). Unlike En-haut (the highlands), which is the place of resistance, the space of the myth of the return of origins, La Folie, where the Inscrutables live, belongs to the alienated, called here the Wanderers. But like En-haut, there are people who in desperation have entered another socioeconomic dy-namic. They are gatherers. They are hunters and fishers who "didn't plant seeds, nor cut sugar cane, nor bought nor sold." And they had a similar contempt for money, so that if they came across a coin they threw it out. The economic separation of society is that which indicates the healing of the deep wound between the living living and the living dead.

Nevertheless, the canefield is to one side, and between madness and sanity. It is a purgatory, a condition obliged by the threat of hell; it is a way of acknowledging the hegemony of the agro-export economy, to declare zombiism the only way out. It is also a way of saying that the being is only economic, and to not be economic is to not be. Desperation leads to the most primitive forms of subsistence. Unproductivity is therefore one of the forms of invisibility.

Within this superimposition of planes and this feminine organization in which work, sensibility, ethnicity, and nation occur simultaneously, there is always place for the lyric discourse that serves to differentiate one type of man from the other. Man, by the way, always inhabits the two spheres, the lyrical-mythical and the social realist: in the first instance, as loved/lover—Jeremiah, Angebert, the first Elie, and Amboise—and in the second, as possessed—Germain, Ti Paille, the second Elie, and Angel Menard—constituted as signs of defeat, of man, of the black of "A Negro? A headless, homeless crab that walks backwards" (*BB*, 58). In La Folie, the angelic representation of man, of the kind of person who is so "kind and gentle" one wondered "what he was doing in this world" (24), is Tic-Tac, a homonym of Angebert, who speaks no word, but with his flute speaks all the languages of the world, who lived in the "dome of the forest," in its "lap," between "spasms," "sighs," "love," without being at all a romantic personage.

But if invisibility is a kind of metaphorization of the loss of faith, of hope in society, the other invisibility isn't self-generated by the rupture of the structure of the personality but rather imposed by society. For Amboise, who has lived seven years in France, the French were "burst bladders that had set themselves up as lanterns" (167). Amboise lived in France when "the blacks were rare in Paris," probably in the years when the first Negritude was gestating, and he worked in a factory. At first he admired the French for "their air of solitude and self-sufficiency, like gods", until he understood he could forswear life,

> disappear at any moment without anyone noticing, because nothing depended on him, he corresponded to nothing either for good or ill. [And] at the end of two or three years he felt as if he were living in a nightmare. . . . As soon as he left the hotel he felt as if he were going through places peopled with evil spirits, strangers to his flesh and blood who watched him go by with complete indifference, as if for them he didn't exist. He spent all his time now warding off invisible blows. (150)

Thus his return was marked by silence.

6 / Gioconda Belli

Urban House/Nation—*Domi Nostre*

Garden/Wilderness

Obsessed with the urgent desire to systematize and catalog, in 1984, a little before he died, Angel Rama wrote in an article on order and disorder, that

> there is no literature more difficult to know and systematize than that called Hispano-American. . . . While . . . the critical panorama of Euro-pean literatures invokes a well-charted and better cultivated garden, the American seems a jungle where roads are plotted with difficulty, and often with the swing of the machete. (17)[1]

The comparison of one culture with order and garden and the other with disorder and wilderness is pertinent, not only to introduce the changes in the notion of *patria* implemented in records of the revolutionary transition, but also to establish borders between notions of 'country as garden explored' in women's literature and 'country as wilderness traversed' in literature by men. It is also pertinent to explore how the latter owes to the nativist novel a notion of the State tied to the exploration of nature.

Although the synchrony Rama points to for the rest of continental literature does not exist in the case of the Caribbean, the process of literary production from the region registers an asynchronic parallelism derived from a "similar process of development . . . which translates into similar urban cultural processes that at the same time explain the difference of plains and levels between one zone and another" (20).

In the decade of the eighties a synchronicity is palpable in Central American literature, for like that of Colombia and Venezuela at the beginning of the century, it shows a marked interest in narrativizing nature as country. The literature of the revolutionary horizon returns to "forest" to mark its own transition. The phrase "the mountain is something more than. . ." signals a break from the narrativization of nature in a liberal nation. I have been arguing that in this "more than. . ." is located the difference between the economic and the insurrectionary concepts of country, the *caudillo* revolts that proposed the takeover of lands and the establishment of power, and the armed insurrection that postulates "the new man." The renarrativization of nature from a revolutionary perspective functions as a takeover. The differences between *testimonios* and nation-building novels also establishes distances.

The replaying of traditions is a road. It is above all the attempt to march from the country into the city. It is to document and entitle the wooded mountain as seized and then march toward the city, without ascribing barbarianism to one and civilization to the other. Those terms have already fallen into disuse. Nature is just: "an immense green steppe." It is not the site of residence of the symbolic savage of the nation, although the indigenous peoples still inhabit it. Its hovels do not yield signs of modernity, and the people "do not know electricity, nor medicines, at most a tablet of Mejoral, never have seen ice, and the ships, the trains, planes, movies, are marvels in which they don't believe" (Ramírez 1989: 87).

In 1982 the mountain is not disorder: it is "power," "myth," "symbol," "site of gestation," "a boot camp," "the new country's uterus." It is as green as Rivera's forest, obscure and unexplored as the nature that houses the economic: "in its mountainous margins abound its wild turkey, deer, elks, mosquitoes, tigers; in the summer leishmaniases swarm, and year-round curious and screaming monkeys eating wild bananas insolently mock the loggers of the rubber forest" (Borge, 144). A no-man's land, the guerrilla eye perceives it for the first time, but the scattered peasant houses recall the hovels and the space where *La Maporita* or *El Miedo* were built. A temporary home, in its structures it shows its transitoriness together with its precariousness and the transmigrating character of its people. It is a humble dwelling on the banks of the river to fish in, to transport groceries, food, commodities, a change of places; where to be human and where to be animal are the same and become interchangeable; where each element and building materials are described in detail because they are uncanny and unique.

Here the insurrection is in the forefront; it is the agency, but with a different signature, with a different sensibility—attempting to identify nation with people, people with nation-state, fighting to invert, to extrapolate from the economic to the social. Theirs is not an insensitive surveillance, no, but one that, although from afar, feels responsible. That is why the new man learns how to treat people, learns the meaning of shyness and of peasant reserve, learns their silences, moods, smiles, and laughter, understanding how

> to cultivate relations among the peasants, to approach them, to break their shyness, their reserve, their distrust toward strangers, their silence, to talk to men, to look for the way of the elders, to draw out the smile in women, to understand children. (Ramírez, 94)

Houses, huts, people, the natural *loci*, mark the moment of articulation with the natural nativism of the nation-building novel, and the place where Rama's theses of synchronic development become visible. In this nature, as in that one, we find only men, men who in their physical appearance signal that they have reached a frontier. They are the famous guerrillas who pass through like phantoms. Seemingly maddened Spanish explorers and conquerors, half-naked, absolutely alone, the guerrillas wander through the unknown latitudes in complete solitude:

> Soaked to the oesophagus, with lips kissed by the mist, with dark circles under the eyes . . . half-naked. . . . Yes, we seemed shipwrecked, vagabonds, dementia escaped from a strait jacket. (Borge, 158)

> . . . drawing strength from my throat to scream orders to nobody, into the wind, already without Claudia and hunted night and day. . . . The barking of trained dogs following me even into dreams, above me the flight of helicopters buzzing the tops of the trees, repression covering the areas like a shroud, fear transfiguring the faces of peasants who saw themselves obliged to receive me and hardly exchanged a word with me. . . . (Ramírez, 133)

There is much of the chronicle of the conquest also. The subject-position adopted is that of the explorer/warrior/guerrilla; he who searches for a site; he who has also mistaken the place; he who, hunted and surrounded by the army of the modern nation, must go. Hence his madness and solitude, a solitude equivalent to seeing the land as it was envisioned by a few; seeing that military victories are rather interminable lists of defeats; seeing that the forces did not exceed fifteen per column and that there were only three of them dispersed in the immense territory of mountain ranges, valleys, rivers, and thick forest . . . , each small group separated from the others by long days' journeys. The rest was a handful of peasants . . . collaborators, couriers, guides. . . . (Ramírez, 78)

In contrast to the narrative of '82, Ramírez does not here postulate the absolute control of the body as a condition of revolutionary strength. In trying to be human, the narrative admits that the body hurts, is hungry and is prey to an "inevitable and compulsive [anxiety], violent as arrogance, persistent as lovesickness, totalitarian as a tropical tyranny. . ." (Borge, 165).

Forest, jungle, nature—as opposed to the orderly garden of European cultures—continues to be an unknown *locus,* a place inhabited by extraordinary beings, the barbarians, the mestizo-indigenous people whose unwritten cultures are unknown but not feared: white-indigenous people, the color of "ripe bananas." Old Rubén Darío and his school of Modernism still lurking in the idea of the bronze Titan, of "mythological strength," who uproots trees. The Centaur is replaced by the Caupolicán: mahogany arms, firm muscles, nerves at the ready.

Toward the end of the decade of the eighties, in 1989, a year before the electoral defeat of the FSLN, testimonial literature leaves records of a march from the country toward the city. The mountain has ceased to be the space from which the new country will be built. The restlessness of living in inhospitable, unexplored, uninhabited, militarized nature is rewritten. Only the consciousness of the precarious situation of man in that space remains:

[T]hey could not continue without weapons, without communications, without a social base, naked, hungry, and crucified by the blisters and leishmaniases, . . . armed struggle required a better development of the subjective conditions . . . a closer relation with the masses was indispensable. . . . (Borge, 183–184)

The march toward the cities cannot be stopped. As in the case of Argentinian literature at the beginning of the century, and underlining the acuity of Rama's thesis, Nicaraguan literature as a narrative of nation-state had to recognize the strength of urbanization and of the city's organization as the precondition for nation-building.

In order to fulfill this objective, which seemed like a distant mountain range, as elusive as a fish that must be captured with raw hands, a struggle that must be fought without immediate expectations of resolution, in that moment we call it prolonged war. This was integral

but its principle form was armed struggle, and within it guerrilla warfare. . . . In practice, this conception, the guerrilla infant, was born
contaminated by the invading evil and did not have, except in our
own wishes and imagination, a supporting base in the interior, not
even a minimum infrastructure in the invaded zone, such as had been
conceived in the initial projects. (Borge, 139)

The dreamed country, the national sphere, is displaced once more in this
literature of horizons to the city, where the new social type will incorporate the masses into himself, and in and among them, women, although the
organizing slogan is all male:

because with friendship we can make comrades of the friends, and
after the friend becomes comrade we can convert him into a brother
in the struggle; and of these brothers in struggle we could draw out a
militant cadre of the FSLN. (Ramírez, 41)

Mountain/City

The new country is predicated on urbanism. In this new topography of city
as nation, woman enters the discussion. In 1988 Gioconda Belli, known
primarily for her poetry, published *La mujer habitada,* a novel which dealt
with the Sandinista revolution in the city. In 1990 she finished her second novel, *Sofía de los presagios,* which reraised questions of origins and
nationality. Her third novel, in process, comes back to questions of country,
nation, and fatherland. It is in these two texts that the feminine Nicaraguan
narrative comes to textualize questions of gender. At the closure of the
horizon of change, the beginning of the proposals of globalization, 1990 is
the year of the electoral defeat of the Sandinista National Liberation Front.[2]

La mujer habitada is a novel plotting the participation of women in
the armed struggles constituting revolutionary nations. The protagonist,
Lavinia, is a young professional educated abroad. She has just obtained
her first job as an architect and is moving into her own place, a house
she has inherited from her aunt Inés, a semiliberated woman who has
totally supported her niece's feelings of independence. At the architectural
firm, Lavinia meets Felipe, and her first professional assignment is the construction of a general's house. It is through Felipe that Lavinia becomes
acquainted with the insurgent Organization, and it is through the construction of the house that she first becomes engaged in the revolution. Thus
political and sentimental engagement work in tandem.

The main question of the novel, however, is the involvement of woman in politics, and the difficulties of becoming part of an organization that favors and privileges the heroism of men. A narrative device comes to help this formation in the guise of the indigenous past. An indigenous woman, Itza, still a presence through the orange tree planted in Lavinia's backyard, comes to inspire her behavior. The orange juice she makes using the oranges from her garden are the source for planting the seeds of rebellion, and make her take opportunities as they come: first to lose her fear of participation, then to learn from another woman, Flor, what women are considered to be during the revolutionary struggle. The construction of the general's house enables her to become acquainted with the army's way of life, and finally, when Felipe dies moments before a decisive maneuver for the Organization, she demands to take his place. Thus woman is plotted into the revolution in a narrative of insurgency and political commitment which questions all ways of thinking, among them being like El Che, an impossibility for women, or being the repose of the warrior, which means waiting at home for the warrior to come back and rest.

In contrast to the militant narrative, *Sofía de los presagios* is a novel more within a feminist, classical mainstream. Sofía is a gypsy, her adopted father a wealthy landlord, her adopted mother a poor woman from the town. Her indomitable nature and unconventional behavior are attributed to her ethnicity. The seeds of woman's rebellion thus lie in her biology. Unfortunately for her, a provincial woman, her destiny is to marry and beget children, and she is affianced to a well-to-do he-man. Sofía, however, disavows all gender roles and on the day of her wedding shames her fiance by insisting on riding her favorite horse to the church and racing it right up to the ceremony. The husband, naturally, takes offense, and promises revenge. He locks her in the house and lets her see no one except her stepmother and stepfather and best friend. Surrounded by maids, she is bored to tears, and in her visits to her father she entertains all sorts of sexual fantasies with her subalterns.

The plot is eventful. Her best friend brings her contraceptives so that she never gets pregnant. She tricks her husband into getting a phone and through telephone conversations she becomes infatuated with another man. She meets a series of witches and necromancers who help her escape the tyranny of patriarchy, and one of the men teaches her the pleasure of sensuality. But the real denouement of the story comes when her father dies and she inherits his fortune, capital which empowers her, giving her all the necessary means to divorce and set up a productive system that increases her power and freedom. She then decides who she hires and fires, how much she pays to her laborers, and what kind of coupling she wishes. In the end she chooses a gay, Paris-educated cousin as her manager; she decides to produce flowers and cocoa for export; and she chooses who the father of her child will be.

A story of woman's liberation thus follows a novel of insurgency. In the earlier novel, the protagonist dies at the hands of the army. In the second, she succeeds as a landowner. Modernization was considered detrimental to the population of the imaginary Faguas, the social landscape of the first novel, while it becomes highly beneficial in the second, instrumental to women obtaining liberal freedom.

In the case of the Sandinista revolution textualized by the novels, especially *La mujer habitada* and, tangentially, by *Sofía de los presagios*, the proposition of the nation is reduced to a smaller expanse: the house in the city, the country estate, and the peasant hut. Mountain and city are still inextricable, but mountain in these narratives bears a closer referent, more a natural park, a botanical garden, a zoo where the sense of social order reigns. The larger space has been seized by male prose and the site of the city, the smaller—but no less important—by feminine prose.

We have already seen that women's presence in men's testimonials occurs in the cities rather than in the mountains. Women couriers, women collaborators, and even militant women appear in the city. With the exception of Gladys Baez, Doris Tijerino, Leticia Herrera, Dora María Tellez, Claudia Chamorro, among the better known and more quoted of the ensemble of testimonials produced in Nicaragua, and a dozen names at most among the less known and more timely—the majority of which are cited by Commandant Rivera—male texts mention only male names in the mountain.

Historical speech in the mountain, history in the mountain, is a male enterprise. History in the city is a different thing. It is an ensemble of disparate events, a mixed history in which everyone, including women, participates. We have already explored the preoccupation with the city and urban insurrection, which comes to be fundamental at the end of the testimonial. City is a reconsideration of revolutionary tactics and strategy, it is an offensive looking for the enemy rather than waiting for it, it is the incorporation of the masses into the struggle. As a discursive contribution of a certain relevance, privileging the urban spaces over the natural ones offers a feminizing perspective on the struggle and the city, as a discursive contribution of certain relevance.

In my reading of Gioconda Belli, I want to emphasize contrasting spaces: smaller ones, like the bedroom and the house, traditionally historicized by women, as spaces of one's own or as recuperated; garden as nation; rural property and *haciendas* as family property, a reformulation of the same nation and then the city. I also want to distinguish the representation of the white oligarchic woman from the representation of other women in the text, and untangle the ways in which gender is the site of the enunciated contracts and the seat of sensibility. In *La mujer habitada,* three discourses are normative: the indigenous (at the moment of resistance to the conquest), the liberal (postindependentist, the moment immediately preceding the projects of modernization in Central America), and the revolutionary (defined here as postmodern in the sense of going beyond the modernity of the liberalization projects). The three are voiced by women. Ethnicity, naturally, resides here as well.

National History Enters the Woman's Bedroom

In Chapter 5 of *La mujer habitada,* the woman's bedroom, a chamber no one enters except the husband and the maids, and beyond that her lovers, is itself suddenly assaulted and taken by two men belonging to "The Organization." From that moment on we can trace a tangent.

One is tender, serene, and reasonable, the other authoritarian, ferocious, and intransigent: the two men coming into the house are obverse and reverse of the image of the revolutionary man seen by a contemporary oligarchic woman. Coming into the bedroom, the two men apologize for having violated privacy, interfered with domesticity, and interjected impromptu national history. Private oligarchic spaces and traditional feminine spaces, proposed as sexually emancipated spaces in this text, become socialized, thus effecting a change in the notion of feminine privacy, at least in the social imaginary of woman.

A genuinely open open-door policy to the clandestine organization is the predominant sensibility. But as we saw in Part One, in masculine guerrilla literature woman comes into the text largely as an erotic, sentimental, or familiar subject. Woman is here at best a sensibility educated by the mass media. Woman is dismissed as "romantic," as in the discursive space of the novel serialized in fashion magazines. However, the social text and armed repression help open wide the door through which the commitment of the white, educated, oligarchic woman can come to reach the bosom of the clandestine organization. The other women, mestizas coming from different social sectors, also begin to jostle to appear as they are, protagonists of the armed insurrection, collaborators or militants in the text of a national history which registers that history as a fundamentally male national insurrection.

While it is true that men's literature from past decades (mainly the writings of Sergio Ramírez and Lizandro Chávez Alfaro, but including those of Chuno Blandón and Orlando Nuñez as well) fictionalized the social spaces of guerrilla struggle, this is the first time that feminine prose enters the debate in Nicaragua. Houses as the sites of domesticity, city spaces, productive spaces, rural property, estates, fields, and mountains are taken over by women, and they no longer have the same meaning. The vision of what has been called the "new man," whose incarnation is Che Guevara, the model of a new subjectivity, is debated by women. Hindsight completes the revision and discussion of the portrait of the ensemble of these men and women and of these spaces signed differently.

Blood on the Linen Sheets

Spaces and protagonists are united in a symbolic, prioritized element: blood. The blood of the wounded, the blood shed by repression, and menstrual blood. The first comes to substitute for the third on the bedsheets. But menstrual blood also stains the male text. Menstruation, which according to Jean Franco's *Plotting Women* is associated with uncleanliness, and therefore with the devaluation of woman, secures a space and undergoes a transformation in *La marca del Zorro*. Rivera witnesses Claudia Chamorro suffering from "a serious problem with her menstruation, heavy bleeding," and since she does not carry Kotex she obtains old rags from the peasant houses which

> she washed in the canals and the rivers to wear them already clean instead of Kotex. And when they were soaked . . . she washed them again, and dried them on the bushes. We waited till they dried, she put them on again, and then we continued the march. She took care of that while I remained on guard with arms ready, far away without disturbing her. On one of those occasions, as she was washing her rags, the guard came upon us, and while she gathered her things, I faced them and we could retreat unharmed. (Ramírez, 130)

Not only is menstrual blood not an object of disgust, not an immediate illustration and referent of feminine weakness and an unequivocal sign

of maternity and reproduction, but it is seen as a natural condition sur-
mounted, a sign of respect for the female subject whose physiological function is not a restriction. Blood here is an "in spite of." In this concrete case,
as in the case of Aramburu, Franco has pointed out, menstrual blood is a
sign of power. Later, it appears in the most illuminated passage of male
guerrilla literature, moments before woman acquires that horizon's highest
medal of honor, an instant before Chamorro, the white oligarchic woman
from Granada, of the traditionally conservative governing families, covers
the withdrawal of the guerrilla commander.

In the novel, the blood of the wounded stains the sheets; in the testimonial, the menstrual blood stains the text. Both signal a counterposition
and reinforce abrupt revisions of meaning. Lavinia, the protagonist of *La
mujer habitada*, hides the stained sheets, signaling complicity. Claudia, the
guerrillera, by necessity, washes the rags with her own hands—certainly
the fine and delicate hands of Modernism. In the novel, the "new man"
thanks the woman for her complicity, with a tender look. In the testimonial, the guerrilla commander, son of a washerwoman, and whom we see
dressed as a woman washing in the first pages of the testimonial, keeps
woman guarded.

The malleability that comes with these writings is noteworthy, for in this
act of rupture the terms of women's and men's literature are separated into
two different camps, women defining *hacienda* and men defining mountain
as primary metaphors of nation. In the former, Belli argues against "tropical Quixotism" and the social changes seen from afar, from European or
Latin American scenarios, or from the very same spaces of the *hacienda*
and property, from the more traditional cities like Granada and León, and
from the prestigious streets like the famous Calle Atravesada in Granada.

At this point it is consistent to remember the distinctions between fiction and testimonial, considering the wise warnings of Gayatri Spivak, and
respect the constitution and structure of the discursive fields, the transactions between history and literature, the value granted to the different
epistemes. For in fact there is a rapprochement between the two fields,
the novel and the work of compilation undertaken by the memoir of the
guerrilla fighter. History and anthropology come closer to the canon that
makes up the social imaginary, leaving them registered in literature, in fiction. That is why "we should rethink the notion of fiction as the negation
of truth"—that is, "the effect of the real" that we grant more to history
than to literature—to the historical fact as a real event recorded by the
testimonial, and to the fictive and the literary event recorded by the novel.[3]

We will note several times that active women are very rarely textualized in these male guerrilla *testimonios,* whose products—proto-agons/ protagonists—are all male. For these reasons, perhaps, what Belli's novel dramatizes for Lavinia is precisely the difficulties of the process of election, of choosing between a given type of socioeconomic advantage and other choices presented as ethical. The historical participation of women in the struggle is only truly narrated through feelings.

Proposing the incorporation of women of higher social stratas into the formation of a revolutionary nation-state defies all prohibitions and contradicts all paradigms. The novel, then, enlists areas of silence or blindness in order to discuss them. First, it introduces as evidence the participation of oligarchic men for whom entrance into the arena of political struggle is not so difficult. After all, the new subjectivity has been predicated on the basis of the male sexual gender: to be like El Che, or to have "balls." Thus the class antagonism of the new horizon is again reconciled in the space of the "male."

In the liberal Neo-Positivistic horizon, social alliances are better understood when they take place among men. As we saw in the nation-building novel of the turn of the century, it was indispensable to eliminate the figure of Woman—doña Bárbara and her kind. All those womanly aspirations, to liberate or to incorporate into herself what had been given to the masculine, had to be punished as an example. In Teresa de la Parra's María Eugenia Alonso, a white woman from the *Mantuana* oligarchy, Neo-Positivism will serve as an example of the place assigned to women of that social milieu and of that ethnicity. María Eugenia will soften up the inter- and intra sectorial social pact that is foisting on her all the implications of the law and the reproduction of conventions.

Under the new paradigm of the modern revolutionary nation-state of Nicaragua, headed by men and (at least theoretically) by women from lower social stratas, the wretched of the earth, or what I will call the ethnonation, the stipulation was to have balls, and in the best of cases having balls delineates the social condition of the guerrilla fighter. In Belli's novel, feminine desire is reawakened to resolve one of the questions set aside by the preceding horizon, namely the incorporation and participation of white oligarchic women in state formations before the state is legally constituted, given that she does this before the interpretation of the spirit of the law prohibits her from doing so. But let it not be a surprise that this aspiration, consigned by the texts in both political horizons, enters the discussion through the only door left open, namely that of affections. The formation of couples and the reproduction of reproduction is mediated by a sentimental tradition suggested by María Eugenia Alonso in her fidelity to romantic performances and postures learned in fashion magazines, here in *La Mode Illustrée*.

In *La mujer habitada* (1988), deliberation on the participation of woman, on the election of woman, is registered in a crosshatching of mass romantic sentimentality and revolutionary sensibility, set in dialogue within the private stance of the house and the bedroom. Love, marriage, passion, the feminine arena of feelings, and reproduction invoked by menstrual blood, in some the social feminine, suppressed or modified by the birth of the mestizo revolutionary nation, come to the table as epistemes to be taken into account in the configuration of the new structures of social formations.

Indigenism/Liberalism/Liberationism

Indigenism, Liberalism, and Liberationism are the three interlocking epistemes. Indigenism is the speech of indigenous and colonial resistance narrated by Itza, the tree-woman. Liberalism is the white, oligarchic discourse of Aunt Inés on gender equality. Liberationism is the discourse of the mestiza Flor, on gender and political participation in the revolution. Enunciative contracts interweave plot and voice. The first, but not the hegemonic, discourse is voiced by the indigenous woman. The hegemonic discourse is mestizo; it is Flor's, placed in Lavinia's mouth.

Initially, in these discursive contracts, two and even three sensibilities are postulated, but that is only an illusion. In reality there is only one sensibility, that which invokes roots to make them serve one's own agenda: a wish to return to the original cultures, a wish which comes to be intertwined in revolutionary postmodernism and to validate the discourse of gender. In this it very much invokes the images of indigenous and black people in postrevolutionary Mexican plastic arts and in Cuban narratives. They make explicit, in their own spheres, the wish to rescue these ethnicities and to incorporate them into the space of the new national reality they hope to constitute.

Three social subjects, the indigenous woman (the place of mythical ancestry), the modern white middle-class woman (place of biological ancestry), and the mestiza (the locus of historical alliances) position women within Nicaraguan revolutionary culture. *Mestizaje* could be understood as a matrilocality, a desired cultural matrix. The white woman as a daughter of the indigenous woman is, in the best of cases, a hyperbolized symbolic transposition: an appropriation together with a wager.

The indigenous voice is the poeticized voice of the political discourse of the conquest, and the white voice that of the realist political discourse liberalized. In this division of discursive work, the indigenous woman is the vegetal, organic mother, and her social meeting space is the garden, curiously the place of the female representation of the liberal nation. Literary and historical topoi are discursive spaces occupied by the revolutionary cultural discourse—fronts oppositional to what is foreign, the blond, the masculine—that in this narrative, as in the former horizon, are represented as synonyms, as the threatening other, Mr. Danger. The indigenous discourse of resistance, the voice of this side of *mestizaje,* is the historical fund, support, counterpoint, commentary, and collective unconscious of the modern revolutionary woman Belli proposes, and whose self-image, the metaphor of the contemporary woman, is a dream retold, the Mountain. Not the Mountain of guerrilla literature but a European peak. At the top of this mountain is the snow: "the snow was another thing: white and cold, inhospitable," like the European winters. On the outskirts are tropical forest: "since her childhood she loved the green, the rebellious tropical vegetation, the stubbornness of plants resisting the intense summers" (Belli, *LMH,* 41), the definition of Faguas/Nicaragua/Latin America. And from that composite Mountain, part European, part Latin American, like *mestizaje,* under the care and support of her grandfather, Belli's protagonist flew.

The wager in favor of the transitional structure against the structures of Modernity (the word appears with surprising frequency in the first chapters of the text), understood as favoring the Central American Common Market, becomes evident in the distancing or in the perspective of the protagonist Lavinia, from the rural, patriarchal, oligarchic, and seigniorial order of the countryside seen through architectural landscapes—different styles of housing and recreational country houses—and through her social relations—mainly mother and father and her friends Sara and Adrián. In spite of Lavinia's devotion and appreciation of this architectural landscape, the unfolding postulation of social networks proposes *mestizaje* in a series of women who constitute the support and service sectors, the social cushion on which she leans.

Despite the possibilities of high society couplings and her friends, the text is made up of women, their alliances constituting the three discursive fields, that of the indigenous woman Itza, the mestiza Flor, and the white Creole Aunt Inés, mentors at distinct levels. Sara and Lavinia are obverse and reverse of the possibilities of the traditional versus the contemporary revolutionary woman of the spatial horizon of the allegorical Faguas. Lucrecia, Mercedes, Silvia, and doña Ñico represent the service sector. With the exception of Inés, Lavinia, and Sara—porcelain women—all the women are women of color, mestizas. The allegorical levels, fundamentally carried by the first three women, fill the heroic space as bearers of the past, present, and future historical discourses. Lavinia is the woman in transition, and the rest are relegated to secondary planes. The novel argues in favor of a post-modernity—defined as constituting a revolutionary order and, therefore, one that goes beyond Modernity, understood as the renovation undertaken by the Central American Common Market, and as a postmodernism drastically different from the postmodernism of developed countries—and of a development encompassing an ample spectrum of the social body, from the oligarchic woman all the way to her subalterns. In this, the proposed enlightened feminine elite (Lavinia/Gioconda Belli) pronounces herself in favor of widening the democratic horizon that Germani speaks of, but admits that in Faguas the bridge is not crossed without recourse to weapons. The narrative is an index of the involvement of the dominant classes in national history and the acceptance of their responsibility in the new social design.

Women of Porcelain/Women of. . . .

"Porcelain," like "nacre" and "alabaster," belongs to the horizon of Rubén Darío's Modernist sensibility at the end of the last century. As we saw in Loynaz or in Teresa de la Parra, in Belli's novels women from the elite are still described with the language of that horizon of the *fin-de-siècle* sensibility: white, of fine feet and hands, porcelain dolls. Women are also adjectivized as "sensitive," but more often "languid," and as regal. Further, the comparison of their countenances and postures with European icons is common. Rhys' Antoinette sees herself reflected in a picture titled "[Miller's] *Daughter*," Loynaz' Bárbara sees herself in Carolsfield portraits, de la Parra's María Eugenia is in the chromotypes of *Paul et Virginie*, and Lavinia in an eighteenth-century lady, or in the

> engraving of one of her favorite children's books: the girl with the straw hat and the diaphanous flower dress, elbows leaning against the ground, her sight toward the infinite horizon and the serpentine plain of wheat fields. And at the bottom of the picture: "The world was mine and everything in it belonged to me." (Belli, *LMH*, 130)

The diaphanous dress, the straw hat, and the serpentine plain of wheat fields, as much as the other images, recall chromotypes of "Little Miss

Muffet," the nursery rhyme representing a white girl dressed like Alice in Wonderland in Hamilton's reader, a text used in Central America to teach English in elementary girls' schools run by nuns, a text which served as model and counterpoint for a local population whose phenotypes and styles of dress were different. These white images of white women and girls are reinforced in a fleeting vision the protagonist has while preparing her ball gown—and suddenly,

> she didn't know by means of what association, Lavinia evoked Scarlett O'Hara in one of the first scenes of *Gone with the Wind*. Lucrecia was the black nanny, spreading Scarlet's ballroom dress on the bed. Only Lucrecia was neither fat nor black. Her brown skin retained the lingering paleness of a hemorrhage that almost killed her. . . . I am remembering a film I saw—said Lavinia. Me too—said Lucrecia—a film called *Sissi* about a princess who marries a king. That is the way you would look when you wear one of these dresses. The two laughed. Lavinia also remembered that film: a fairy-tale romance. It had caused a ruckus when she went to school. Everyone, in those days, wanted to look like Romy Schneider. (Belli, *LMH*, 167)[4]

Like her literary ancestors, Lavinia is also under the weight of ethnic social relations and of preformed stereotypes, of the desire to be like, longing for the purity of blood and princess-like aristocracy to which Orientalist Modernism was given, and beset by liberal fears whose projects aimed to whitewash the race. Perhaps that is the displaced fear her parents feel about her independence. Lavinia speaks of the injustices, the accident of being born into metaphors of skin: change is "a deep skin very hard to yank out; she will endure her original skin, secretly hidden, behind the sought after identity" (180). But neither does she hide the pleasure of seeing herself beautiful in front of the mirror, "the red color contrasting with the white skin and the dark hair over her shoulders" (182).

In contrast to ideological discursivity, the discourse of beauty resides in the white phenotype evident in her body, for instance in the beauty of her "aristocratic" feet. In fact, distinctions between poor and rich, between participants and nonparticipants, is evidenced in two or three instances by feet and shoes, as much as by manners: in her feet and in her "spoiled rich-girl manias"; she is an "only daughter, [a] spoiled, rich girl," or a "well-dressed white girl," as she knows the others see her, the peasants, The Organization, Felipe, Sebastian, Flor.

The writing that describes phenotype constricts and, up to a certain point, is unworthy of the discursive contracts. For, being who she is, Lavinia is born within consumption, frivolity, the free use of time to which porcelain women accede through birth, a liberal education (European or North American style) through which she can negotiate alternative forms of behavior, wish for, and entertain the possibility of change. This education, as a formal discipline—manners and social graces, manners and readings—gave her access to nontraditional forms of thought, taking them out of the conservative frameworks of her class. The contact with transnational modernism, the English Sufragettes in the case of de la Parra's María Eugenia Alonso (1935) and via Natalia Vásques in the case of Lavinia (1988), allows them to transcend their local circumstances. Lavinia's seclusion with Jerome, on the other hand, gave her an alternative vision of the possible relations between herself and her body. These protagonists represent in women what it meant to men in the narratives of the turn of the century to learn through travel to foreign lands. That is why the first postulate is to pronounce oneself against the traditional goals of women: immediate, prescribed, and arranged marriages among power elites and the reproduction of the species.

Like María Eugenia, who could very well play the role of the great aunt Inés, Lavinia insists on moving away from marriage, taking her distance and practicing her profession. Clearly situated in the liberal horizon, in which women of porcelain have already gained the right of access to the socioproductive professions, she has now to conquer another two spheres: the free exercise of her sexuality, and her incorporation into the circles of state power—a practice that in the allegorical Faguas is achieved only through associating oneself with the Great General or by affiliating oneself with "The Organization." And this last is the means she will fight for.

Whether to live alone or with company is a choice that Rhys' Christophine, at the abolition of slavery in 1838, proposes to her pupil Antoinette: "Have spunks, and do battle for yourself." "Get up, girl, and dress yourself. Woman must have spunks to live in this wicked world," she advises her (Rhys, *CW,* 528, 518). And Loynaz takes Christophine's advice, living in a nevertheless strange solitude, as if fashioned out of nothingness, leaving her protagonist Bárbara orphaned from every social relation, including the most elemental social and blood ties. Schwarz-Bart places the whole dynasty of Lougandor women in matrilocality, dispersed in the woods, assuming their own lives without coupling permanently. In Belli it is different; for her, Lavinia is still a prisoner of what she considers attributes of romance that she discards and disqualifies but clings to nevertheless, placing her Lavinia in a position of relative independence—that is, alone with respect to the traditional concept of the family, but together with a man in her heart. Lavinia exercises her sexual freedom together with her abilities as a free thinker.

But the free practice of her sexuality comes coupled with proposals for national liberation. For this reason, she chooses to couple with a professional man, grey-eyed, educated in Europe though middle-class, and deeply committed to the urban insurgency. Her liberal attitude leads to her involvement in the revolutionary transition. And it is also because of such circumstances that her mentors are on one hand Inés, the great aunt and on the other Flor, the mestiza, a member of "The Organization." But gender formation in transition involves a discussion of feminist tactics and strategies, to which each one of her protagonists subscribes.

Traditional marriage and the advantages and disadvantages of domesticity are discussed through Sara, her alter ego, and the other oligarchic woman, since she cannot discuss them with a woman like Mercedes, Lucrecia, or even Flor. In Mercedes, a secretary, Belli explores the use and abuse of a woman office clerk as a means of satisfying sexual desire but also as a means to upward mobility by a woman through the use of her body. In her, then, is virginity; in Lucrecia, abortion, the unwanted children, the impossibility of coupling and domesticity for the lower strata; and in Flor, incest, the uncle's sexual abuse of his niece. In the elaboration of gender issues, the text reveals aspects of the *roman à clef,* given that the conflicts have not been worked out within the psyches of characters, as attributes of self, but rather are presented as illustrations of vices to combat. And even the protagonist's own development shows artifice in the dialogues between her and her lover Felipe which sound as if they were lifted from a manual. The idea that a woman must be the resting place of the warrior, the brook of his river, the other side, has the flavor of the artificiality of something read rather than lived.

Thus porcelain women and earthen women, the whites and the mestizas, serve as illustrations of the formation of new types of women whose preferred attributes are diction, courage, rebellion, controlling their own lives, and establishing economic, political, and social independence.

The Decay of the Seigniorial Order

In the description of the construction of houses, especially the country house, as nowhere else, the decrepitude of the seigniorial order and the

irruption of modernity is evident. Even if the issue is modernization, described as disloyal competition, as a litigation between the Greens, "the
aristocracy," "lineage," "pedigree," and the military caste, it is in the arena
of the construction of housing and the design of space that the struggle for
power is discussed.

The evolution of the traditional, paternalistic regime of the *hacienda* can
be seen in the sketch of the grandfather, a spoken portrait of the landlord
of the country estate, with his "long nose and small, clear, and penetrating eyes . . . [the] transparency of his skin, [the] fine and red veins" (46),
dressed in khaki like any other English explorer of the nineteenth century,
proposing different degrees of modernization:

> for the grandfather, a follower of liberal and socialist ideas, a fierce
> opponent of the dynastic regime of the great generals, had established
> before the Labor Code the eight-hour work day, social benefits, and
> labor security. (47)

We are not here before the idealization of natural or moral economies,
nor before the idea that property comes from nothing, without origins,
without labor, struggle, or litigation, as is the case in Teresa de la Parra's
defense of property in the earlier transition. On the contrary, we are facing
support for projects of liberalization, of social identification, where property is a kind of republic, with regulating and protecting laws but also with
laws for ordering and managing labor, for the idea of property coexists
with the violence characteristic of property relations. As Raymond Williams proposes, speaking against the idealization and romanticization of
the countryside of the famous Golden Age:

> There is no innocence in the established proprietor. Very few prop-
> erty titles can endure human investigation. The "old stock" to which
> we are sentimentally referred, are ordinarily only those families which
> have oppressed and exploited their neighbors longer. (Williams, 50)

The cracks in dual economies with their democratic and autocratic poles
are also raised, the diverse groups being the dynamic pole that includes
the Greens, but also the Blue army, linked to foreign capital. The speaking
voice belongs to a woman from the Greens who asks for her way out. There
is the advanced technology, notorious in Belli's text, signaled by mechanization, electric steps, elevators, movable walls, and all the italicized foreign terms to describe a certain kind of consumption, from the breakfast
with pancakes and Aunt Jemima syrup to the aquamarine kimono that the

protagonist wears to receive more or less the wounded guerrilla and the guerrilla lover. In this cheap and conspicuous consumption, as much as in the bad taste of the members of the repressive Blue party, foreign influence gains notoriety.

The disparate degrees of modernization in the social subtext, mainly in agro-export and in the expansion outward to the exterior, have been sufficiently documented in the texts of the social sciences. Modernization brought about changes, albeit limited, in the traditional, paternalistic *hacienda,* exemplified in the text, and it brought about the change in property relations that had an impact on the characteristic split between urban and rural, center and periphery, archaic and modern, democrat and autocrat. Within the novel, bureaucratic rationalization, the centralization and bureaucratization of the nation-state, visible in the army, is narrated through the ruling order of the inner corridors of the garrison, and the way in which the schedule is followed, and in General Vela's daily routine, so useful to the Movement.

I believe that within the popular movement, in the ever-growing formation of the middle strata, the possibilities of bureaucratization—the active life of the protagonist as much as her participation in social struggles—can be seen. Within this context I want to highlight the importance of the representation of the social order through the architectural and structural forms visible in all the spaces of the house that the novel depicts, where it is found that the construction of the house operates as a metaphor for the construction of the nation and for the historical contribution of women to the history of their social, national, and provincial environment.

The first house I want to highlight in this sense is the one that appears at the end, the old country house that has been lent by a collaborator for training guerrilla cadres in urban struggle, and that has been vacated precisely because its owners built a new one:

> Finally they reached an open space where an old country house rose up. . . . It was part of a farm belonging to some collaborators. They built a new one and no one comes around, for the peasants say that the house is haunted. . . . After lunch they came into the house and closed the doors. Through the windows, the pale evening light lit the thick-walled space. Inside the high ceilings of the house it was cool. Lavinia knew this type of typical Spanish architecture. The thick walls did not let heat in. The high ceiling allowed the steam to rise up above their heads, leaving a fresh, habitable space. In the colonial houses of the

cities, the living quarters closed in on themselves, open only toward an inner garden and galleries. The country house, conceived for country living, obeyed another design tradition: an interior only for resting, and the veranda facing the country, where everyday activity took place and where, in times past, in ornamented rattan rocking chairs, ladies and gentlemen would have rocked in the afternoon contemplating the plantations. (Belli, *LMH*, 224–226)

As we can see, the shift not only from new to old, but also from the functions originally assigned to the structure, the edifice, from those who served colonial society—bypassing the questions of plantations, labor, and service constructed as landscape—to the future army that would use it as a warehouse, demarcates the borders between the archaic and the modern.

It is the thawing of pastoral sensibility, archaic and rural; the internal transformation of these new types of society; the direction toward capitalist agrarian development and beyond. In the center of the modern structure of sensibility, there is a kind of counter-pastoral proposal to the horizon of the previous sensibility, to the aesthetic centered on the estate and the peons of the Nicaraguan Vanguardismo who constructed the republic as *hacienda*. Besides, in each house there is a model couple, a gendered nation side by side with an ethnic nation. The use of the structure expresses certain moral and social values and, naturally, the formation of feminine fantasy, informed by the advance of gender.

The first house described is the protagonist's, a place inhabited by Aunt Inés and passed on to Lavinia as an inheritance. It is located in a seigniorial neighborhood inhabited by old people who emerge at sunset to sit in their old, white wicker rocking chairs to wait for death. Again the house evokes the horizon of the old landed order. Lavinia's own house is dilapidated and in need of repair. In this it looks somewhat like Coulibri, the plantation house in Rhys' *Wide Sargasso Sea* (1966), which is repaired before being burned during a black uprising. Lavinia's house is "a reduced version of the enormous colonial mansions thrown toward the inner courtyard," which, significantly, she has "transformed into wilderness" (12).

In this enormous house—an adjective that will be repeated in describing Sara's house and the house where the protagonist goes to be trained to take part in a revolutionary operation—in the great age of the structure and of the old people living in it, deterioration and repair are signs of change. A new, Modern generation of oligarchs, made up of estate owners, merchants, and members of the Green party, has remodeled the social tenor and fully occupied the social space. Sara's house is "an old house, with four galleries and ample bedrooms with oval windows. In the inner garden, . . . a flamboyant tree . . . grew over the rooftop and gave shade to the interior . . . and [which] she, its owner, covered with ferns, begonias, marigolds, and roses" (Belli 1988: 226). The same flowers appear reproduced, in pots and miniaturized, along a veranda in Flor's house.

These material structures, these houses/homes, declare the social relations among the characters and the relationship between couples. In the first house we cited, the last mentioned in the text, the relations between couples are not blood relations; neither are they sanctioned by law. They are the relations of the social family understood as an unequal guerrilla group in the process of formation and all of whom relate on the basis of false names. In Lavinia's house, on the contrary, the relationship proposed is that of equals, and in Sara's, the traditional.

All the constructions are counterposed to the main structure, General Vela's house. In the construction of this house converge the political training and professional training of the protagonist, who since childhood had "dreamed of constructing buildings, leaving her mark." And the construction of the house of insurrection as a nation/gender-house is little by little being prepared. In this ambiance the guerrilla woman is no longer coupled. In fact, in this house the first mission assigned to her by the Movement and the first blueprint she is assigned to produce in her job converge. Beginning with the design and the construction of the house, her professional dexterity, together with the daily routine of a high-ranking army official, will be recognized. That is how, in the construction of the house, the two agendas mentioned above are fulfilled: the professionalization and bureaucratization of woman and her participation in the construction of a new nation-state.

Initially Lavinia's relations are only with the women of the house. Together with the women, she begins to design the spaces, but at the end of the project, she has to talk to the General. The meeting place is a transitional house where bad taste and Faguas' modern mentality coincide:

> a mixture of styles, each one vying with the other, disparate and high sounding, bright and ostentatious: mirrors with gilded, spiraled frames, coordinated tables built into the wall, heavy furniture upholstered with shiny fabrics, chrome chairs and tables, enormous and flowery vases, rugs of strange pastel colors, reproductions of landscapes on the walls, paintings of gigantic and artificial waves. (208)

The conversation between the guerrillera/architect and the General is made up of generalities but turns essentially on the construction of the movable wall for the armory:

> The wall would be made of three wooden panels, each with an iron support, resting on individual pivots mounted in a metal railing. A mechanism fixed to a wall will permit one to fix or free them so they will turn. On one side, the panels will display the collection of arms, fixed across the surface with wall mounts; on the other side, the panels will simply present a mahogany wall, in a beautiful shade. . . . Due to the rotation area required by the panels to construct the illusion, the General can also count on a space behind the wall, a sort of "secret chamber" which could be utilized as a warehouse for other weapons, the accessories necessary to clean them. . . . (213)

Lavinia copies this device from the house of William Randolph Hearst.

Reading on the axis of architecture and the constructions of houses divides society into three different camps. First, there are the landowners—some, like her grandfather, members of the illustrious elite (socialists and liberals at the end of the century)—and merchants like Lavinia, Sara, and Florencia, women described with adjectives borrowed from Modernism (porcelain) and from the iconic European woman of the eighteenth century, adjectives which Belli uses in two instances, once to refer to Sara and the other time to refer to Lavinia. This group at large is classified as the Greens. They are part of the ruling elite but do not hold state power. Their power resides in prestige and in the partial control of the economy through land. They are the productive/nonproductive, landed oligarchy who are becoming a modern merchant "bourgeoisie." José Coronel Urtecho's *Tres conferencias a la empresa privada* is a classic that narrates this shift.

Second, there are the Generals, who resemble the house Vela inhabits, as much as the one he is building. These are the Blue generals, controllers of state power and despised as *nouveau riche*. And third, there are the insurgents and the poor people, seen through the house of Flor but mainly through that of Lucrecia, who lives in a house built of wood,

> the roof without a ceiling, the electric cables crossing the zinc planks and only one light bulb, swinging tied to a pole. Hanging mattresses folded over a shelf . . . a chair falling apart in one corner . . . a small room which seemed to serve as living room and bedroom at the same time; on one side of the room, behind a wooden separation and a

dirty, unraveling drape, she heard the voice of Lucrecia. . . . The place smelled of dirty rags and mould. (143)

To the landowners are ascribed almost all the foreign terms which sprinkle the text, an index of "fine" dining, "good" table manners and "good" food, of consumption and dress—Aunt Jemima, pastas, trattoría, Sevres and Limoges porcelain, invitations à la Emily Post, pantyhose, jeans, hard rock, *allegro ma non tropo.* . . . Since there is an explicit critique of taste, to which the bad taste of the *nouveau riche,* the governing Generals, is contrasted, there is also that "unkept modernity," that "uncouth artifice," as it is called, displayed in decorator magazines like *House and Garden* and *House Beautiful,* badly understood and poorly interpreted, seen in the list of the ornaments in the house. Consequently, there is in the references to food and European porcelain a contrast to the notions of good and bad taste of the *fin-de-siècle* oligarchies.

In this opposition past/present, giving a vote of confidence more to European taste and sensibility than to modernization North American style, Belli repeats, at a different level naturally, Teresa de la Parra's María Eugenia Alonso, and this is reminiscent of the pronouncement on Modernism by Octavio Paz, whose sensibility continues to denote a counterpart to mercantile developmentism. This "cultural phenomenon lacking an organic base" will make us think, consequently, of a "baroque without [the] counterreformation, [a liberalism] without the bourgeoisie, [a] positivism without industry, and [a] modernism without modernization" (Paz, 184). Hedonism, dilettantism, and refined consumption are still responses to the utilitarian and senseless ethics of consumerisms. But in this counterposition we can see political boundaries side by side with poetic ones. If by the end of this century the attitude of the aesthetics of Modernism is irreconcilable with scientific Positivism and Monetarism, at present, aesthetics turns against cheap capitalism in Central America.

This counterproposal of one aesthetic for another could be tied to the poetic and political ideas understood as national affirmation. Poetics in the text center around the historical reproduction of the indigenism espoused by Itza, the orange-tree woman whose commanding voice as a mentor and as an exemplar comments on each action of the protagonist. It is indigenous culture, understood as autochthonous, that this woman's voice speaks, to which the difference of gender is added. It is the indigenous in gender that is recaptured, and it is, in turn, the articulation of place preoccupations in defense of what is one's own speaking ethnicity in the voice of the prior horizon, and gender in that the voice simultaneously speaks preoccupations which women share.

The poet Belli shines through in these lyric passages, in which the political ideas do not turn out to be analogous to the aesthetics of socialism or the socialist realism through which other revolutionary circumstances have been narrated. But, in turn, what is strictly political—and the plot is entirely constituted of historically faithful anecdotes—in its allegorization makes language lose its merely descriptive and referential attributes and places it in a mediated, signifying plane. For those familiar with the daily history of the Organization and the schemes and points of reference in the city, it is not difficult to make the historical correlations for Faguas, the Great General, the Tago volcano, Las Brumas, General Vela, and so on, and neither would it be difficult to localize the models for Lavinia, Flor, Sebastian, and Felipe.

But as the reading of the text is not only national—and in fact the popularity of the novel in Germany makes it an internationalizable text—the allegorical aspects come to add another dimension to the reading that we will come back to in the end. But, as a matter of course, in reference to history as a marketable fact—that is, saleable and exportable—the text, placed within the transnational circuit, calls attention to itself in words such as Citlalcoatl, Yarince, Maribios, Tenoztle, Ticomega, Maguatega, Quiote-Tlaloc, and Tamagastad, which more than reinforces the allegorical functions, holding the same attraction for German readers as the foreign words in the text hold for Latin American.

The Return to the *Hacienda*

Sofía de los presagios (1990) seems to share many of the ideational structures of the nation-building novel. Blood, *hacienda*, peons, and productive agriculture are rearranged in a narrative that marks the return to the land as property. *Hacienda* as big, landed property, Schwarz-Bart's Belle-Feuille, Rhys' Coulibri, and Belli's El Encanto are major preoccupations of the feminist literate consciousness.

Here, in a different horizon, what in *La mujer habitada* we have called the decrepitude of a seigniorial order and a proposal of a "small country" is taken up again: the productive country, the *hacienda* country comes to be plotted anew. In *Ti Jean L'Horizon*, "small country" has France as a comparative term. It is in relation to France that the country textualized in *Sofía* is called "small." It is not, however, Schwarz-Bart's mini-nation, for

Guadeloupe, after all, is a department of France. But the remaking of country is related to France, as in de la Parra at the beginning of the century, to the degree that France continues to be the referent of enlightenment par excellence.

The "small country," then, I want to argue, is a small republic or proto-nation and *hacienda,* with extractive economies, as well: a banana republic. To the degree that what is plotted is a productive space in relation to gender formation, and that the feminine is simultaneously incarnated in a productive and reproductive relation, the *hacienda* is the only country the woman without a country, the gypsy "of nowhere," has in the novel. "You were born [says Eulalia, her adoptive mother] in an arid place and without volcanoes [that is, not in Nicaragua] in times of heat, but your country does not exist. . . ." (Belli, *SP,* 102).

The replaying that articulates gender, country, and manor also brings memories of Gallegos to the extent that there is a correlation between the masculine and the productive that is incarnate in Sofía, the protagonist. Masculine fears of the feminine that are embodied in the image of woman as "the devil's daughter," Sofía, or doña Bárbara, the woman who has a pact with the devil, are articulated here again in a prose that also invokes the spirit of the law to settle disputes. And the written letter of the law protects, in this case, woman, as in the previous case it protected men, for property and property titles finally remain in her hands.

The feminine united to the masculine appears, on the other hand, tied to antiquity and to modernity: "Sofía's office is a mixture of the old and the modern, of woman's things and of man's things" (166). In her house, in the kitchen, a preliminary phrase makes us see, in a traditionally feminine room, the coincidence of "the old and the modern . . . a wooden stove fore-telling times when . . . liquid cooking gas was scarce in the country" (90).

Without question, on the part of the feminine narrative we are before an investment, before an expropriation of a masculine argument regarding national epistemes. Again and again, in questions pertaining to economic development, we come back to Rama's postulate of sychronicity or asyn-chronicity. At the close of the century, the cycles run by the larger nations of the continent are perhaps followed by the smaller ones, and the nationalist spirit comes to them coupled with social revolutions, socialist style. Only in this way can we explain the reproduction of Neo-Positivist perceptions in the revolutionary horizon—the intuition that productive sites are the ones that give meaning to the nation and not, as was thought, the construction of the political-institutional units of government. The idea that the nation is relative to its territorial extension, to the number of inhabitants, to the possibilities of financing their projects, is already in effect.[5]

But there are also notorious turns within this commonsense narrative of history as progress and development, dominant macronarratives in the text. The first, without doubt, is the attempt to renegotiate the idea of the feminine, to make the paradigmatic figure of doña Bárbara cross the liminal borders and appropriate for herself the value assigned to the *hacienda*. The return to the masculine as a principle incarnated in the feminine, as well as the recuperation of the figure of woman as participatory in the process of national formation, is expressed as desire in the consciousness of woman in the new revolutionary nation. The revindication of this fortitude and the postulate that both principles coexist in each of the genders nevertheless reveals its difficulties.[6]

In the ethnic horizon, the national-feminine echoes the transformation of indigenous people into mestizos and the displacement of the indigenous from the plane of the real to that of the symbolic. The disparity of the indigenous cultures from the order of the real was already a structural part of the first text, where the indigenous was a counterpoint. In *Sofía*, the indigenous is invoked as wisdom from the millennium: as magic, witchcraft, destiny, knowledge of herbs—in sum, as the esoteric and obscure, the indecipherable, the forbidden, the marginal, but endowed with power and assimilated into Mesopotamian and Egyptian cultures of Eastern European gypsies to Orientalism. It is globalized and denationalized. At a subliminal level, ethnic groups from all continents establish their pacts and place their wisdom at the service of the feminine incarnated in Sofía. An ensemble of minor figures—Samuel, doña Carmen, Xintal—oscillate between *mestizaje* and the spirit of the ancestors, a kind of minor, specialized peons, like the Brujeador in *Doña Bárbara,* who place their knowledge of herbs and of the invocation of the beyond at the service of the future proprietress.

These barely visible beings are relegated to the margins; they live in what would come to be the feminine representation of the masculine representation of the forest, in the Mombacho, a modernized border: in "its green skirt of thick vegetation . . . an unexplored planet, narrow tracks mount, loosing themselves towards coffee and cocoa farms" (140). The paradox of uniting what is unexplored to what is productive, and of situating the margins at the center distinguishes the writers. The attempt to draw the limits of a space saturated with productivity incorporates elements of the imaginary from Guadeloupan Schwarz-Bart, in the description of hovels in which these witches/peons/mestizos live, beautifying misery. Xintal, the witch, for instance, has a hovel

chameleon-colored which hides itself among the bushes and cente-
nary trees, whose tops give a perennial shade. The rustic dwelling has
walls of rough wood, the roof of old clay shingles, and over the stones
which serve as a stove a bougainvillea vine creeping across the roof
peeks through the gaps in the windows. At times, when it is windy,
purple flowers season the rice and vegetable porridge. (*SP,* 145)

As in Schwarz-Bart, the peasant hovel of the mini-nation is very precarious, in contrast to *El Encanto,* where Sofía is going to come to live "like
a queen." *El Encanto,* on the other hand, is a junctural, gliding term: by
it is understood the center, the productive place, the factory of meaning.
Inasmuch as it will generate capital, it gives meaning to Sofía's life, to her
independence, but it also refers to the golden dreams of queens and princesses whose very remote referent is again Rubén Darío's Modernism, very
au courant in Nicaragua, and to the idea that the protagonist is a gypsy
who knows, by blood, the mysteries of destiny and can invoke them as
rules that will govern incantation. Incantation is charm, grace, wisdom,
and capital.

Peons, on the other hand, are also objects of sexual desire, and are desire
itself, a veiled insinuation of social pacts which, as in the horizon of modernization at the beginning of the century, recurs to the body to realize
them. Erotic desires that Fernando, her peon custodian, awakens in Sofía,
and her talk of the sweetness of the flesh that Samuel, the sorceror, makes
possible are not only literary learnings or bookish inspirations, but take
from their matrix the fecund spirit eroticism has. In *Lady Chatterley's
Lover,* as in "Little Red Riding Hood," the history of the relations with
The Other has its double edges of eroticism, rape, and fecundity. The desire
for or fear of the offspring begotten by such unions does not manifest itself
here as biological children incarnated but only as expressions of the exercise of willpower, free will, and, in sum, freedom and imagination. It is a
learning of self-government and of the dominion of alterity which realizes
itself at a subliminal level, very related to the rejection of erotic relations
between husband and wife, seen as a perpetual rape; it is the relation with
Jerónimo, Sofía's attorney, whose function is only the reproduction of the
species; or it is the relation with Fausto, her gay cousin, where homosexuality and consanguinity make possible the establishment of the best of
relations.

Naturally, a contemporary reading cannot evade the borders between
this rejected sexuality and what the mythology of big penises represents:
phallocentrism and lesbianism. As in *Doña Bárbara,* the expression of "the

masculine" in a woman regularly projects itself in an unexpurgated dimension and therefore tends to access tracks of established signification. The rejection of the phallus is automatically interpreted as an attraction to women's bodies, just as the free expression of eroticism locates itself within the circuit of whoredom. They are, it is understood, nuclei of meaning from other circuits which are carried over and incorporated into the new.

There is not, therefore, a location for the symbiosis of the two principles, masculine and feminine, in only one being. In *Sofía*, what is postulated is the productive management of the country estate, coupled with the management of the reproduction of her body, interpreted as antagonistic. If the new nation is predicated on equality, it seems to say, it is necessary to accept an alternative typology, not only in which women are socially productive and own their own bodies, but also in which the principle of "the feminine" in men, in this case Fausto's open homosexuality, is recognized and accepted as a commonplace. Although it might seem paradoxical, the representation of Sofía as "the masculine" is as problematical as that of Fausto as "the feminine," except that the latter has in this narrative an obviously simplistic and homophobic textualization.

The "Three C's" of Success:
Cara/Cuerpo/Capital (Face/Body/Capital)

In *Sofía de los presagios*, Woman's realization is postulated as the absence of blood family and the death of social family. What a pity that only the woman without biological or adoptive parents, without husband, can realize herself as a social being. If biological parents are necessary for the reproduction of the species, this reproduction is a totally accidental fact. If social parents are necessary to educate and raise them, in adult life they turn out to be a nuisance. Marriage is also ballast for woman, and the husband only the reinstallation and reproduction of patriarchy within the domestic sphere.

In *Sofía*, to be a woman is to come from an unknown country; it is not to have history or memory. The past is an invention of mestizo medicine men and the people are in charge of giving them a history, identifying them with the exotic beauty of gypsies. In this trinity, face and body are two important aspects, but they are less important than capital, for it is of capital that woman wishes to take hold.

Teresa de la Parra argued in *Ifigenia* that it is only when the paterfamilias dies and women are left an inheritance that they can realize a series of emancipatory acts, the first in dealing with the state. They can, in the first instance, count on the services of a trained interpreter of the law to disentangle them from previously contracted duties (like marriage) and immediately unfasten the affective legal tie to insure the legal ownership of land, which she secures under her maiden name, taking possession of the property.

There is not, then, in *Sofía* the same dynamic as in the plains, nor the conflict of the peons and other contestatory national beings and of property, for the obscure (mestizos and women), in the displaced figure of the gypsy, have by an act of imaginative will taken control and power. The horizon of labor however, is still a problem. But to the degree that the principle of social justice in the revolutionary horizon appears as wage adjustment it is modified. In this sense, Gioconda Belli's proposal is more modern than Gallegos', for her search for social harmony rests in sharing profits.

The third C of success is capital; "it was invested in land and property, which she was not ready to abandon" (Belli, *SP*, 119). The concept of investment and her desire to know "the legal status of her possessions, the list debtors, taxes that have been paid annually, the bill for paying off past crops" (126) essentially distinguishes Sofía from María Eugenia Alonso and from the representations of the other porcelain women, for whom property was rent, ornamentation, or land without labor—garden. The mediation of the spirit of the law, which in the prior horizon was a prerogative of men, is here assumed by the energetic hand of a woman who asks that "everything be written in her maiden name . . . within a month, and [who makes] the demand of a divorce from [her] husband" (127). Still filled with resentment, she proposes the continuation of man/woman relations on different grounds as well: the husband has so much experience in the management of land that he can, if he wishes, accept a job as administrator. Doña Bárbara would never have asked Santos Luzardo to be the manager of her property. Gallegos' liberalism was patriarchal. Belli, on the contrary, makes it clear not only who is in command but that the subordination of man is a woman's desire.

To take things by the reins means, then, a consciousness of investments, of property and of legislation, but also of recouping what is most productive in land and selling the least. Within the revolutionary horizon, this principle of economic woman also needs the other—more doubtful—consent of "honest labor."

In order to begin understanding the difference, honest labor is the labor of don Ramón in the manor and of doña Carmen in the bar. Honest labor and professional labor are synonyms. The love potions, the work of doña Carmen, are professional; that is, she deceives no one and distributes to each the philters they need. To be honest and professional in both cases is not to trespass the limits, not to want to be what one is not, not to steal what belongs to someone else, not to wish what is alien, not to envy, not to try to occupy another's place. Twisting destiny, so much proclaimed in the philters of witchcraft and magic, only succeeds in putting things in their place: Sofía in the *hacienda* and Gertrudis, as the salaried worker, in the agency and married to the man Sofía proposes as her administrator. Her ex-husband is, it seems, a rancher of lesser import than don Ramón, and, now, than Sofía.

But, at the beginning, the hegemonic order and harmony of this social horizon is located in the settlement of wages. The workers still hold the mentality of serfs and, according to the author, are "obliged by the love of a whole life without knowing anything but obedience and loyalty" to the boss, to serve the child (159). But where there is no love, money mediates, "for in times of poverty and economic difficulties, few could reject the wages she thought of paying" (ibid.).

Knowing how to handle money and knowing the laws that regulate competition structure a dialogue within the text in which the other ranchers complain of the high wages and predict bankruptcy for the estate. Not only was she certain "to spoil the workers," but these same workers "will take advantage of her and the costs of the crops will effect dwindling earnings" (189).

The discussion of prices and wages, markets, and property management are tied to the concept of the rotation of the crops and the planting of cocoa and flowers in the Mombacho to be exported to Costa Rica (ibid.). Mombacho, the mountain, thus comes to be a place of dominion: the witch's home, her friends and protectors, her mentors, and cocoa plantations to make her future.

In contrast to the forest represented in the mountain, the mountain of El Mombacho is a civilized place: half zoo, half botanical garden, where some domesticated animals, "nocturnal, silent, and surprising birds," "blue birds," "the most unusual spectacle of congo monkeys," some orderly young trees, "a world of enormous and green-hued and dazzling vegetables," "flowers . . . of mauve and steel . . . the silenes red with their tall stems, the janizary and laurel trees, the majestic ceibos"—all of which constitute part of the knowledge handed down from mother to daughter (ibid.). In contrast to the guerrilla mountain, here there are "main roads," "peasant living quarters" and "working tools." But the verdure continues to be immense and the spectacle unusual. This, however, is also a country, a place of gender training, which pretends, like witches and gypsies, to control nature to better control the future and destiny.

The first signs of change we see in taking possession of property, however, occur in the domestic sphere: the house is not transformed into a home but into a garden, where, according to Sofía, the pleasure principle will be realized.

> In a few days Sofía revolutionizes the time of El Encanto. . . . [T]he peon women . . . scrape the floor and clear the cobwebs, for she has promised to pay them, and before, only their husbands were paid. Carpentry brigades change the roof and the termite-eaten boards. . . . [There is also talk] of the economic bonanza that Sofía's largesse with her new fortune will bring to those who work for her in the town. . . . From don Pascual she purchased all the vases and you'll see how she keeps the inner garden. It seems she bought the Mombacho! . . . In the great house, Sofía has remodeled her old single room as an office. (161–165)

When she decides to reproduce herself, however, the girl she will engender out of her own will and to whom she decides to give no father, is born within the bosom of landowning social relations. The reproduction of the child is articulated as the reproduction of the estate, and the variation in crops introduced: that which produces juicy rents, surplus value.

It is necessary to add that the heterosexual couple, so devalued, and utilized only to reproduce the species, is predicated differently, since the relationship that exists between Fausto and Sofía is the only one that is not disrupted and is understood as functional. It is not only a business relationship in which Fausto acts as administrator; they are also relatives. The feminization of the masculine tied to blood relations and to his skills as an administrator of people and of money is what makes this anodyne appearance of the fierce Sofía of prophecy compatible, to which her author makes her confess that contact with "the enormous sums of money [the famous *morocotas* in *Doña Bárbara*] is sensual and revivifying" (171). And,

> if there is something that has fascinated her in handling the property, aside from the challenge . . . to the property owner . . . [it] is that a homosexual and a woman can obtain as good or better crops than theirs. (190)

Woman Has No Country

If there is something surprising about these narratives by women, it is their consciousness of the negation of a feeling of nationality that we had taken for granted. Situated in a crisis between English and Caribbean, white and black, masters and freedmen, Antoinette negates herself, inquiring of her being: "I often wonder who I am and where is my country and where do I belong and why I was ever born at all" (Rhys, 519). Allegorized as a gypsy, woman in *Sofía de los presagios* descends from the gypsies, and "the gypsies . . . have no fixed place, no land, no place to return" (366). Abject before the verdicts of the law that do not protect her, de la Parra's María Eugenia Alonso wonders what kind of social organization Venezuela will produce. Loynaz' Bárbara is simply situated in a nameless land to which all the coordinates of a generic island are given, and Schwarz-Bart chooses a male protagonist to plot the search for nation.

The denationalization of the representation of woman in these narratives is the consequence of their exclusion as subjects of law in liberal republics, and of plotting the construction of nation as a series of male acts. It is the consequence of having been sold to the highest bidder through lavish dowries, of being relegated to the marginal spaces of poverty. In this symbolic sense, Fanotte, the woman who serves as a model for Télumée, and the rich landowner, Sofía, being women, are in the same signifying plane. And the destitute Antoinette, whose dowry only serves to enrich the English gentleman, together with the recluse María Eugenia are regarded as victims of patriarchy and people without recourse or appeal to the law. In these senses, the only one who can claim to belong is the gypsy, because jurisdiction as a landowner is recognized in her, or, paradoxically, the destitute Télumée, for she has absolutely nothing to claim. To national origins and feelings of country, to the transformation of the macrospace into a microspace, and to the evasion of the great national narratives, the last, yet-unpublished pages written by Gioconda Belli are added, where, almost predictably, exile and a country of one's own are unmentionable. Living in a generic atmosphere, which could be identified as Spain, the ancient "mother country" governed by the socialists, woman worries about the preservation of the species. In this return to Spain, the global circuit closes itself, a present episteme whose embryonic paradigms we are already within. But there is in her a return to her origins: the reclassification of the species, the striving to reorder and reclassify everything, from the most remote geographic expanse to the vanishing frontiers of the nation-state.

It is predictable that in the twilight of the national formations the interest in historicizing them awakens. It is also ironic that woman claims country at the moment of her departure and, even more disturbing, that in facing the vanishing structures of national reference, the utopias begin to be constructed anew. Resuscitated spaces. A return to the fountains. To the architecture and the most ancient structures of the psyche: house, garden, nation.

Notes

Throughout this book, all translations are by Ileana Rodríguez and Robert Carr, except where a work appears as a translation in the Bibliography.

Introduction

1 [As a Virginia state legislator] Jefferson sought and secured abolition of the laws of primogeniture and entail in Virginia in order to discourage concentration of property in the hands of a few great landowners. He believed that property was among the natural rights to which man was born and that it meant the right to a decent means of subsistence. After observing the economic conditions in France . . . , he wrote: "Whenever there is in any country, uncultivated lands and unemployed poor, it is clear that the laws of property have been so far extended as to violate natural right. The earth is given as a common stock for man to labour and live on. If for the encouragement of industry we allow it to be appropriated, we must take care that other employment be provided to those excluded from the appropriation. If we do not the fundamental right to labour the earth returns to the unemployed." (*Encyclopedia Britannica*, 15*th* ed., vol. 10, p. 127).

1 Transitions

An earlier version of this chapter appeared in the *Latin American Studies Center Series*, No. 4 (University of Maryland at College Park) 1992.

1 In the Latin American literary tradition of nineteenth-century Modernism, a "woman of porcelain" is a lily-white Victorian woman, and a black woman is a "woman of ebony." I have chosen "earthen woman" (i.e., "mujer de la tierra") to describe mestizas.

2 In his article "Populism and Nationalism: Some Reservations," (in Rodríguez & Zimmerman, eds.), John Beverley argues that Gallegos offers the mestizo three routes: in the marriage between Santos and Marisela, the idea that he can be part of the new capitalist society; for the peons, that they can aspire to intermediate positions; and for the masses, labor relations based on just labor contracts. I entirely agree with this reading.

3 In Manuel Díaz Rodríguez' novel, the patrician lineage is also very much taken into account. *Sangre Patricia,* which takes place entirely in Europe, offers a typology of this class of Venezuelan society, and it even insinuates that madness is an end result of *Independentista* history. Díaz Rodríguez refers to the "hispano/yanqui" war defending the rights of the Spaniards and seeing Spain as race, as opposed to what he already calls the Dollar Empire. Furthermore, he suggests that the next war will not be "from people to people," but from "race to race." See Díaz Rodríguez, *Sangre Patricia.*

4 The moment of publication of Jean Rhys' *Wide Sargasso Sea* coincides with the period of the awakening of nationalist consciousness in the Caribbean and the discussion of the Commonwealth. Cf. Knight 1978.

5 Cf. Capote, *Memorias de una cubanita.*

6 Cintio Vitier, *Ese sol del mundo moral* and *Lo cubano en la poesía.*

7 Apparently Sandino did not have a concept of the State. His proposal for indigenous peasant communities along the Coco river did not presuppose either a political force to ensure their existence or a legislative force—much less an army. The Army to Defend the National Sovereignty had as a goal to expel the U.S. army from Nicaragua. The peace agreements did not contemplate the situation of legal negligence of his economic program. It could be supposed that he trusted the "gentleman's agreement." See Ramírez, *El pensamiento vivo de Sandino.*

8 See Halperín Donghi, *Hispanoamérica después de la independencia.*

9 See the anthology by Mejía Sánchez.

10 See Payeras, *Los días de la selva y el pueblo resistirá las pruebas,* and Burgos Debray, *Me llamo Rigoberta Menchu.*

11 See Lienhard, "Escritura y poder en la conquista de América," and *La voz y su huella.*

12 See Ileana Rodríguez, *Registradas en la historia: Diez años de quehacer feminista en Nicaragua.*

13 See the film as well as the book by Edmundo Desnoes, *Memories of Underdevelopment* (*Memorias del subdesarrollo*).

14 See his "Stages of Modernization in Latin America."

15 See Berman, *Todo lo sólido se desvanece en el aire: La experiencia de la modernidad.*

2 Teresa de la Parra

1 See Herbert Graig, "Teresa de la Parra y la introducción de Marcel Proust en Hispanoamérica."

2 See Francine Masiello, "Texto, ley, transgressión: Especulación sobre la novela (feminista) de vanguardia."

3 See David Viñas, *Literatura argentina y realidad política.*

4 See Burgin and Caplan, eds., *Formations of Fantasy.*

5 See Foucault, *History of Sexuality.*

6 See Lemaitre, *Mujer ingeniosa: Vida de Teresa de la Parra.*

7 See Doris Meyer and Margarita Fernández Olmos, eds., *Contemporary Women Authors of Latin America: Introductory Essays.*

8 See Irigaray, *Speculum de l'autre femme.*

9 See Showalter, *Sexual Anarchy: Gender and Culture at the Fin-de-Siècle.*

10 Cf. Bosh, *La lengua viva de Teresa de la Parra.*

3 Dulce María Loynaz

An early version of this chapter was published in *Other Women's Voices Other Americas,* ed. Georgiana Colvile (Lewiston, NY: Edwin Mellen Press) 1993.

1 Very few critical essays have been written about this novel. Among them see Aurelio Boza Masvidal, "Dulce María Loynaz: Poesía, ensueño y silencio"; Miguel Angel Carbonell y Rivero, "Esquema de Dulce María Loynaz de Alvarez Cañas"; Aída Cuéllar de la Paz, "Ala y raíz en el *Jardín* de Dulce María Loynaz"; Juan Ramón Jiménez, "Dulce María Loynaz: Españoles de tres mundos"; and Antonio Martinez Bello, "Dulce María Loynaz, *Jardín:* Novela lírica"—in *Dulce María Loynaz: Valoración múltiple,* ed. Pedro Simón.

2 In his "Asuntos de familia: clase, linaje y política en Nicaragua," Carlos Vilas points out that when speaking about families, one refers to the notable families, those whose social prestige is backed up by their economic power and their political authority. If it is true that the study refers to Nicaragua, the familiar articulations he points out, and the differentiation between class in itself and for itself, are evident in the case of Cuba at the beginning of the century. The political formation of the Somoza family, which subordinated the conservative fractions of the gentry, a class that always saw Somoza as a newcomer and despised him for his obscure origin, is a mental structure whose perception can also be seen in Cuba at the beginning of the century. For the familiar relation in prerevolutionary Cuba, see Alfred Padula, *The Fall of the Bourgeoisie: Cuba, 1959–1961.*

3 See Bakhtin, *Speech Genres and Other Late Essays.*

4 Bakhtin, *Speech Genres.* Although Bakhtin's categories are ample and flexible, the overwhelming use of the pronoun "he" and the male centering of the definition make it very problematic to apply or to adjust to women writers.

5 Cf. Bettelheim, *The Uses of Enchantment: The Meaning and Importance of Fairy Tales.*

6 The more complete compilation of criticism on Loynaz is Pedro Simón's *Dulce María Loynaz: Valoración múltiple.*

7 See Oakley, *Sex, Gender and Society.*

8 Guerra, *passim.*

9 Cf. Said's *Orientalism.*

10 Cf. Gilman, *passim.* I have in mind the novels, say, of William Faulkner.

11 Cf. Juliet Mitchell, *What is Feminism? A Re-examination.*

12 The most documented case of a Caribbean protagonist marrying a foreign suitor is Jean Rhys' Antoinette, a character in dialogue with Charlotte Brontë's *Jane Eyre.* For more information see Elgin W. Mellon, *Jean Rhys: A Descriptive and Annotated Bibliography of Works and Criticism.*

13 Cf. Modleski, *Loving with a Vengeance: Mass-produced Fantasies for Women.*

4 Jean Rhys

1 Cf. works such as Nancy Brown, "England and the English in the works of Jean Rhys"; Codaccioni, "L'Autre vie de Bertha Rochester"; Corhay-Ledent, "Between Conflicting Worlds: Female Exiles in Jean Rhys' *Voyage in the Dark* and Joan Riley's *The Unbelonging Cross/Cultures;* and Mona Fayad, "Unquiet Ghosts: The Struggle for Representation in Jean Rhys' *Wide Sargasso Sea.*"

2 See Elgin W. Mellown, *Jean Rhys: A Descriptive and Annotated Bibliography of Works*

and Criticism. This annotated bibliography is not complete. Further, several studies have been published between 1984 and 1990. But this volume contains all the necessary references to the polemics between West Indian and English and North American literary critics.

3   I think here of works like Arnold E. Davidson's *Jean Rhys;* Teresa O'Connor's, *Jean Rhys: The West Indian Novels;* Deborah Kelly Kloepfer's, *The Unspeakable Mother: Forbidden Discourse in H.D.;* Helen Nebeker's, *Jean Rhys: Woman in Passage;* and Thomas F. Staley's, *Jean Rhys: A Critical Study.*

4   Bettina Knapp's "Jean Rhys: *Wide Sargasso Sea:* Mother/Daughter Identification and Alienation"; Deborah Kelly Kloepfer's "*Voyage in the Dark:* Jean Rhys' Masquerade for the Mother"; Judith Moore's "Sanity and Strength in Jean Rhys' West Indian Heroines"; and Barbara Nelson's *The Anatomy of the Madwoman.*

5   Cf. Wyndham, *The Letters of Jean Rhys, 1931–1966.* Also see Pierette Frickey, "The Dominican Landscape: In Memory of Jean Rhys"; and Missy Dehn Kubitschek, "Charting the Empty Spaces of Jean Rhys' *Wide Sargasso Sea.*"

6   Cf. Stephanie Branson, "Magicked in the Place: Shadow and Substance in *Wide Sargasso Sea*"; Charlotte Bruner, "A Caribbean Madness: Half Slave and Half Free"; Nancy Brown, "England and the English in the Works of Jean Rhys"; Mona Fayad, "Unquiet Ghosts: The Struggle for Representation in Jean Rhys' *Wide Sargasso Sea*"; Pearl Hochstadt, "From Vulnerability to Selfhood: The Pain-Filled Affirmations of Jean Rhys"; and Eva Klein, "Ancho Mar de los Sargazos: Las Antillas desde dentro."

5   Simone Schwarz-Bart

1   See Mary Louise Pratt, *Imperial Eyes: Travel Writing and Transculturation.*

6   Gioconda Belli

1   See Rama, in Mejía Sanchez, *La critica de la novela Iberoamericana.*
2   Cf. Beverley and Zimmerman, *Literature and Politics in the Central American Revolutions.*
3   See Spivak, "Can the Subaltern Speak?" and Carr, "Re(-)presentando el Testimonio: Notas sobre el cruce divisorio Primer Mundo/Tercer Mundo."
4   Gayatri Spivak, "A Literary Representation of the Subaltern" in her *In Other Worlds: Essays in Cultural Politics.* See also previous note.
5   See Tania Modleski, *Studies in Entertainment: Critical Approaches to Mass Culture.*
6   See Toril Moi, *Sexual/Textual Politics: Feminist Literary Theory.*

Selected Bibliography

Abbott, Keith. 1985. "Some Thoughts on Jean Rhys' Fiction." *The Review of Contemporary Fiction* 5, no. 2 (Summer): 112–114.

Acevedo, Ramón Luis. 1990. " 'Cenizas de Izalco' de Claribel Alegría y Darwin Flakoll o la armonización posible." *Cisalpino* 21: 77–88.

Achugar, Hugo. 1981. "Modernización, europeización, cuestionamiento: El lirismo social en Uruguay entre 1895–1911." *Revista Iberoamericana* 47, nos. 114–115 (Enero–Junio): 7–32.

Acker, Bertie. 1988. "Ifigenia: Teresa de la Parra's Social Protest." *Letras Femeninas* 14, nos. 1–2 (Spring–Fall): 73–79.

Aizenberg, Edna. 1985. "El bildungsroman fracasado en Latinoamerica: El caso de *Ifigenia*, de Teresa de la Parra." *Revista Iberoamericana* 51, nos. 132–133 (July–December): 539–546.

Albertazzi, Silvia. 1988. "*Quartet* di Jean Rhys: Un minuetto in trascrizione jazzistica." In Illa Maria Crisafulli Jones and Vita Fortunati, eds., *Ritratto dell'artista come donna: Saggi sull'avanguardia del Novecento*. Urbino: Quattro Venti.

Alegría, Claribel and D. J. Flakoll. 1983. *No me agarran viva: La mujer salvadoreña en lucha*. México: Ediciones Era.

———. 1984. *Para romper el silencio: Resistencia y lucha en las cárceles salvadoreñas*. México: Ediciones Era.

Amuso, Teresa Rose. 1987. "Crises of Survival: The Precarious 'I' in the Worlds of Elizabeth Bowen and Jean Rhys." *Dissertation Abstracts International* 48, no. 2 (August).

Anderson, Benedict. 1991. *Imagined Communities: Reflections on the Origins and Spread of Nationalism*. London, New York: Verso.

Angier, Carole. 1985. *Jean Rhys*. London: Penguin.

Anon. 1828. *Marly, or the Life of a Planter: Comprehending Characteristic Sketches of the Present State of Society and Manners in the British West Indies and an Impartial Review of the Leading Questions Relative to Colonial Policy*. Glasgow: R. Griffin.

Arenal, Electra. 1981. "Two Poets of the Sandinista Struggle." *Feminist Studies* 1: 19–27.

Armas, Ramón de. 1975. *La revolución pospuesta*. La Habana: Ciencias Sociales.

Ashcom, Jane Neide. 1988. "Two Modernisms: The Novels of Jean Rhys." *Jean Rhys Review* 2, no. 2 (Spring): 17–27.

Asturias, Miguel Angel. 1967. *Obras completas*. Madrid: Aguilar.

Auerbach, Erich. 1957. *Mimesis: The Representation of Reality in Western Literature*. Garden City, New Jersey: Doubleday.

Bakhtin, M. M. 1981. *The Dialogic Imagination: Four Essays*. Austin: University of Texas Press.

————. 1986. *Speech Genres and Other Late Essays*. Austin: University of Texas Press.

Baldanza, Frank. 1987. "Jean Rhys on Insult and Injury." In Biles and Kramer 1987.

Baltodano Egner, Charlotte. 1988. *Entre el fuego y las sombras*. Managua: CIRA.

Baralis, Marta. 1972. *Ifigenia de Teresa de la Parra*. Buenos Aires: Universidad de Buenos Aires, Facultad de Filosofía y Letras.

————. 1976. *La mujer en las letras venezolanas*. Caracas: Imprenta del Congreso de la República.

Belli, Gioconda. 1988. *La mujer habitada*. Managua: Vanguardia.

————. 1990. *Sofía de los presagios*. Managua: Vanguardia.

Bender, Todd K. 1987. "Jean Rhys and the Genius of Impressionism." In Biles and Kramer 1987.

Berger, Gertrude. 1985. "Rhys, De Beauvoir, and the Woman in Love." *The Review of Contemporary Fiction* 5, no. 2 (Summer): 139–145.

Berman, Marshal. 1989. *Todo lo sólido se desvanece en el aire: La experiencia de la modernidad*. México: Siglo XXI.

Bettelheim, Bruno. 1977. *The Uses of Enchantment: The Meaning and Importance of Fairy Tales*. New York: Vintage.

Beverley, John, and Marc Zimmerman. 1990. *Literature and Politics in the Central American Revolutions*. Austin: University of Texas Press.

Biles, Jack I., ed., and Victor A. Kramer, foreword. 1987. *British Novelists since 1900*. New York: AMS.

Boersner, Demetrio. 1978. *Venezuela y el Caribe: Presencia cambiante*. Caracas: Monte Avila.

Borge Martínez, Tomás. 1989. *La paciente impaciencia*. La Habana: Casa de las Américas.

Borinsky, Alicia. 1985. "Jean Rhys: Poses of a Woman as Guest." *Poetics Today* 6, nos. 1–2: 229–243.

Bosch, Velia. 1978. *La lengua viva en Teresa de la Parra*. Caracas: Comité Venezolano Coordinador del III Congreso Interamericano para el Estudio de la Obra de las Escritoras.

Boudon, Raymond. 1986. *L'Idéologie, ou, l'origine des idées reçues*. Paris: Fayard.

————. 1986. *Theories of Social Change: A Critical Appraisal*. Berkeley: University of California.

Brandmark, Wendy. 1986. "The Power of the Victim: A Study of *Quartet*, *After Leaving Mr. Mackenzie* and *Voyage in the Dark* by Jean Rhys." *Kunapipi* 8, no. 2: 21–29.

Branson, Stephanie. 1989. "Magicked by the Place: Shadow and Substance in *Wide Sargasso Sea*." *Jean Rhys Review* 3, no. 2 (Spring): 19–28.

Brathwaite, Edward K. 1971. *The Development of Creole Society in Jamaica, 1770–1820*. Glasgow: Oxford University Press.

Brontë, Charlotte. 1980. *Jane Eyre*. Boston: Twayne Publications.

Brown, Nancy Hemond. 1987. "England and the English in the Works of Jean Rhys." *Jean Rhys Review* 1, no. 2 (Spring): 8–20.

————. 1987. "On Becoming a Butterfly: Issues of Identity in Jean Rhys' *After Leaving Mr. Mackenzie.*" *Jean Rhys Review* 2, no. 1 (Fall): 6–15.

Bruner, Charlotte H. 1984. "A Caribbean Madness: Half Slave and Half Free." *Canadian Review of Comparative Literature/Revue Canadienne de Litterature Comparée* 11, no. 2 (June): 236–248.

Burgin, Victor, James Donald, and Cora Kaplan, eds. 1986. *Formations of Fantasy.* London and New York: Methuen.

Burgos Debray, Elizabeth. 1983. *Me llamo Rigoberta Menchú.* La Habana: Casa de las Américas.

Cabezas, Omar. 1982. *La montaña es algo más que una inmensa estepa verde.* La Habana: Casa de las Américas.

————. 1989. *Canto de amor para los hombres.* Managua: Vanguardia.

Campbell, Elaine. 1986. "The Unpainted Pastel Portrait." *Jean Rhys Review* 1, no. 1 (Fall): 13–15.

Carpentier, Alejo. 1974. *El siglo de las luces.* La Habana: Editorial de Arte y Literatura.

Carr, Robert. 1992. "Re(-)presentando el Testimonio: Notas sobre el cruce divisorio Primer Mundo/Tercer Mundo." *Review/Revista Interamericana* 36, no. 18 (Spring): 36. Special Issue: *La voz del otro: Testimonio, subalternidad y verdad narrativa,* ed. John Beverley and Hugo Achugar.

Carrera, Julieta. 1956. *La mujer en América escribe.* México: Ed. Alonso.

Carrera Suarez, Isabel, and Esther Alvarez Lopez. 1990. "Social and Personal Selves: Race, Gender and Otherness in Rhys' '*Let them Call It Jazz*' and *Wide Sargasso Sea.*" *Dutch Quarterly Review of Anglo-American Letters* 20, no. 2: 154–162.

Carvalho, José Murilo de. 1982. "Political Elites and the State Building: The Case of Nineteenth-Century Brazil." *Comparative Studies in Society and History* 24, no. 3: 378–399.

Cayetano Carpio, Salvador. 1982. *Secuestro y capucha.* Salvador: Ed. Universitaria Centroamericana.

Cerna, Lenín. 1981. *Y se rompió el silencio.* Managua: ENN.

Certeau, Michel de. 1985. *Heterologies: Discourse on the Other.* Minneapolis: University of Minnesota Press.

Chartier, Delphine. 1986. "Jean Rhys: L'Auto-Censure créatrice: Analyse des versions successives de la nouvelle '*Rapunzel, Rapunzel*'." *Jean Rhys Review* 1, no. 1 (Fall): 15–29.

Chatterjee, Partha. 1993. *Nationalist Thought and the Colonial World: A Derivative Discourse.* Minneapolis: University of Minnesota Press.

Clausewitz, Carl von. 1984. *On War.* Translated and edited by Michael Howard and Bernard Peter Paret. Princeton: Princeton University Press.

Clifford, James, and George E. Marcus, eds. 1986. *Writing Culture.* Berkeley, Los Angeles, and London: University of California Press.

Codaccioni, Maria-José. 1984. "L'Autre vie de Bertha Rochester." In Actes du Congres de Poitiers, ed., *Société des Anglicistes de l'Enseignement Supérieur.* Paris: Didier Erudition.

Conde, Maryse. 1979. *Essais sur des romanciéres des Antilles de langue française.* Paris: L'Harmattan.

————. 1988. *A Season in Rihata.* London: Heinemann.

Contribución a la bibliografía de Teresa de la Parra 1895–1936. 1970. Caracas: Universidad Católica Andrés Bello.

Corhay-Ledent, Benedicte. 1990. "Between Conflicting Worlds: Female Exiles in Jean Rhys' *Voyage in the Dark* and Joan Riley's *The Unbelonging* Cross/Cultures." In Geoffrey V. Davis and Hena Maes-Jelinek, eds., *Crisis and Creativity in the New Literatures in English*. Amsterdam: Rodopi.

Coronel Urtecho, José. 1974. *Tres conferencias a la empresa privada, y epílogo en memoria de Joaquín Zavala Urtecho*. Managua: El Pez y la Serpiente.

Curtis, Jan. 1985. "The Room and the Black Background: A Re-Interpretation of Jean Rhys' *Good Morning, Midnight.*" *World Literature Written in English* 25, no. 2 (Autumn): 264–270.

———. 1987. "Jean Rhys' *Voyage in the Dark:* A Re-Assessment." *The Journal of Commonwealth Literature* 22, no. 1: 144–158.

———. 1990. "The Secret of *Wide Sargasso Sea.*" *Critique: Studies in Contemporary Fiction* 31, no. 3 (Spring): 185–197.

Darío, Rubén. 1952. *Poesías Completas*. Madrid: Agvilar, S. A. de Ediciones

Davidson, Arnold E. 1985. *Jean Rhys*. New York: Frederick Ungar Publishing Co.

Defromont, Francoise. 1988. "Mémoires hantées: De *Jane Eyre* à *Wide Sargasso Sea.*" *Cahiers Victoriens Edouardiens* 27 (April): 149–157.

Delourmé, Chantal. 1984. "Jean Rhys: Perte, retour: Égarements." *Fabula* 3 (March): 65–76.

———. 1989. "La Mémoire fécondée: Réflexions sur l'intertextualité: Jane Eyre, *Wide Sargasso Sea.*" *Études Anglaises: Grande-Bretagne, États-Unis* 42, no. 3 (July–September): 257–269.

———. 1989. "*Voyage in the Dark:* Deuil d'un mythe." *Jean Rhys Review* 3, no. 2 (Spring): 12–19.

Desnoes, Edmundo. 1968. *Memorias del subdesarrollo*. Buenos Aires: Galerna.

Díaz/Diocaretz, Myriam, and Iris M. Zavala, eds. 1984. *Women, Feminist Identity, and Society in the 1880's*. Amsterdam, Philadelphia: Benjamins.

Díaz Rodríguez, Manuel. N.d. *Sangre Patricia*. Madrid: Biblioteca Andrés Bello.

Díaz Sánchez, Ramón. 1954. *Teresa de la Parra*. Caracas: Ediciones Garrido.

Dinesen, Isak. 1963. *Out of Africa*. New York: Time.

Drake, Sandra. 1990. "All that Foolishness/That All Foolishness: Race and Caribbean Culture as Thematics of Liberation in Jean Rhys' *Wide Sargasso Sea.*" *Critica: A Journal of Critical Essays* 2: 97–112.

Duncan, Quince. 1975. *El negro en la literatura costarricense*. San José: Ed. Costa Rica.

Eagleton, Terry, Fredric Jameson, and Edward W. Said. 1990. *Colonialism and Culture*. Minneapolis: University of Minnesota Press.

Emery, Mary Lou. 1985. "The Paradox of Style: Metaphor and Ritual in *Good Morning, Midnight.*" *The Review of Contemporary Fiction* 5, no. 2 (Summer): 145–150.

Erwin, Linda Lee. 1988. *Gender, Time, and Narrativity in the Novels of Jean Rhys*. Dissertation Abstracts International 49, no. 1 (July).

———. 1989. " 'Like in a Looking-Glass': History and Narrative in *Wide Sargasso Sea.*" *Novel: A Forum on Fiction* 22, no. 2 (Winter): 143–158.

Euripides. 1978. *Iphigenia at Aulis*. Translated by W. S. Merwin and George E. Dimock, Jr. New York: Oxford University Press.

Fayad, Mona. 1988. "Unquiet Ghosts: The Struggle for Representation in Jean Rhys' *Wide Sargasso Sea.*" *Modern Fiction Studies* 34, no. 3 (Autumn): 437–452.

Febres, Laura. 1984. *Cinco perspectivas críticas sobre la obra de Teresa de la Parra*. Caracas: Editorial Arte.

Felman, Shoshana. 1985. *Writing and Madness*. Ithaca, New York: Cornell University Press.

Ferracane, Kathleen K. 1987. *Images of the Mother in Caribbean Literature: Selected Novels of George Lamming, Jean Rhys and V. S. Naipaul*. Dissertation Abstracts International 48, no. 2 (August): 398A.

Foucault, Michel. 1978. *The History of Sexuality*. New York: Pantheon Books.

———. 1979. *Discipline and Punish: The Birth of the Prison*. New York: Vintage Books.

Fraginals Moreno, Manuel. 1976. *The Sugarmill: The Socioeconomic Complex of Sugar in Cuba, 1760–1860*. New York: Monthly Review Press.

Franco, Jean. 1989. *Plotting Women: Gender and Representation in Mexico*. New York: Columbia University Press.

Frickey, Pierrette. 1988. "The Dominican Landscape: In Memory of Jean Rhys." *Jean Rhys Review* 3, no. 1 (Fall): 2–10.

Friedman, Ellen G. 1989. "Breaking the Master Narrative: Jean Rhys' *Wide Sargasso Sea*." In Ellen G. Friedman and Miriam Fuchs, eds., *Breaking the Sequence: Women's Experimental Fiction*, 117–128. Princeton: Princeton University Press.

Fromm, Gloria G. 1985. "Making Up Jean Rhys." *The New Criterion* 4, no. 4 (December): 47–50.

Gaines, Nora. 1986. "Bibliography." *Jean Rhys Review* 1, no. 1 (Fall): 29–35.

———. 1987. "Bibliography." *Jean Rhys Review* 2, no. 1 (Fall): 15–20.

———. 1988. "Bibliography." *Jean Rhys Review* 3, no. 1 (Fall): 14–20.

Gallegos, Rómulo. 1977. *Doña Bárbara*. Caracas: Ayacucho.

García Márquez, Gabriel. 1983. *El asalto*. Managua: ENN.

García Marruz, Fina. 1991. "Aquel girón de luz. . . ." In Pedro Simón, ed., *Valoración múltiple: Dulce María Loynaz*, 163–175. La Habana: Casa de las Américas.

Gardiner, Judith Kegan. 1989. "The Exhilaration of Exile: Rhys, Stead, and Lessing." In Mary Lynn Broe and Angela Ingram, eds., *Women's Writing in Exile*. Chapel Hill: University of North Carolina Press.

———. 1989. *Rhys, Stead, Lessing, and the Politics of Empathy*. Bloomington: Indiana University Press.

Garrels, Elizabeth. 1986. *Las grietas de la ternura*. Caracas: Monte Avila.

———. 1988. "Layo y Edipo: Padres, hijos y el problema de la autoridad en el *Facundo*." *La Torre* 2, no. 7 (Julio–Septiembre): 505–526.

Gates, Henry Louis, ed. 1986. *"Race," Writing, and Difference*. Chicago: University of Chicago Press.

———. 1988. *The Signifying Monkey: A Theory of Afro-American Literary Criticism*. New York: Oxford University Press.

Gellner, Ernest. 1983. *Nations and Nationalism*. Ithaca: Cornell University Press.

Germani, Gino. 1972. "Stages of Modernization in Latin America." In Stefan A. Halper and John R. Sterling, eds., *Latin America: The Dynamics of Social Change*. New York: St. Martins Press.

———. 1974. *Política y sociedad en una época de transición: De la sociedad tradicional a la sociedad de masas*. Buenos Aires: Paidos.

———. 1981. *The Sociology of Modernization: Studies on its Historical and Theoretical Aspects with Special Regard to the Latin American Case*. New Brunswick, New Jersey: Transaction Books.

Gilbert, Sandra M., and Susan Gubar. 1979. *The Madwoman in the Attic: The Woman Writer and the Nineteenth-Century Literary Imagination.* New Haven and London: Yale University Press.

———. 1988. *No Man's Land: The Place of the Woman Writer in the Twentieth Century.* New Haven and London: Yale University Press.

Givner, Joan. 1988. "Charlotte Brontë, Emily Brontë and Jean Rhys: What Rhys' Letters Show About That Relationship." In Alice Kessler-Harris and William McBrien, eds., *Faith of a (Woman) Writer.* Westport, Connecticut: Greenwood.

Gordimer, Nadine. 1973. *The Black Interpreters: Notes on African Writing.* Johannesburg: Spro-Cas/Ravan.

———. 1988. *The Essential Gesture: Writing, Politics and Places.* New York: Knopf.

Graig, Herbert. 1990. "Teresa de la Parra y la introducción de Marcel Proust en Hispanoamérica." In Felix Menchacatorre, ed., *Ensayos de literatura europea e hispanoamericana.* San Sebastián: Univ. del País Vasco.

Gregg, Veronica Marie. 1987. "Jean Rhys and Modernism: A Different Voice." *Jean Rhys Review* 1, no. 2 (Spring): 30–46.

———. 1988. *Jean Rhys, Europe and the West Indies: A Literary Study.* Dissertation Abstracts International 49, no. 3 (September).

Groves, Robyn Kaye. 1988. *Fictions of the Self: Studies in Female Modernism: Jean Rhys, Gertrude Stein and Djuna Barnes.* Dissertation Abstracts International 49, no. 5 (November).

Guerra y Sánchez, Ramiro. 1964. *Sugar and Society in the Caribbean: An Economic History of Cuban Agriculture.* New Haven: Yale University Press.

Guha, Ranajit. 1983. *Elementary Aspects of Peasant Insurgency in Colonial India.* Delhi: Oxford University Press.

———. 1988. "The Prose of Counter-Insurgency." In Spivak and Guha 1988.

Gutierrez, Joaquín. 1975. *Puerto Limón.* San José: Ed. Costa Rica.

Hagley, Carol R. 1988. "Ageing in the Fiction of Jean Rhys." *World Literature Written in English* 28, no. 1 (Spring): 115–125.

Halperín Donghi, Tulio. 1972. *Hispanoamérica después de la independencia: Consecuencias sociales y económicas de la emancipación.* Buenos Aires: Paidos.

Hanson, Clare. 1988. "Each Other: Images of Otherness in the Short Fiction of Doris Lessing, Jean Rhys and Angela Carter." *Journal of the Short Story in English* 10 (Spring): 67–82.

Harris, Richard L., and Carlos Vilas, eds. 1985. *Nicaragua: A Revolution under Siege.* London: Zed Books.

Harris, Wilson. 1973. *The Palace of the Peacock.* London: Faber and Faber.

Harrison, Nancy R. 1988. *Jean Rhys and the Novel as Women's Text.* Chapel Hill: University of North Carolina Press.

Hiriart, Rosario. 1980. *Más acerca de Teresa de la Parra.* Caracas: Monte Avila.

———. 1981. "Dos cartas de Gabriela Mistral." *Insula: Revista de letras y ciencias humanas* 36, no. 415 (June): 4, 10.

Hirsch, E. D. 1967. *Validity in Interpretation.* New Haven: Yale University Press.

Hite, Molly. 1989. *The Other Side of the Story: Structure and Strategies of Contemporary Feminist Narratives.* Ithaca: Cornell University Press.

Hobsbawm, Eric J. 1990. *Nations and Nationalism: Programme, Myth, Reality.* New York: Cambridge University Press.

Hochstadt, Pearl. 1987. " 'Connais-tu le pays?' Anna Morgan's Double Voyage." *Jean Rhys Review* 1, no. 2 (Spring): 2–7.

———. 1987. "From Vulnerability to Selfhood: The Pain-Filled Affirmations of Jean Rhys." *Jean Rhys Review* 2, no. 1 (Fall): 2–6.

Huang, Yaunshen. 1987. "The Portrayal of Women in *The Flight from the Enchanter* and *After Leaving Mr. Mackenzie.*" *Waiguoyu* 2, no. 48 (April): 36–40.

Irigaray, Luce. 1973. *Le langage des déments*. The Hague: Mouton.

———. 1974. *Speculum de l'autre femme*. Paris: Minuit.

James, Louis. 1978. *Jean Rhys*. London: Longman.

Jameson, Fredric. 1991. *Postmodernism or, The Cultural Logic of Late Capitalism*. Durham: Duke University Press.

Kaplan, Cora. 1975. *Salt and Bitter and Good: Three Centuries of English and American Women Poets*. New York: Paddington Press.

———. 1986. *Sea Changes*. London: Verso.

Kappers-den Hollander, Martien. 1987. "A Gloomy Child and Its Devoted Godmother: Jean Rhys, Barred, Sous les verrous and In de Strik." *Jean Rhys Review* 1, no. 2 (Spring): 20–29.

———. 1988. "Measure for Measure: *Quartet* and *When the Wicked Man.*" *Jean Rhys Review* 2, no. 2 (Spring): 2–17.

Kavanaugh, Desmond. 1989. "Jean Rhys and God." *Durham University Journal* 81, no. 2 (June): 275–280.

Kesteloot, Lilyan. 1967. *Les Écrivains noirs de langue française: Naissance d'une litterature*. Bruxelles: Université libre de Bruxelles.

———. 1968. *Negritude et situation colonial*. Yaonde: Editions Cle.

Klein, Eva. 1987. "*Ancho Mar de los Sargazos:* Las Antillas desde dentro." *Plural: Revista cultural de Excelsior* 16, no. 12 (192) (September): 49–51.

Kloepfer, Deborah Kelly. 1985. "*Voyage in the Dark:* Jean Rhys' Masquerade for the Mother." *Contemporary Literature* 26, no. 4 (Winter): 443–459.

———. 1989. *The Unspeakable Mother: Forbidden Discourse in Jean Rhys and H. D.* Ithaca: Cornell University Press.

Knapp, Bettina L. 1986. "Jean Rhys: *Wide Sargasso Sea:* Mother/Daughter Identification and Alienation." *Journal of Evolutionary Psychology* 7, nos. 3–4 (August): 211–226.

Knight, Franklin. 1978. *Caribbean: The Genesis of a Fragmented Nationalism*. New York: Oxford University Press.

Kubitschek, Missy Dehn. 1987. "Charting the Empty Spaces of Jean Rhys' *Wide Sargasso Sea.*" *Frontiers: A Journal of Women's Studies* 9, no. 2: 23–28.

Lai, Look Wally. 1984. "The Road to Thornfield Hall: An Analysis of Jean Rhys' *Wide Sargasso Sea.*" In John La Rose, ed., *New Beacon Review*. London: New Beacon Books, Ltd.

Leigh, Nancy J. 1985. "Mirror, Mirror: The Development of Female Identity in Jean Rhys' Fiction." *World Literature Written in English* 25, no. 2 (Autumn): 270–285.

Lemaitre, Louis Antonine. 1987. *Mujer ingeniosa: Vida de Teresa de la Parra*. La Muralla.

Lessing, Doris. 1962. *The Golden Notebook*. London: Michael Joseph.

———. 1981. *African Stories*. New York: Simon and Schuster.

Lienhard, Martin. 1989. "Escritura y poder en la conquista de América." *Casa de las Américas* 29, no. 174: 128–129.

———. 1990. *La voz y su huella*. La Habana: Casa de las Américas.

Liscano, Juan. 1968. *Rómulo Gallegos*. México: Novaro.

———. 1969. *Rómulo Gallegos y su tiempo*. Caracas: Monte Avila.

Long, Edward. 1970. *The History of Jamaica*. London: Frank Cass & Co.

Loynaz, Dulce María. 1951. *Jardín*. Madrid: Aguilar.

————. 1955. *Ultimos días de una casa*. In *Obra lírica*. Madrid: Aguilar.

Machado, Antonio. 1989. *Poesía y prosa. Tomo II: Poesías completas*. Madrid: Fundacíon Antonio Muchado.

Mackinnon, Catharine. 1987. *Feminism Unmodified: Discourse on Life*. Cambridge, Massachusetts: Harvard University Press.

————. 1989. *Toward a Feminist Theory of the State*. Cambridge, Massachusetts: Harvard University Press.

Madden, Richard. 1970. *A Twelve Months Residence in the West Indies, During the Transition from Slavery to Apprenticeship, with Incidental Notices to the State of the Society, Prospects and Natural Resources of Jamaica and Other Islands*. Westport, Connecticut: Negro University Press.

Magarey, Kevin. 1986. "The Sense of Place in Doris Lessing and Jean Rhys." In Nightingale, Peggy, ed., *A Sense of Place in the New Literatures in English*. Lucia: University of Queensland Press.

Magnus, Mörner. 1970. *Race and Class in Latin America*. New York: Columbia University Press.

Marroni, Francesco. 1986. "*Voyage in the Dark:* Jean Rhys e le stanze dell'esilio." *Il Lettore di Provincia* 17, no. 67 (December): 78–91.

Martí, José. 1963–1965. *Obras completas*, T. 8. Ed. Nacional de Cuba. La Habana.

Martinegro, Allessandro. 1967. *L'itinerario di Teresa de la Parra verso il mondo criollo*. Pisa: Giardini.

Martínez, José de Jesús. 1982. *Mi general Torrijos*. La Habana: Casa de las Américas.

Masiello, Francine. 1985. "Texto, ley, transgresión: Especulación sobre la novela (feminista) de vanguardia." *Revista Iberoamericana* 51, nos. 132–133 (July–December): 807–822.

McPherson, Diane M. 1990. *The Character Who Represents Herself: Self-Portraiture and Metatextuality in the Fiction of Jean Rhys*. Dissertation Abstracts International 51, no. 1 (July).

Meckier, Jerome. 1988. "Distortion versus Revaluation: Three Twentieth-Century Responses to Victorian Fiction." *Victorian Newsletter* 73 (Spring): 3–8.

Mejía Sánchez, Ernesto, ed. 1984. *La crítica de la novela Iberoamericana contemporanea-antología*. México: Instituto de Investigaciones Filológicas, Centro de Estudios Literarios, UNAM.

Mellown, Elgin W. 1984. *Jean Rhys: A Descriptive and Annotated Bibliography of Works and Criticism*. New York and London: Garland Publishing, Inc.

Méndez Capote, René. 1990. *Memorias de una cubanita que nació con el siglo*. La Habana: Pueblo y Educación.

Meyer, Doris. 1983. " 'Feminine' Testimony in the Works of Teresa de la Parra, María Luisa Bombal, and Victoria Ocampo." In Doris Meyer and Margarita Fernandez Olmos, eds., *Contemporary Women Authors of Latin America: Introductory Essays*. Brooklyn: Brooklyn College Press.

Meyers, Robert A., and J. Gill Holland. 1983. "The Theme of Identity in the Works of Jean Rhys." *Revista/Review Interamericana* 13, nos. 1–4: 150–158.

Mezei, Kathy. 1987. " 'And It Kept Its Secret': Narration, Memory, and Madness in Jean Rhys' *Wide Sargasso Sea*." *Critique: Studies in Modern Fiction* 28, no. 4 (Summer): 195–209.

Miller, Beth. 1983. *Women in Hispanic Literature: Icons and Fallen Idols.* Berkeley: University of California Press.

Mistral, Gabriela. 1988. *Cartas a Lydia Cabrera.* Madrid: Torremozas.

Mitchell, Juliet, and Ann Oakley, eds. 1986. *What is Feminism? A Re-examination.* New York: Pantheon Books.

Modleski, Tania. 1982. *Loving with a Vengeance: Mass-produced Fantasies for Women.* Hamden, Connecticut: Archon Books.

———. 1986. *Studies in Entertainment: Critical Approaches to Mass Culture.* Bloomington: Indiana University Press.

Moi, Toril. 1985. *Sexual/Textual Politics: Feminist Literary Theory.* London and New York: Methuen.

Moore, Judith. 1987. "Sanity and Strength in Jean Rhys' West Indian Heroines." *Rocky Mountain Review of Language and Literature* 41, nos. 1–2: 21–31.

Morrell, A. Carol. 1984. *The Rhetoric of Space and Place: A Study of the Use of Symbolic Analogy, Circular Patterning, and Romance Conventions as Persuasion in Certain Modern Commonwealth Fictions.* Dissertation Abstracts International 45, no. 6 (December).

Moya-Raggio, Eliana. 1988. "El sacrificio de Ifigenia: Teresa de la Parra y su visión crítica de una sociedad criolla." *La Torre: Revista de la Universidad de Puerto Rico* 2, no. 5: 161–171.

Nance, Kimberly Ann. 1990. "Pied Beauty: Juxtaposition and Irony in Teresa de la Parra's *Las memorias de la mamá blanca.*" *Letras Femeninas* 16, nos. 1–2 (Spring-Fall): 45–49.

Nebeker, Helen. 1981. *Jean Rhys: Woman in Passage: A Critical Study of the Novels of Jean Rhys.* Montreal: Eden Press.

Nelson, Barbara A. 1987. *The Anatomy of the Madwoman.* Dissertation Abstracts International 47, no. 12 (June).

Nelson, Cary, and Laurence Grossberg, eds. 1988. *Marxism and the Interpretation of Culture.* Urbana: University of Illinois Press.

Niesen de Abruna, Laura. 1988. "Jean Rhys' Feminism: Theory against Practice." *World Literature Written in English* 28, no. 2 (Autumn): 326–336.

Nieto Caballero, Luis Eduardo. 1929. *Colinas inspiradas.* Bogotá: Ed. Minerva.

Nudd, Donna Marie. 1984. "The Uneasy Voyage of Jean Rhys and Selma Vaz Dias." *Literature in Performance: A Journal of Literary and Performing Art* 4, no. 2 (April): 20–32.

Nuñes, Maria Luisa. 1982. "Becoming Whole: Literary Strategies of Decolonization in the Works of Jean Rhys, Frantz Fanon, and Oswald de Andrade III." In Anna Balakian et al., eds., *Proceedings of the Xth Congress of the International Comparative Literature Association/Actes du Xe congres de l'Association internationale de litterature comparee.* New York.

Nuñez, Orlando. 1990. *Sábado de Gloria.* Managua.

Nuñez-Harrell, Elizabeth. 1985. "The Paradoxes of Belonging: The White West Indian Woman in Fiction." *Modern Fiction Studies* 31, no. 2 (Summer): 281–293.

Oakley, Ann. 1972. *Sex, Gender and Society.* London: Maurice Temple Smith Ltd.

Oates, Joyce Carol. 1985. "Romance and Anti-Romance: From Brontë's *Jane Eyre* to Rhys' *Wide Sargasso Sea.*" *Virginia Quarterly Review: A National Journal of Literature and Discussion* 61, no. 1 (Winter): 44–58.

O'Connor, Teresa F. 1985. *The Meaning of the West Indian Experience for Jean Rhys.* Dissertation Abstracts International 46, no. 3 (September).

————. 1986. *Jean Rhys: The West Indian Novels*. New York and London: New York University Press.

Padula, Alfred. 1974. *The Fall of the Bourgeoisie: Cuba, 1959–1961*. Dissertation Abstracts International (December).

Parra, Teresa de la. 1965. *Obras completas*. Caracas: Ed. Arte.

————. 1986. *Ifigenia: Diario de una señorita que escribió porque se fastidiaba*. México: Colección Biblioteca.

Parry, Benita. 1988. "Problems in Current Theories of Colonial Discourse." *Diacritics* (Fall): 65–77.

Payeras, Mario. 1982. *Los días de la selva y el pueblo resistirá las pruebas*. Managua: Editorial Nueva Nicaragua.

Paz, Octavio. 1974. *Los hijos del limo: Del romanticismo a la vanguardia*. Barcelona: Seix Barral.

Perus, Francoise. "El 'otro' del testimonio." *Casa de las Américas* 39, no. 174: 134–136.

Piedrahita, Carmen. 1981. "Literatura sobre la problemática femenina en Latinoamérica." *Cuadernos Americanos* 236, no. 3: 222–238.

Pietri, Arturo Uslar. 1948. *Letras y hombres de Venezuela*. México: Fondo de Cultura Económica.

Pinto, Anibal. 1962. *Chile: Un caso de desarrollo frustrado*. Santiago de Chile: Editorial Universitaria.

Pratt, Mary Louise. 1992. *Imperial Eyes: Travel Writing and Transculturation*. London: Routledge.

Quintana, Emilio. 1967. *Bananos: La vida de los peones in la yunai*. Managua: Ed. Central.

Ragatz, Lowell. 1976. *The Fall of the Planter Class in the British Caribbean, 1763–1833: A Study in Social and Economic History*. New York: Octagon Books.

Raiskin, Judith L. 1990. *Unruly Subjects: Nationhood, Home and Colonial Consciousness in Olive Schreiner and Jean Rhys*. Dissertation Abstracts International 50, no. 12 (June).

Rama, Angel. 1970. *Rubén Darío y el modernismo (Circunstancia socio-económica de un arte americano.)* Caracas: EBUC.

————. 1984. *La ciudad letrada*. Hannover: Ediciones del Norte.

Ramchand, Kenneth. 1969. "Terrified Consciousness." *Journal of Commonwealth Literature* 7 (July): 8–19.

————. 1970. *The West Indian Novel and Its Background*. London: Faber and Faber.

Ramírez, Sergio, ed. 1983. *El pensamiento vivo de Sandino*. Managua: Editorial Nueva Nicaragua.

————. 1987. *Las armas del Futuro*. Nicaragua: Editorial Nueva Nicaragua.

————. 1989. *La marca del Zorro: Hazañas del Comandante Francisco Rivera Quintero contadas a Sergio Ramírez*. Managua: Editorial Nueva Nicaragua.

Review of Contemporary Fiction. 1985. Vol. 5, no. 2 (Summer) Special issue on Jean Rhys.

Rhys, Jean. 1974. *My Day: Three Pieces*. New York: F. Hallman.

————. 1985. *The Complete Novels*. New York and London: W. W. Norton and Co.

Rivera, José Eustacio. 1982. *La Vorágine*. La Habana: Casa de las Américas.

Riverend, Julio le. 1975. *La República*. La Habana: Ciencias Sociales.

Rodríguez, Ileana. 1986. "El concepto de cultura nacional durante los años de formación del Frente Sandinista de Liberación Nacional." In *Literatura y crisis en Centroamérica*. San José: Instituto Centroamericano de documentación e investigación social.

————. 1991. *Registradas en la historia: Diez años de quehacer feminista en Nicaragua.* Managua: Vanguardia.

Rodríguez, Ileana, and Marc Zimmerman, eds. 1983. *Processes of Unity in Caribbean Ideologies and Literature.* Minneapolis: Institute for Ideologies and Literature.

Rodríguez, Maria Cristina. 1987. "Men and Women Interacting in the Novel and in the Film Version of Jean Rhys' *Quartet.*" *Imágenes: Publicación semestral de teoría, técnica, crítica y acerca de la imágen en movimiento* 3, no. 1: 24–27.

Roe, Sue. 1987. "'The Shadow of Light': The Symbolic Underworld of Jean Rhys." In Sue Roe, ed., *Women Reading Women's Writing.* Brighton, England: Harvester.

Romero García, Manuel Vicente. 1976. *Peonía.* Caracas: Monte Avila.

Rubin Suleiman, Susan. 1986. *The Female Body in Western Culture.* Cambridge, Massachusetts: Harvard University Press.

Sage, Lorna. 1986. "The Available Space." In Moira Monteith, ed., *Women's Writing: A Challenge to Theory.* Sussex and New York: Harvester, St. Martins.

Said, Edward. 1978. *Orientalism.* New York: Pantheon Books.

————. 1983. *The World, The Text and The Critic.* Cambridge, Massachusetts: Harvard University Press.

Schiller, Herbert. 1989. *Culture, Inc.* Oxford: Oxford University Press.

Schwarz-Bart, Simone. 1972. *Pluie et vent sur Télumée miracle.* Paris: Du Seuil.

————. 1981. *Ti Jean L'Horizon.* Paris: Points.

————. 1982. *The Bridge of Beyond.* London: Heinemann.

Showalter, Elaine. 1985. *Female Malady: Women, Madness and English Culture, 1830–1980.* New York: Pantheon.

————. 1985. *The New Feminist Criticism: Essays on Women, Literature and Theory.* New York: Pantheon.

————. 1990. *Sexual Anarchy: Gender and Culture at the Fin-de-Siècle.* New York: Pantheon.

Simon, José G. 1985. "Teresa de la Parra, pionera del movimiento feminista." *Circulo: Revista de cultura* 14: 85–89.

Simón, Pedro. 1991. *Dulce María Loynaz: Valoración Múltiple.* La Habana: Casa de las Américas.

Smilowitz, Erika. 1984. *Critical Issues in West Indian Literature: Selected Papers from the West Indian Literature Conference 1981–1983.* Parkersburg, West Virginia: Caribbean Books.

————. 1986. "Childlike Women and Paternal Men: Colonialism in Jean Rhys' Fiction." *Ariel: A Review of International English Literature* 17, no. 4 (October): 93–103.

Sommer, Doris. 1991. *Foundational Fictions: The National Romances of Latin America.* Berkeley and Los Angeles: University of California Press.

Spivak, Gayatri Chakravorty. 1985. "Three Women's Texts and a Critique of Imperialism." *Critical Inquiry* 12, no. 1 (Autumn): 243–261.

————. 1987. *In Other Worlds: Essays in Cultural Politics.* New York: Methuen.

————. 1988. "Can the Subaltern Speak?" In Cary Nelson and Lawrence Grossberg, eds., *Marxism and the Interpretation of Culture.* Urbana and Chicago: University of Illinois Press.

Spivak, Gayatri Chakravorty, and Ranajit Guha, eds. 1988. *Selected Subaltern Studies.* New York: Oxford University Press.

Stacey-Doyle, Michele. 1987. *Jean Rhys: A Sense of Place a Sense of Self.* Dissertation Abstracts International 48, no. 3 (September).

Staley, Thomas F. 1979. *Jean Rhys: A Critical Study.* London: Macmillan.

Stallybrass, Peter, and Allon White. 1986. *The Politics and Poetics of Transgression.* London: Methuen.

Subercaseaux, Bernardo. 1989. *Fin de siglo: La época de Balmaceda.* Santiago de Chile: CENECA.

Summers, Marcia A. 1985. "Victimization, Survival and Empowerment in *Wide Sargasso Sea* and *Daughter of the Earth.*" Selected Proceedings of the University of South Dakota's 1st Annual Women's Research Conference. In Karen Hardy Cardenas, Susan Wolfe, and Mary Schneider, eds., *Woman's Place.* Vermillion: University of South Dakota, Women's Research Conference.

Tarozzi, Bianca. 1989. "The Turning Point: Themes in *Good Morning, Midnight.*" *Jean Rhys Review* 3, no. 2 (Spring): 2–12.

Teresa de la Parra, bibliografía y otros trabajos. 1980. Caracas: La Casa de Bello.

Thompson, Irene. 1985. "The Left Bank Aperitifs of Jean Rhys and Ernest Hemingway." *The Georgia Review* 35, no. 1 (Spring): 94–106.

Torrealba Lossi, Mario. 1951. *En torno a la novela de Teresa de la Parra.* Caracas: Avila Gráfica.

Toureh, Fanta. 1986. *L'Imaginaire dans l'œuvre de Simone Schwarz-Bart.* Paris: L'Harmattan.

Trebilcot, Joyce. 1983. *Mothering: Essays in Feminist Theory.* Totowa: N.J.N. Rowman and Allanheld.

Uslar Pietri, Arturo. 1948. *Letras y hombres de Venezuela.* México: Fondo de Cultura Económica.

——. 1978. *Letras y hombres de Venezuela.* Madrid: Mediterraneo.

Vanouse, Evelyn Hawthorne. 1988. "Jean Rhys' *Voyage in the Dark:* Histories Patterned and Resolute." *World Literature Written in English* 28, no. 1 (Spring): 125–133.

Vargas, Oscar René. 1991. *Adonde va Nicaragua.* Managua: Nicarao.

Vidal, Hernán. 1989. *Cultural and Historical Grounding for Hispanic and Luso-Brazilian Feminist Literary Criticism.* Minnesota: Institute of Ideologies and Literature.

Vilas, Carlos. 1986. *The Sandinista Revolution: National Liberation and Social Transformation in Central America.* New York: Monthly Review Press.

——. 1989. *Transición desde el subdesarrollo: Revolución y reforma desde la periferia.* Caracas: Nueva Sociedad.

——. Forthcoming. "Asuntos de familia: Clase, linaje y política en Nicaragua."

Viñas, David. 1971. *Literatura argentina y realidad política.* Buenos Aires: Ed. Siglo XX.

Visel, Robin. 1988. "A Half-Colonization: The Problem of the White Colonial Woman Writer." *Kunapipi* 10, no. 3: 39–45.

Vitier, Cintio. 1970. *Lo cubano en la poesía.* Habana: Instituto Cubano del libro.

——. 1975. *Ese sol del mundo moral.* México: Siglo XXI.

Webb, Ruth. 1988. "Swimming the Wide Sargasso Sea: The Manuscripts of Jean Rhys' Novel." *The British Library Journal* 14, no. 2 (Autumn): 165–177.

Wheelock, Jaime. 1974. *Raíces indígenas de la lucha anticolonialista en Nicaragua, de Gil Gonzalez a Joaquín Zavala, 1523 a 1881.* México: Siglo XXI.

Williams, Raymond. 1975. *The Country and the City.* New York: Oxford University Press.

——. 1983. *Culture and Society 1780–1950.* New York: Columbia University Press.

——. 1990. *The Politics of Modernism: Against the New Conformist*. London, New York: Verso.

Wilson, Lucy. 1986. " 'Women Must Have Spunks': Jean Rhys' West Indian Outcasts." *Modern Fiction Studies* 32, no. 3 (Autumn): 439–448.

——. 1989. "European or Caribbean: Jean Rhys and the Language of Exile." *Frontiers: A Journal of Women's Studies* 10, no. 3: 68–72.

Wolfe, Peter. 1980. *Jean Rhys*. Boston: Twayne Publishers.

Wyndham, Francis, and Diana Melly, eds. 1984. *The Letters of Jean Rhys, 1931–1966*. New York: Viking.

Y se rompió el silencio. 1981. Managua: ENN.

Index

Africa, 18, 29, 119, 123, 129, 130, 133, 135, 136, 137, 142, 143–50, 152, 158, 159
Aidoo, Ama Ata, 146
Altamira, 26, 33, 141
Anderson, Benedict, 3, 5, 9, 14, 16, 31
Anderson, Imbert, 30
Anexionistas, 11
Arauco, 33, 35, 83
Argentina, 13, 168
Arguedas, José María, 7
Aristocracy (aristocratic, aristocrats), vxii, 27, 29, 65, 71, 88, 98, 139, 179, 182; Aristos, 29
Armas de, Ramón, 5, 7, 11, 12
Asturias, Miguel Angel, 141
Austin, Jane, 69

Baez, Gladys, 171
Bakhtin, Mikhail, 14
Balls, 38–41, 42, 45, 175
Baltodano, Mónica, 41
Banderas, Quintín, 12, 89
Barbarian(ism) 9, 24, 26–27, 35, 74, 84, 95, 96, 101, 122, 142, 166, 168
Bedroom, 45, 94, 98, 137, 140, 152, 157, 172, 176, 179, 185, 186
Belli, Gioconda, xviii, 1, 6, 7, 8, 14, 17, 18, 19, 30, 32, 45, 47, 48, 52, 53, 54, 80, 85, 91, 134, 148, 155, 156, 169–197, 172, 175, 177, 179, 188, 193

Benítez-Rojo, Antonio, 14
Bhabha, Homi, 141
Black, 4, 11, 14, 16, 18, 30, 53, 73, 80, 81, 82, 89, 94, 100, 106, 107, 110, 112, 113, 115–120, 122–124, 126–131, 143, 145-148, 155–164, 176, 179, 184, 196; blackness, 144, 150, 158, 162
Blandón, Chuno, 173
Blood (bloodness, bloodshed, bloodlines), 16, 17, 18, 24, 26, 60, 65, 81, 97, 98, 110, 111, 119, 120, 121, 127, 129, 134, 144, 147, 164, 173–174, 176, 179, 180, 185, 188, 191, 192, 195; menstrual blood, 173, 176
Bolívar, Simón, 5, 29, 71, 98, 148
Borge, Tomás, 16, 36, 166–169
Brathwaite Kamau, Edward, 130
Brazil, 4, 141
Bridge of Beyond, The, 132, 133, 135–137, 142, 151, 158, 163
Brontë, Charlotte, 108, 116, 117, 121, 125, 130
Bush (bushland), 32, 36, 37, 55, 99, 102, 103, 112, 114, 122, 124, 128, 130, 142, 173, 191

Cabezas, Omar, 16, 36, 37, 41, 43, 44, 46
Cabrera, General, 29
Cacique, 2, 34
Calibán, 110, 111
Campos, Gloria, 41

Cane, 3, 38, 45, 99, 102, 136, 138, 155, 156, 157, 159, 162, 163

Capital, xvii, xviii, 2, 3, 4, 9, 10, 13, 24, 26, 32, 34, 48, 54, 60, 64–68, 74, 101, 128, 139, 170, 182, 191; capitalism, 11, 28, 30, 49, 187; capitalist, 4, 27, 54, 64, 96, 105, 184

Capote, José María, 12

Cardenal, Ernesto, 10

Carolsfield, xvii, 104, 178

Carpentier, Alejo, 103, 115, 136, 155

Carrión, Javier, 6

Casanaré, xvi, 31, 141

Caupolicán, 168

Cebreco, Agustín, 12

Cerna, Lenín, 6, 8

Césaire, Aimé, 147

Céspedes de, Carlos Manuel, 7

Chamorro, Claudia, 44, 171, 173

Chamorro, Pedro Joaquín, xvii

Chamorro, Violeta, xvii–xviii

Chaos, 26, 50, 55, 91, 102, 114

Chávez Alfaro, Lizandro, 7, 173

Child, xv, 11, 52, 65, 71, 83, 90, 93, 103, 104, 112, 127, 129, 133, 142–144, 150, 152, 153, 167, 170, 171, 178, 181, 191, 194, 195; boy, 44, 112, 144, 145, 149; childhood, 45, 92, 113, 177; daughter, xvii, 6, 23, 41, 54, 61, 62, 65, 77, 105, 108, 110, 111, 113, 124, 133, 143, 155, 156, 176, 178, 179, 189, 194; girl, xvii, 41, 43, 44, 54, 62, 66, 78, 103, 104, 105, 112, 113, 114, 129, 152, 155, 156, 161, 178, 179, 180, 195; son, xvii, 3, 31, 115, 122, 127, 133, 140, 162, 174

Chile, 4, 12

Cisneros, Salvador, 12

Civilization, 2, 3, 4, 8, 15, 24–26, 36, 60, 71, 74, 84, 90, 96, 142, 166, 194

Class, xvi, xviii, 3, 9, 11, 15, 25, 28, 30, 42, 43, 49, 50, 52–54, 63, 73, 81, 88, 94–96, 113, 120, 121, 125, 144, 175, 176, 178, 180, 181; declassé, 65, 66, 90, 98; polyclassist, 48, 30

Clausewitz, Carl von, 5

Colombia, 2, 30, 66, 86, 141, 165

Colonialism, 3, 4, 5, 11, 65, 109, 110, 120, 126, 128–131, 141, 142, 145, 147, 158, 159, 176, 183, 184

Conde, Maryse, 137

Coronel Urtecho, José, 186

Coupling (couple), 41, 52, 61, 69, 78, 86, 90, 94, 99, 100, 103, 104, 113, 115, 137, 162, 171, 176, 177, 180, 181, 184, 185, 195

Creole, 4, 12, 13, 60, 65, 74–77, 80, 109, 110, 113, 117, 120, 121, 122, 124–131, 138, 177

Cuadra, Joaquín, 7

Cuba, 1, 10, 11, 12, 14, 17, 29, 43, 113, 136, 155, 176

Cunavichero, xvi, 34, 35

Custom, 16, 24, 38, 48, 66, 84, 157

Darío, Rubén, 18, 29, 61, 76, 85, 89, 168, 178, 191

de la Parra, Teresa, xvii, xviii, 1, 2, 8, 9, 18, 23, 27, 28, 30, 32, 37, 52, 53, 54, 59–87, 89, 91, 93, 94, 96, 98–100, 106, 134, 139, 148, 155, 156, 160, 175, 178, 180, 182, 187, 192, 196; Gregoria, 17, 80, 82, 100, 160; Ifigenia, 27, 54, 61, 84, 94, 97, 192; María Eugenia, 28, 60–87, 98, 101, 175, 176, 178, 180, 187, 193, 196; Mercedes (Galindo), 23, 28, 29, 75–78

Democracy, 7, 10, 13, 15, 16, 17, 25, 28, 30, 48, 50, 51, 53, 68, 73, 81, 114, 178, 182, 183

Deshón, Roger, 6

Development, 2, 4, 6, 7, 8, 9, 10, 15, 25, 28, 33, 42, 45, 48, 49–50, 51, 53, 54, 60, 61, 72, 77, 86, 90, 91, 94, 97, 101, 154, 165, 167, 178, 184, 189, 190; developed, 24, 25, 28, 29, 97; developmentist, 98, 187; underdevelopment, 25, 50

Díaz Rodríguez, Manuel, 32,

Dowry, xvii, 29, 61, 65, 68, 81, 196

Drake, Sandra, 121

Duncan, Quince, 141

Economic (economy), economist, xv, 2, 3, 4, 7, 9, 10, 11, 15, 25–28, 34, 35, 38, 42, 48–51, 53–55, 60, 64, 67, 70–73, 75, 83, 84, 86, 94, 95, 97–99, 101, 102, 106, 109,

110–116, 118, 120–122, 126, 135, 136,
138–142, 148, 149, 156–160, 163, 166,
167, 181, 182, 186, 189, 193, 194, 195;
socio-economic, 10, 48, 163, 175
Eden, 41, 55, 100, 115, 117, 123, 128, 146
El Che, 16, 41, 42, 44, 170, 173, 175
El Dorado, 123, 124, 128
Ellison, Ralph, 162
Ethnicity, xv, xvii, 1, 3–8, 10, 12, 15–18, 22–
27, 30–34, 38, 39, 41, 42, 48, 50, 52–54,
60, 70, 77, 79, 80, 82–84, 94, 95, 97, 98,
101, 107, 109, 110, 117–119, 121–123,
125–127, 130–133, 135, 137, 138, 143,
145–149, 157, 159–161, 164, 170, 172,
175, 176, 179, 184, 190; ethnolinguistic,
33; ethno(s/ia), 16, 38, 50, 52, 55, 70, 81,
110, 138, 141, 146, 175; ethnology, 18,
110, 149; interethnic, 48, 94, 127, 129,
138, 159; multiethnic, xviii, 31, 52, 96, 97,
107; socioethnic, 94
Europe, 18, 28, 33, 60, 62–64, 67, 72, 73, 74,
77, 78, 79, 82, 83, 85, 86, 90, 95, 98, 101,
109, 117, 120, 121, 123, 126, 134, 165,
168, 174, 177, 178, 180, 181, 186, 187, 190

Family, xvii, 3–7, 13, 26, 31–34, 41, 48,
51–55, 60, 63–68, 72, 74, 76, 80–82, 85,
86, 89, 90, 93, 98, 100–103, 124, 133,
134, 137, 142, 146, 160–162, 172, 174,
181, 182, 185, 192; founding family, 43,
59–87, 148, 155
Fanon, Frantz, 28, 127
Father, 52, 65, 71, 89, 131, 137, 149, 152, 170,
171, 177
Feminine, xvi, 15, 16, 23, 32, 35, 39, 40–43,
46, 51, 52, 55, 59, 60, 62, 68, 70, 72, 76,
80, 83, 91, 93, 96, 97, 101–103, 107, 120–
122, 124, 125, 132, 135, 139, 146, 149,
150–155, 164, 169, 171–173, 175, 176,
178, 184, 189, 190, 192
Franco, Jean, xiv, 60, 91, 98, 131, 173, 174
Frente Sandinista de Liberación Nacional
(FSLN), xvi, xvii, 7, 45, 168

Gallegos, Rómulo, 2, 3, 8, 12, 14, 16, 23–25,
27, 30, 33, 39, 47, 64, 70, 71, 84, 96, 106,
122, 136, 140, 153, 189; *Doña Bárbara*,
24, 27, 33–35, 97, 103, 140, 190, 191, 195;
doña Bárbara, xvi, xviii, 25, 27, 35, 42,
43, 86, 95, 96, 122, 153, 175, 189, 190,
193; Marisela, 25; Mr. Danger, xvi, 86,
95; Santos (Luzardo), 24–26, 33–35, 42,
73, 77, 87, 96, 193
García Márquez, Gabriel, 100
García Marruz, Fina, 90
Garcilaso de la Vega, el Inca, 6
Garden, 6, 19, 23, 31, 33, 52, 53, 55, 88, 89,
92, 109, 112, 114, 117, 122–124, 128, 131,
133, 139, 141, 155, 165, 168, 170–172,
177, 184, 185, 187, 193–195, 197
Garrels, Elizabeth, 9, 70, 71, 73, 86
Germani, Gino, 47, 50, 51, 64, 178
Gilbert, Sandra, and Gubar, Susan, 110,
124, 125
Glittering Coronet of Isles, The, 123, 130
Goldmann, Lucien, 14
Gómez, Máximo, 12, 89
González, Eduardo, 14
Gordimer, Nadine, 146
Guerlaine, 62, 66
Guha, Ranajit, 14
Gutiérrez, Joaquín, 141
Granada, 7, 44, 174
Guadeloupe, 1, 29, 133–64, 189, 190
Guiraldes, Ricardo, 16, 23, 30
Gunder Frank, André, 15

Hacendataria, (class), xvii, xviii, 23
Hacienda(s), xvii, 4, 9, 13, 52–54, 63, 64,
83, 85, 97, 98, 113, 155, 172, 182, 183,
188–190, 194
Haitian Revolution, 116
Halleslevens, Omar, 6
Harnecker, Marta, 41
Harris, Wilson, 130
Herrera, Leticia, 171
Hidalgo, Miguel, 5
History, xv, xviii, 4, 5, 7, 24, 26, 27, 30, 31,
33, 39, 53, 60, 63–65, 70, 73, 78; historico
geographic, 49
Hobsbawm, Eric, 24, 33, 50, 128
Hombres de maíz, 8

Hortus Conclusus, 4, 55, 100, 108
House, 19, 31, 32, 36, 38, 40, 48, 53, 55, 60,
    65, 67, 72, 75,76, 83, 85, 88–90, 92–94,
    99–103, 107, 112–126, 133, 135, 137, 138–
    140, 150, 152, 155, 160, 162, 166, 167, 169,
    171–173, 176, 177, 181, 183, 187, 189,
    195, 197; Great House, 3, 54
Husband, 52, 69, 82, 105, 111, 125, 170, 172,
    191, 192, 193, 194, 195

Independentist, 2, 3, 27, 54, 64, 81, 84, 89,
    92, 99–101, 107, 113, 118, 155
Indigenous peoples ("Indian"), xv, 4, 6, 8,
    10–11, 14, 17, 18, 24, 26, 30–32, 36–39,
    42, 43, 48, 51–52, 74, 80, 97, 102, 120,
    121, 132, 160, 166, 168, 170, 172, 176,
    177, 187, 190
Infante, Tita, 41
Ingenio, El, 114

Jameson, Fredric, xviii, 4, 5, 90
Jane Eyre, 109, 120, 124, 125
Jardín, 1, 29, 88–95, 103, 115, 125, 155
Jungle, 23, 55, 122, 140, 165, 168

Kaplan, Cora, 125

Ladino, 8, 15, 16
Latifundia(o), 4, 8, 9, 35, 63
León, 7, 174
Le Riverend, Julio, 12, 13, 92
Lerner, Daniel, 11, 25, 48
Lessing, Doris, 146
Lienhard, Martin, 8, 40
Lineage, 4, 5, 6, 7, 31–32, 55, 64, 71, 77, 81,
    97, 119–20, 121, 132, 134, 140, 143, 144,
    155, 162, 163, 182
Liscano, Juan, 73
Loynaz del Castillo, Enrique, General, 6, 13,
    29, 88
Loynaz, Dulce María, 1, 6, 13, 18, 19, 29,
    40, 52, 55, 80, 81, 88–107, 108, 113, 115,
    117, 125, 134, 148, 155, 156, 178, 180, 196;
    Bárbara, 88–107, 178, 180, 196; Laura,
    17, 80, 81, 89, 90, 100
Ludmer, Josefina, 13

Macaques, 15
Maceo, Antonio, 5, 12, 89, 148
Maceo, José, 5, 12
Machado, Antonio, xiv, 39
Machismo, xvii, 49, 101, 102, 108
Mackinnon, Catharine, 12, 18
Madness, 99, 110, 111, 114, 119, 121, 122,
    126, 127, 128, 129, 138, 163, 167
Manley, Norman, 122
Maporita, 31, 36, 141, 166
Marca del zorro, 173
Market, xvi, 1–2, 7, 9, 25, 27, 38, 51, 66, 77,
    95, 99, 102, 122, 177, 178, 188, 194
Maroon(ing), 30, 53, 116, 128, 129, 133, 134,
    135, 151
Marriage, xvii, xviii, 18, 23, 27, 52, 61, 65,
    66, 68, 69, 74, 77–78, 79, 82, 90, 96, 99,
    100, 112, 127, 176, 179, 180, 181, 192,
    193, 194
Martí, José, 5, 9, 10, 11, 12, 29, 92, 100, 148
Martínez, Ana Guadalupe, 43
Martínez, José de Jesús, 38, 39, 42, 43, 48,
    49
Martinez Pelaez, 5
Martinique, 109, 137
Marxism, xvi, 1–2, 9, 28, 49
Masculine, xvi, xvii, 1, 3, 15, 23–52, 63, 64,
    68, 71, 72, 83, 105, 119, 120, 134–136,
    139–142, 147, 149, 151–154, 172, 175,
    177, 189, 190, 192, 195
Masiello, Francine, 13, 63, 72
Mejía Sánchez, Ernesto, 30
Memorias de la mama blanca, 54, 61, 70,
    71, 155
*Memorias de una cubanita que nació con el
    siglo*, 155
Menchú, Rigoberta, 38, 160
Méndez, (Méndez-Capote), General, 29
Méndez Capote, Renée, 155
Mestizaje, xviii, 7, 17, 68, 86, 96, 119, 137,
    138, 145, 150, 153, 154, 156, 158, 176, 177,
    190, 193
Mestizo(a), 6, 14–17, 24, 26, 30, 32, 35, 37,
    40, 42, 43, 61, 72, 74, 75, 77–81, 83, 98,
    102, 119, 120, 121, 140, 168, 172, 176–
    178, 181, 190, 192, 193; mestizo republic
    79, 97, 122

Milanés, Pablo, 1, 12
Miller's (*Daughter*), xvii, 113, 124, 156, 178
Modern(ity), xvii, 1, 23–55, 59, 60, 62–64,
72–75, 76, 84, 85, 99, 102, 148, 172, 177,
178, 182, 187, 189
Modernism, xvii, 2, 5, 23–55, 61, 62, 63, 76,
85, 91, 95, 96, 97, 100, 104, 105, 106, 115,
142, 168, 174, 178, 179, 180, 186, 187, 191
Modernization/modernizing, 3, 4, 5, 7, 60,
64, 85, 92, 93, 95, 113, 136, 145, 148, 154,
171, 172, 182, 183, 187, 191
Mode Illustrée, La, 61, 95, 176
Montonero, 2, 34
Morazán, Francisco, 5
Morelos, José María, 5
Moreno Fraginals, Manuel, 114
Mother(hood), 18, 41, 52, 74, 82, 94, 103,
108, 110, 111, 119, 140, 141, 143, 153, 154,
159, 170, 177, 194, 196
Mujer habitada, La, 1, 169, 171, 172, 174,
176, 188
Mulatta(o), 15, 16, 17, 53, 54, 61, 74, 75, 77,
81, 82, 84, 89, 110–115, 118–124, 126,
127, 128, 137, 143, 154
Murilo de Carvalho, José, 4

National bourgeoisie, 2, 3, 4, 7, 8, 9, 10, 15,
47
Nationalism, xvi, 7, 10, 48, 77, 78, 94, 95,
109, 117, 124, 130, 155, 189
Nation-building(-state), 1, 2, 4, 5, 8, 10, 14,
30, 38, 35, 39, 128, 136, 141, 166, 167, 168,
175, 188
Neo-colonial, 4, 147
Neo-historicism, 2
Neo-imperialism, 4
Neo-liberal, xvi, xvii xviii, 2, 9
Neo-positivism, xvi, 1, 2, 3, 13, 14, 15, 24,
38, 39, 53, 84, 85, 86, 90, 91, 98, 99, 115,
175, 189
Nicaragua, xv, xvi, xviii, 1, 2, 6, 7, 9, 10, 13,
15, 38, 134, 163–195
Nuñez, Orlando, 173

Orientalism, 18, 190

Pastor, Beatriz, 15

Patria, 5, 7, 38, 60, 165
Patriarch, 7, 32, 54, 60, 62, 67, 71, 83, 84, 97,
99, 106, 107, 111, 120, 131, 146–150, 153,
154, 170, 177, 192, 193, 196
Paul et Virginie, 66, 178
Payeras, Mario, 37, 38, 41
Paz, Octavio, 187
Peón, 24, 25, 26, 32, 36, 42, 52, 54, 55, 72,
188, 190, 191, 193, 195
Perez, Pedro A., 12
Perus, Francoise, 36
Perry, Benita, 123
Pinto, Anibal, 4
Plantocracy, 3, 5, 23, 55, 81, 94, 95, 112, 113,
121, 128
Platt Amendment, 89
Plotting women, 173
Pluie et vent sur Télumée miracle, 1, 132, 133
Positivism, 10, 72, 73, 187
Postmodernism, xviii, 2, 110, 116, 124, 172,
176, 178
Pratt, Mary Louise, 16
Productive, xviii, 5, 9, 24, 25, 28, 30, 31, 32,
34, 49, 54, 72, 74, 83, 91, 93, 95, 96, 97,
114, 122, 141, 154, 170, 173, 186, 188–193
Productivity, 2, 3, 8, 14, 25, 28, 34, 48, 62,
63, 68, 72, 74, 76, 142, 156, 162, 190
Progress, 2, 3, 4, 15, 24, 25, 26, 28, 33, 36,
78, 91, 190
Property, 2, 3, 5, 7, 10, 13, 14, 24, 30, 34, 35,
42, 49, 52, 53, 55, 60–63, 73, 77, 82, 85,
96, 97, 114, 115, 127, 131, 153, 172, 173,
174, 182, 183, 188, 189, 193, 195

Quezada, Juan José, 6
Quintana, Emilio, 141

Ragatz, Lowell, 95
Rama, Angel, xvi, 2, 28–30, 165, 189
Ramchand, Kenneth, 109
Ramírez, Sergio, 2, 10, 11, 13, 15, 166–
169, 173
Reform, xv, 3, 8, 11, 15, 28, 36, 50, 70, 95,
99, 100, 111, 117, 118, 120, 172
Retamar, Roberto Fernández, 110
Revolution, xv, 2, 3, 5, 6, 8, 11, 12, 13, 14,

Revolution (*continued*)
16, 19, 24, 28, 36–47, 48, 49, 52–55, 64, 69, 81, 82, 102, 155, 165–195
Reyes, Alfonso, 10
Rhys, Jean, 3, 15, 17, 18, 29, 32, 52, 55, 69, 80, 89, 90–94, 96, 100, 102, 108–131, 134, 148, 156, 178, 180, 184, 188; Antoinette, 3, 69, 82, 99, 101, 103, 108–131, 178, 180, 196; Christophine, 17, 18, 69, 80, 82, 90, 100, 109, 112, 113, 116, 118–120, 122–124, 127–131, 148, 180
Rivera, Francisco (El Zorro), 38, 44, 46, 173
Rivera, José Eustasio, 2, 3, 16, 23, 30–32, 36, 102, 103, 136, 166; Alicia, xvi, 32; Arturo (Cova), xvi, 31, 32
Rodríguez Monegal, Emir, 30
Romanticism, 61, 62, 66, 68, 73, 76, 83, 86, 116
Romero García, Manuel Vicente, 72

Said, Edward, 18
Saint Pierre, Bernardin de, 76
Sandinista, xiv, 9, 13; administration, xiv, 6, 7
Sandinismo, 13
Sandino, 6, 7, 9, 148
Sangre Patricia, 32
San Martin, Jose de, 5
Savage, 101, 127, 129, 134, 142, 166
Schiller, Herbert, 25
Schneider, Romy, 179
Schwarz-Bart, Simone, 1, 3, 15, 17, 19, 35, 43, 47, 51, 52, 53, 55, 80, 81, 84, 91, 100, 123, 132–164, 180, 188, 190, 191, 196; Queen without a Name, 17, 123; Télumée, 18, 80, 132–164, 196; Victoria, 18; Wademba, 18
Segundo Sombra, Don, 103
Senghor, Leopold, 147
Servants, 52, 53, 55, 79, 80–82, 100, 112, 113, 114, 122, 124, 156, 160
Serrat, Joan Manuel, xiv
Siglo de las luces, El, 155
Simón, Pedro, 93, 155
Sissi, 179
Slave, 1, 5, 51, 53, 67, 69, 81, 89, 106, 112,

115, 118, 121, 126, 129, 131, 137, 139, 143, 145, 146, 147, 148, 149, 150, 157, 158, 180
Sofia de los presagios, 1, 54, 169, 170, 171, 188, 192, 196
Solitude, 19, 23, 32, 45, 52, 68, 90, 91, 94, 96, 99, 100, 101, 114, 116, 164, 167, 180
Sommer, Doris, 14
Somoza, Anastasio, 15
Sosnowski, Saul, xiii
Spivak, Gayatri, 110, 120, 123, 130, 131, 174
State, xv, xvi, xviii, 1, 2, 6, 7, 8, 9, 13, 14, 15, 16, 19, 20, 23–25, 30, 47–55, 60, 69, 71, 79, 83, 86, 93–95, 99, 102, 105, 109, 112, 114, 120, 122, 128, 131, 132, 134, 138–141, 158, 165, 166, 168, 175, 180, 183, 185, 186, 193, 196
Subercaseaux, Bernardo, 27, 29
Suffragette movement, 67, 180

Tecún Umán, 8
Tellez, Dora María, 171
Territoriality, 4, 9, 31, 32, 35, 42, 115, 124, 132, 133, 135–155
Territorialization, 112, 135–155, 162
Testimonial/*testimonio*, 14, 28, 36–47, 48, 102, 134, 139, 140, 141, 160, 166, 171
Ti Jean L'horizon, 1, 132, 134–139, 148, 150, 152, 157, 162, 188
Tijerino, Doris, 41, 171
Torriente, Lolo de la, 93
Torrijos, Omar, General, 38, 39, 41, 42, 45, 48
Transaction, 60–65, 97, 157, 160, 174
Transition, xv, xvi, xvii, 1, 2, 3, 15, 16, 23–55, 61, 72, 83, 92–101, 114, 115, 121, 148, 165, 166, 177, 178, 181, 182, 185
Tres conferencias a la empresa privada, 186

Ultimos días de una casa, Los, 155
Uslar Pietri, Arturo, 70, 71, 75

Valignano, Alexander, 16
Valle, María Esperanza, 41
Vargas, Oscar Rene, 2
Venezuela, 1, 2, 23–30, 59–87, 93, 94, 98, 99, 141, 165, 196

Viglietti, Daniel, 5
Vilas, Carlos, 6, 28, 49, 51, 55
Violeta, doña, xvi, xvii, xviii
Voragine, La, xvi, 17, 18, 30, 31, 35, 37, 97, 142, 163

Watteau, Antoine, 66, 76

Wheelock, Jaime, 8
Wide Sargasso Sea, 1, 94, 112, 113, 119, 128, 134, 184
Williams, Eric, 147
Williams, Raymond, 5, 89

Zea, Leopoldo, 10

Ileana Rodríguez is Associate Professor in the Department
of Spanish and Portuguese at Ohio State University. She is a
specialist in the centro-Caribbean area and has written
extensively on the literature and culture of the island and
mainland nations.

Library of Congress Cataloging-in-Publication Data
Rodríguez, Ileana.
House/garden/nation : space, gender, and ethnicity in
postcolonial Latin American literatures by women / Ileana
Rodríguez ; translated by Robert Carr and Ileana
Rodríguez.
Includes bibliographical references and index.
ISBN 0-8223-1450-9 (alk. paper). — ISBN 0-8223-1465-7
(pbk. : alk. paper)
1. Caribbean literature—Women authors—History and
criticism. 2. Caribbean literature—20th century—
History and criticism. 3. Women in literature. 4. State,
The, in literature. 5. Ethnicity in literature. 6. Feminism
and literature. I. Title.
PN849.C3R7 1994
809'.89287'09729—dc20 93-42502 CIP